Henry G

I hope this book will answer some of your questions about the history of the Schwegm family & the company.

Bill Schwegm

The Schweizer brothers: the author, William (Bill) at left, Paul A. and Ernest took places in Schweizer sailplane number 1,000. The aircraft, a 2-32 model, held many United States and world records, including a distance run of 505 miles. Production of the 2-32 ended in 1976, but the craft remains much in demand.

SOARING WITH THE SCHWEIZERS

The Fifty-Year History of Their Aviation Adventures

WILLIAM SCHWEIZER

RIVILO BOOKS

Manufactured in the United States of America
First Edition

5 4 3 2 1

LIBRARY OF CONGRESS CATALOGING-IN-PUBLICATION DATA

Schweizer, William (Bill) 1917–
Soaring with the Schweizers: The fifty-year history of their aviation adventures.
Includes Index
1. United States—Aviation History
2. Sail Plane Manufacturing and related activities

Published by Rivilo Books, Falls Church, Virginia

The paper in this book meets the guidelines for permanence and durability of the Committee on Production Guidelines for Book Longevity of the Council on Library Resources, Inc.
ISBN 0-9630731-0-9

CONTENTS

PREFACE

It's no wonder that my father encouraged the Schweizer boys to come to Elmira, New York to set up a little company to manufacture sailplanes back in 1939—he knew a good thing when he saw it. This book is about the history of the Schweizer Aircraft Corporation.

In the case of Schweizer Aircraft, a preface must convey a sense of family. There is no finer example of family than the Schweizers. They are a close-knit and talented group, and their varied personalities have meshed to create and build a small and unusual industrial company, one whose name is known and respected worldwide.

The unique character of the company is a reflection of its family owners. Singly and jointly, they are the embodiment of hard work, honesty, integrity and steadfast purpose. The "senior brothers" have established themselves in global aviation, particularly in soaring and gliding. Ernie has been the engineer, the designer—from sophisticated sailplanes to beautiful sculpture—Paul, the financial manager, salesman and pilot, with an international reputation for soaring skills, dedicated to the art of soaring and the author of its history in the United States; and Bill, the youngest, the manufacturing manager and a salesman of considerable talent who can persuade prospective buyers of their need for the company's products—and a renowned story teller as evidenced in this manuscript.

The "younger generation" is becoming equally well-recognized. Les is the engineer and designer, as his father has been. Bill's son, Stuart, is demonstrating organization skills in manufacturing and production, and his brother, Paul H., specializes in finance and worldwide sales.

The friendliness and helpfulness of all the Schweizers have endeared them to a large numbers of employees through the years. Certainly one of the advantages of a small company is this "one-on-one" relationship.

The family would not be complete without the Schweizer women. Each wife of the six Schweizers has been and is strongly supportive of her husband and has added appropriate dimension to the success of the company.

Since their arrival in Elmira in 1939, our Chemung Valley area has been blessed with Schweizer enthusiasm and leadership, and we are a better community for their presence.

May the next many years be as exciting and as challenging to the Schweizers and their company as were the first fifty!

Boyd McDowell II
Chairman of the Board
Chemung Canal Trust Company

ACKNOWLEDGMENTS

I wish to acknowledge the generous assistance of several individuals who made significant contributions to the telling of the Schweizer aviation story. First, I am indebted to Mary E. Patterson for preparing the manuscript and to Barbara J. Tweedt for her editorial assistance. My special thanks to Susan K. Dove, Doris L. Loud, Emma R. Novotny, Diane Sonner and Kevin Proaper for their support in obtaining historical photographs and preparing exhibits and illustrations.

I am also indebted to Terrell P. Kirk and Wayne Myers, and to Bill and Peggy Gallagher for their critical reading of the manuscript and for their constructive comments. I am grateful to members of the Schweizer Family for their help with this project, especially my brothers, who read the manuscript as a check on my memory. All surviving errors are my responsibility. Last but not least, I must say a special thank you to my wife Peggy. Not only was her proofreading helpful, but her encouragement kept me going.

1

THE BOYS IN THE SCHWEIZER BARN 1930–1935

We were three teenaged boys who spent most of our spare time building model airplanes and gliders (*Figure 1*). Our fascination with aviation was kindled by Lindbergh's flight across the Atlantic in 1927 and by a 1929 *National Geographic* article about gliding and soaring. Ernie, Paul and I never dreamed that sixty years later we would be reminiscing about our years in the aviation industry, or that I'd be writing the history of the Company that evolved from our teenage hobby—the story of Schweizer Aircraft Corp.

In 1929, the three of us, along with five of our friends from our model airplane club, designed and constructed the first Schweizer glider—which made its maiden flight in June, 1930. We met nearly every day after school in our father's barn, which was our workshop, to build the primary-type glider made of wood with fabric covering. It was later named the SGP 1-1. At that time, Ernie, the designer, was 18; Paul, the organizer, was 17; and I was 12 years old.

The Schweizer family lived on a six-acre country estate on the outskirts of Peekskill, 45 miles north of New York City (*Figure 2*). The large barn made an ideal home for the glider construction project. My father, "Papa" Schweizer, purchased the home in 1923 and named it "Bonnie Brook" for the meandering brook that ran through the property. He had two thoughts in buying Bonnie Brook. He wanted to move his young family out of the New York City area, and he felt that Bonnie Brook would be an ideal site for a resort restaurant.

Papa, a chef trained in France and England, came to this country from his native Switzerland in 1906. During the time the first glider was being built, Papa operated The Carnegie Hall Restaurant (from 1916 to 1932) at the world-famous concert hall in New York City. When he started, there were no local, state or federal income taxes; therefore, at the end of each week, he and his partner just divided the money. Papa commuted to New York City six days a week, leaving early in the morning and returning late at night; so the family did not see much of him except on Sundays.

Our mother, Emma Bader Schweizer, had emigrated from Switzerland in 1908. She was kept very busy with five children, three boys and two girls: Helen, Ernie, Paul, Emily and me. Unfortunately, Mother died of cancer in December, 1924 when she was only 40 years of age. I was six years old and had a difficult time adjusting to this tragedy, but from a family standpoint, it drew us closer together into a stronger unit. Papa hired a live-in couple (Joe and Pauline Heimers) to look after the Schweizer children and our home. In 1932, Papa left the Carnegie Hall Restaurant and opened the Bonnie Brook Inn, a resort restaurant at our Peekskill home, so he could be closer to his family.

Ernie and Paul were the prime movers on the first glider project and supplied most of the $135.00 required to buy materials to build the craft. They saved their allowances and ran to school (two miles away) to save their bus fares to help fund the project.

The frame of the first glider was made completely of wood. It had a few metal fittings where bolts and nuts were used to attach the wings and tail to the fuselage. This made the wings and tail detachable, so they could be built and transported independently. We read various articles on glider construction, which served as our construction and quality guides. Home builders were warned to use aircraft-grade lumber (wood with a fine straight grain and no knots) for strength and reliability. The nearest source for the spruce and birch that we needed was an Ohio firm, Yo Ho & Hooker. Ernie decided to use the Clark

Y airfoil section. This was the same airfoil used on the "Spirit of St. Louis" which Lindbergh had flown from New York to Paris. Our glider's wing span was 34 feet with a constant width. Its wings were covered with cotton muslin and coated with nitrate dope to make the surface air-tight. The wood fuselage was varnished, and the wings and tail were painted yellow and green.

In early June, 1930, we assembled the glider in the barn's second floor hayloft. Papa, who was home all day only on Sunday, very seldom came into the barn and did not know we were building a glider. He was not interested in sports or mechanical things. His main interest, after caring for his family, was working in his flower gardens when he was home. The Heimers were aware of the glider under construction, and Joe probably talked to Papa about it, but they assumed it would not be completed and flown.

Late in June, 1930, a week before Ernie was to graduate from high school, the glider assembly was finally completed. That Sunday Papa came upstairs in the barn while we were working on the craft. He walked around it, looked it over and left without saying a word. He did not even ask, "How are you going to get it out?" We took this as a signal that he was aware of what was going on and that we could fly the glider. Interestingly, Papa did not allow us to ride bicycles because he thought they were too dangerous.

The 1-1 was disassembled in the barn and then reassembled outside (*Figure* 3). It rained on Monday and Tuesday of that week, so the first flight wasn't made until Wednesday, June 19th. We chose to use our neighbor's field, which was flatter and larger than ours. The glider attracted a large crowd and resulted in a front-page article in the next day's "Peekskill Evening Star." (*Figure* 4) We used the shock cord method to launch our glider. This required a twelve man ground crew, a shock cord and a tail rope. A shock cord was a 150 foot rope with a ⅝ inch diameter and a rubber band core. The glider had an inverted "C" shaped hook attached to its nose, and the shock cord had a two inch steel ring attached at its midpoint. To launch the glider, the shock cord was laid in the shape of a "V" with its midpoint at the nose of the glider, and the ring was fastened to the nose hook. Five men held each end of the shock cord and two men held the tail rope. Upon the pilot's command, the men on the tail rope dug in their heels and held their rope firmly while the men on the shock cord started to walk and then run forward. Upon the pilot's signal, "release", the men on the tail rope released their grip and the glider catapulted forward into the air (*Figure 5*). As the glider passed over the shock cord, the ring on the cord dropped off the "C" hook on the glider.

The 1-1 was classified as a primary glider because its fuselage had no enclosure around the pilot. The drag caused by the fuselage gave the ship a high sink rate. Its glide angle was about 1 to 8. This meant that with a five-foot high shock-cord launch, the ship would go 40 feet forward before it touched the ground. (Modern sailplanes have a glide angle in the range of 1 to 40.) The pilot in our original glider sat in the open on a small wooden seat with a lap safety belt and two basic controls: a stick for elevator and aileron control and a rudder bar for turns.

All club members flew the new glider during the first two days, and there were no mishaps. The neighbor's field was relatively small, about 500 feet long, so flights were more or less ground skids about two to six feet off the ground and up to 100 feet in distance.

Now that we had some experience, we decided to move flight operations to Todd Field, which was about a mile from our home and was occasionally used by airplane barnstormers as Peekskill's local airport. There were two adjacent fields, each about 1500 feet long; one had a gentle slope to the south and the other to the north. This allowed us to pick the proper field each day so flights could be made into the wind for lower take-off and landing speeds. Todd Field also made higher and longer flights possible. A trailer was built to transport the glider when it was disassembled. On our first trip to Todd Field, the trailer was pulled by hand because we had not obtained an automotive trailer license. A local policeman who was driving up the road offered a tow, which we gratefully accepted.

We taught ourselves to fly by taking very gradual steps, since there was no opportunity for dual instruction in a single-place glider, and besides, there was no one to instruct us. The flight training procedure was as follows: First, low straight flights—then higher straight flights—next, mild turns and finally 180 degree turns which resulted in an down-wind and uphill landing. During that summer, we incorporated Bellanca-type lift struts which improved the stability and glide angle of our aircraft.

In the fall of 1930, flight operations stopped, and it was back to school. Ernie entered New York University to study aeronautical engineering. On the Friday after Thanksgiving, the glider was taken to Todd Field once again. It was a cold fall day with gusting winds of 20 miles per hour. The wind was so strong that a shock-cord launch was not required. The glider was towed by hand with a rope tied to each wing strut. On the second flight of the day, Paul reached a height of 15 feet and was flying at zero forward airspeed because of the strong wind. A gust of wind hit him from the side and the glider went into the ground, wing first. The crashed glider looked like a pile of kindling wood, but Paul walked away with a few scratches and bruises. Important lessons were learned that day; avoid gusty air, but if you can't, have extra airspeed.

During the winter, the glider was rebuilt with numerous improvements and was ready for operations by the next summer. The fuselage structure and cockpit were enclosed, and it was redesignated the SGU 1-1A (*Figure 6*). The enclosed fuselage resulted in less air drag and a noticeable improvement in the glide angle. It also provided a sense of security and comfort to the pilot.

Primary gliders became quite popular among aviation enthusiasts in the early 1930's because airplanes were not readily available and were very expensive to own or rent. During the depression, many aircraft manufacturers added home built, primary glider kits to their product lines in order to boost sales. No FAA (then CAA) certification of pilots or gliders was required. The only requirement was a CAA identification number on the ship. During that time period, some serious accidents occurred as a result of numerous structural failures in flight and from a general lack of knowledge or experience in building and/or flying gliders.

Elmira, New York was chosen as the site for the First National Soaring Meet, which was held in September, 1930. The area resembled the Wasserkuppe, the center of glider activity in Germany. The Wasserkuppe had ridges running in several different directions with large, flat areas between them. Dr. Wolfgang Klemperer, an outstanding German glider pilot in the 1920's, was a dirigible engineer for Goodyear. On his frequent trips from Akron, Ohio, to New York City, he drove through the Elmira area. Klemperer strongly recommended this area to the National Glider Association as the perfect site for the 1930 competition.

In August, 1931, the Schweizer brothers made their first visit to Elmira to attend the Second National Glider Meet. The trip was made in our 1929 Model A Ford. It took over eight hours to cover the 200 miles from Peekskill, New York to Elmira. Most of the trip was made on old Route 17, which was a narrow, winding road that hit the center of every town and city on the way. The YMCA on Church Street provided our Elmira accommodations at a rate of $.50 per person per day. (At that time a dollar would buy 11 gallons of gas and ice cream was $.30 a quart.)

The meet headquarters were at Caton Avenue Airport in Southport (which became building lots in 1934). Thermal and cloud flying were in their infancy in 1931, so contest flying was principally ridge soaring. Ridge lift is caused by wind hitting a ridge and being deflected upward. The pilot attempts to fly in the up-current in front of the ridge. If the up-current is of sufficient strength, the glider can maintain or gain altitude. Six take-off sites on ridges running in different directions were established in the Elmira area. The ridge used would depend on the direction of the wind that day. The stronger the wind and the more directly it hit the ridge, the better the up-current.

Most of the contest flights were made on South Mountain ridge, which is located one mile south of the Caton Avenue Airport. The ridge is 700 feet above the valley and faces the Northwest. Flights of over eight hours in duration and distance of up to 20 miles were made during the 1931 contest. Franklin (Bud) Iszard, co-owner of Iszards Department Store in Elmira, made a flight of over eight hours that year and finished in second place.

The most memorable event for the Schweizer boys happened as we approached the airport on the first day. An ambulance raced by and we found out later it was carrying an injured glider pilot. Upon our arrival at the field, we saw the crashed glider. It was reported to us that the glider had taken off from South Mountain and as he was approaching the airport, the pilot discovered he was too low to fly over the obstructions along the road. The pilot dived at the ground to pick up speed, hoping he could pull up over the obstructions. However, when he pulled up, he tore the wings off the fuselage. This accident made us think about the importance of structural integrity and quality control in aircraft construction. Attending this meet had been a great education for Ernie, Paul and me. And at the same time, it had reinforced our interest in aviation and soaring. I also learned to hate root beer. I saw a sign at the airport which read, "As much root beer as you can drink for 5 cents," and I accepted the challenge.

In the fall of 1931, my brother Paul entered New York University, also to study aeronautical engineering. Every day Ernie and Paul commuted 45 miles by train to New York City. This was a rigorous schedule for both of them. Glider design and construction were pretty much put on the back burner during the school year, but New York University had a glider club and some of the members occasionally came home with Paul and Ernie on the weekends.

The German glider designs that we saw on our first visit to Elmira were an influence on Ernie's next design, the 1-2. This utility glider had a long, straight wing (40 foot span) and was built from wood with plywood and fabric covering. The construction started in the spring of 1932 and required more man-hours of wood craftsmanship than expected. It was put aside that summer and construction began on a simpler and faster ship to build, the SGU 1-3 (*Figure 7*). This design was similar to the 1-1A, but was an improved version with enclosed fuselage and a 36 foot constant-cord wing.

Ernie received a welding outfit for his birthday in April, 1933. He was anxious to learn to weld because this technique was needed to build safe, modern aircraft. In past designs, welding had been kept to a minimum and had been done by our local blacksmith, who was not a good welder. Ernie became concerned about the quality of welds on our original ship. On a flight in the late summer of 1930, he experienced a loss of aileron and elevator control due to a weld failure. Being big and strong, he let go of the control stick and grabbed a wing strut with each hand. It looked as if he manhandled the ship to a safe landing.

The SGU 1-3 was ready by the summer of 1933 and proved to be a good flyer with a positive, responsive control system. The glide angle was not as good as expected because of a poor choice of airfoil. In a dive the glider did not pick up much speed and would sink rapidly due to the shape of the airfoil. Although it was nicknamed "The Brick," this glider was flown successfully for the next three years.

The all-wood SGU 1-2 was completed during the summer of 1934 and taken to Elmira. It had a beautiful varnished mahogany fuselage with yellow wings and was nicknamed the "Yellow Peril" for good reason. The ship was slow to respond in flight, so we used to kid about taking a "ride" rather than "flying the ship." Because we were not happy with the flight characteristics, we set it aside. In fairness to Ernie, the glider was an outgrowth of too many ideas from too many people. Construction began before the design was complete, and the airfoil was a poor choice.

1

2

1. Ernie, Bill and Paul A. Schweizer stand together in 1925, shortly after the death of their mother.
2. The Schweizer home "Bonnie Brook" in Peekskill, New York, where the brothers first planned and realized their aviation adventures.

3

4

VOL. IX NO. 145 TWO SECTIONS 14 PAGES PEEKSKILL, NEW YORK, FRIDAY, JUNE 20, 1930

Peekskill Now Has Its Own Glider Club

Local "Lindberghs," After Months of Toil, Bring Out Their 32-Foot Machine and Give It a Taste of the Air---Big Crowd Witnesses Launching --- Saved Bus Money for Materials

Using their "spending money" together with other funds, and putting in many hours a day for the past eight months, the Peekskill Airplane Model Club last night put into use a new primary type glider airplane which they constructed in the barns of Mr. Schweitzer, of East Main Street, proprietor of the "Bonnie Brook Inn." The young men used the plane on a flat field in order to test out and to get accustomed to the use of the controls. Later, when they have perfected the handling of the machine, it is expected that they will use it in flights in the vicinity of Peekskill. Hundreds of people watched the exhibition flights last night on the property of Enoch J. Tompkins, East Main Street, near the LaBarron property.

Club Formed Last Year

The Peekskill Airplane Model Club, a member of the Airplane Model League of America which is sponsored by the American Boys' Magazine, was granted a charter on July 24th, 1929. The charter members are Aron Yellott, William Yellott, Paul Schweitzer, Ernest Schweitzer, William Schweitzer, Alfred Wilson, Travis Williamson, James Pettit, Arthur Samson and Vincent Samson.

The framed charter is hung in the clubrooms in the Schweitzer barn, East Main Street.

The Schweitzer boys were instrumental in forming the Airplane Model Club. Ernest graduates next week from the Peekskill High School. His father, who was an interested spectator last night, said that his son would take a course in New York University and would study airplanes and aeronautics.

Saved Bus Money

Mr. Schweitzer said that his son had always been interested in airplanes, which he termed "the coming thing," and said that he was glad to assist his sons in their hobby. Ernest is 18 and Paul 17 years old. The boys, who reside on East Main Street, received money regularly from their father to ride on the bus. However, they pocketed this money and ran to school. During the past year Ernest was a member of the track team of the High School. The money thus saved was later spent in purchasing material for the glider

PEEKSKILL BUSINESS COLLEGE HOLDS ITS COMMENCEMENT

Twenty-seven Students of Local Institution Receive Diplomas at Guardian Hall

OVER 400 IN ATTENDANCE

William Slawson Addresses Graduates on Subject "Service and Fidelity"

More than 400 persons attended the graduation exercises of the class of 1930, Peekskill Business College, which was held in the Guardian Recreation Hall last evening. This was the largest attendance in the history of the institution. Professor Joseph Kuhn, principal of the school, presided. Twenty-seven students received diplomas.

William Slawson, of Lake Oscawana, but formerly of Peekskill, gave an interesting address to the graduates. He spoke on "Service and Fidelity." Mr. Slawson urged the graduates to be true to their work. "Nothing is done by one executive now, as was done years ago," the speaker said. A great part of important work, he said, is being done by assistants, and employers ar erelying on their help. He urged them to remain faithful, in order that they may reach some of the higher positions which are offered these days.

A fine program, in charge of Miss Della Mead and Miss Elsie M. Agor, was enjoyed by the audience.

Following the exercises, diplomas and gifts were presented. Mr. Kuhn was presented with a writing set by the class; Miss Henrietta Dietz, an instructor at the school Miss Wanda Knizeski and Mr. Slawson received bouquets of flowers.

HOSPITAL DIRECTORS VOTE TO BUY X-RAY MACHINE FOR $2,299

Apparatus, of Snook Manufacture, Is Said to be of Latest Design, in Every Detail

NO RESIDENT DOCTOR YET

Board Also Defers Action on Proposed New Kitchen Until Fall

A modern X-ray machine, the last word in that line, will soon be added to the equipment of the Peekskill Hospital. The proposition, which was presented at a meeting of the Board of Dorectors of the Peekskill Hospital last night, was approved and the machine will be ordered. It will be a Snook X-ray apparatus, and is to cost $2,299.10.

The committee in charge of securing a resident physician for the hospital reported progress.

Fifteen members of the Board of Directors were present, with President Carl G. Pfeiffer presiding.

The treasurer's report was received and filed.

There was a short discussion on the proposed new kitchen, but the matter was left on the table until after the Summer vacation. The Board then adjourned for the Summer months. It will next meet on the second Thursday in September.

The Board of Directors gave permissio nto Dr. Highland Millman and Dr. Frederick Rauch, of Lake Mohegan, to treat their patients at the hospital.

The treasurer's report showed that the hospital had operated at a loss during the past month. The balance shown was made possible by reason of subscriptions.

Treasurer's Report

The treasurer's report was as follows:

Cash on Hand May 1st		$ 380.06
Receipts—		
Income from patients		5,131.24
Inc. from X-ray, lab. & amb.		671.00
Inc. from investments		357.50
Subscriptions		1,738.16
		$8,277.06
Disbursements—		
Salaries & wages	$4,476.29	
Kitchen, laundry & supplies	715.19	
Gen. expenses	165.69	
Int. on mortgage	1,651.60	7,008.77

MONTROSE BOY WINS GOLD MEDAL IN STATE-WIDE ESSAY CONTEST

Edwarw Karlin, a Member of Eighth Grade of Hendrick Hudson J. H., Gets Prize

OFFERED BY NAT. D. OF R.

Nearly 600 Persons Attend Closing Exercises Held Last Night---Play on Program

About six hundred persons attended the Hendrick Hudson Junior High Program given in the school auditorium last evening. A fine program, featuring a play "Always in Trouble" and a balloon dance, was given. The cast of characters for the play were especially well selected.

Edward Karlin of the Eighth Grade received a gold medal which was offered by the National Council of the Daughters of the Revolution for the best essay on "The Women of the Revolution."

There were 189 schools in the State of New York entered the contest and 1,000 papers were submitted. Mrs. Margaret M. Robinson, of Paulding Street, who is regent of the Van Cortlandtville Chapter, Daughters of the Revolution, made the presentation.

The program was as follows:

Address—Thomas F. Nolan, Member, Board of Education.

Presentation of History Essay Gold Medal—Mrs. Margaret Robinson.

Presentation of Earned Awards—Supervising Principal, Frank G. Lindsey.

Presentation of Promotion Certificates—Principal, Leroy J. Lucy.

The Cast for "Always in Trouble":

Misery Moon, a hoodoes coon—William Alexander.

Gideon Blair, a millionaire—Ellis Travis

Tom Rissle, as slick as a whistle—William Nielsen.

Hiram Tutt, an awful nut—Ronald Hoffman.

Patrick Keller, a ticket seller—Samuel McMahon.

Samantha Slade, a poor old maid—Nina Francis.

(Continued on page four)

PEEKSKILL PUPILS GET LEGION MEDALS

3. The Schweizer brothers and friends S. Ernest Whidden, Ernest Whidden, Aaron Yellott and Atlee Hauck get ready to hand launch the first glider, the SGP 11, on June 19, 1930. ***4.*** *Its flight was reported in the* Peekskill Evening Star. Peekskill FTA

5

6

7

5. First flight of a Schweizer glider, Ernie at the controls of the SGP 1-1. ***6.*** *An improvement on the original design, with a cockpit.* ***7.*** *"The Brick," SGU 1-3, of 1933 flew much better than its nickname suggests.*

2

SCHWEIZER METAL AIRCRAFT CO. 1936–1939

Ernie graduated from college in 1934 and Paul in 1935. There were practically no aeronautical engineering jobs available at that time, so they worked part-time in my father's restaurant and started Schweizer Metal Aircraft Co. in our barn. Their first project was the SGU 1-6 (*Figure 8*), the first all-metal gliders in the world. The fuselage had a pod and tail boom configuration that was intended to make it simpler and cheaper to build. The ship had a 38 foot wing span with a constant cord (width) to simplify tooling and construction. The wing airfoils used on the first three ships were copied from other gliders, but Ernie and Paul now had training, so the airfoil for the SGU 1-6 was carefully selected after studying government and university wind-tunnel reports on various sections. This paid off. This design won third prize in the 1937 design contest sponsored by the Soaring Society of America. In spite of the good flight characteristics, however, the design was a little ahead of its time. The aviation public was not quite ready to accept an all-metal glider or sailplane. It was finally sold to some members of the Harvard Gliding Club in 1938.

Until this time, we had identified our gliders by name, such as "The Brick," but we realized that we needed a logical identification system. We devised a system which is still in use in 1991. For example, the SGU 1-6 breaks down as follows: The

S stands for Schweizer, the G for glider, the U for utility, the first number (1) stands for the number of persons it is designed to carry and the second number (6) for the place of the model in the series of Schweizer designs. Other letters used in later models included the following: P for primary glider, S for sailplane, M for motor glider and A for airplane. We used this identification system for all designs, even though a few of them (SGU 1-4 and SGU 1-5, for example) were never built.

The 1-6, our first all-aluminum glider turned out to be an uneconomical product for the new Company to manufacture. It required more fabricating equipment and tooling than available or than the Company could afford. It was, however, a valuable learning experience because the aircraft industry was moving to all-aluminum monocoque construction. With this concept, the metal skin carried part of the structural load as opposed to fabric covering which did not. This new approach made fabric covered wood and steel tube welded structures obsolete for high-performance aircraft. In order to fabricate some of the 1-6 parts, such as leading edge nose ribs, Ernie designed and built a drop hammer and a foundry in the basement of our barn. The equipment, used to make male and female dies, remained in Peekskill after the Company moved to Elmira in December, 1939, so all three Schweizer boys had to make frequent trips to Peekskill during the next few years.

In 1936, during the construction period of the SGU 1-6, brother Paul became an active participant in the Soaring Society of America (SSA). (He is still a very active SSA member and a director of SSA). In 1936, the SSA leaders felt there was a need and ready market for a replacement to the Franklin Utility Glider which was now out of production. This ship had been the backbone of the U.S. soaring movement from 1930 to 1935. Approximately 40 ships were built by R. E. Franklin, Professor of Aeronautics at the University of Michigan. With this encouragement, we decided to start a Franklin replacement. It became obvious during the construction of the all-metal 1-6 that this ship was too expensive to build as a Franklin replacement, so the SGU 1-7 (*Figure 9*) was designed, and construction started while the 1-6 was still being built. This glider was designed for low-cost production and so that it could be built with a minimum of fabrication equipment and production tooling. The new 1-7 had an all-aluminum wing structure with fabric covering aft of the spar, constant-cord wing and a welded steel tube fuselage, and tail surfaces covered with fabric. This concept set the design philosophy for Schweizer training and utility gliders for the next twenty years. (The Schweizer high-performance sailplanes became all-aluminum structures right after WWII.)

The question is often asked, "What is the difference between a sailplane and a glider?" According to *The American Heritage Dictionary*, "A glider is a light engineless aircraft designed to glide after being towed aloft or launched by a catapult. A sailplane is a light glider that is used especially for soaring." My definition is: A sailplane is a glider that can maintain or gain altitude by utilizing light up-currents found in normal weather. We considered our aircraft beginning with the SGU 1-6 to be sailplanes.

The 1-7 flew well and had a better glide angle and more positive controls than did the Franklin. It also had a higher stall speed which some of the gliding public thought was too high for a single-place training glider. (Even by today's standards, the 1-7 is still a good trainer.) At that time, the Piper J2 Cub sold for $999, which was about the same price my father paid for a new 1937 Ford sedan. The sales price of the 1-7 was $595.

In June, 1937, I graduated from high school. I received an award as the most outstanding graduate in terms of athletics, scholarship and character, which resulted in a tuition scholarship to Syracuse University. My father did not want me to take aeronautical engineering because my brothers had not been able to find jobs in the field. The aircraft industry was then small and depressed. Airplanes were toys for rich playboys and movie actors. Commercial aviation was in its infancy, and no transcontinental or transatlantic flights were being made. Military aircraft budgets were minimal. However, what happened in the next four years with the World War II build up is a good example of how educational guidance is often out-of-step with the real world. Nevertheless, I majored in science at Syracuse. This gave me a number of job options plus a fall-back position as a high school science, physics or chemistry teacher. During my college years, I spent summers working in the family restaurant and helping out at Schweizer Metal Aircraft Co.

The first 1-7 was sold to the Hudson Valley Gliding Club,

Wurtsboro, New York. The second glider sale was to the Altasaurus Club of North Conway, New Hampshire. It was actually consummated before the Hudson Valley sale and thus was the first glider sold by the new Company. The Altasaurus Club was made up of a spirited group of young M.I.T. and Harvard graduates who lived in the Boston area. Its leader was Eliot Noyes, who later became a world-famous architect and was credited with creating the IBM corporate image in the late 1940's. Eliot was on the Army Air Corps staff in Washington which directed the U.S. Military Glider program during WWII.

The Altasaurus Club members fell in love with the 1-7 and were very enthusiastic flyers. Another member was Dr. Henry Hyle who later became a world-famous neurosurgeon. One day he was flying at Conway and strayed too far from the field. He landed in the top of a tree in a heavily wooded area. After recording the accident with photographs, some of the club members climbed the tree, took the ship apart, lowered the parts with ropes, carried the parts back to the field and reassembled the glider. The next day they flew it.

(Dr. Hyle was stationed in England during WWII and was pictured in *Life* Magazine performing advanced neurosurgery on wounded soldiers. I lost track of him after the war. Thirty years later, when my sons were at Dartmouth, I learned quite by accident that Dr. Hyle was teaching at Dartmouth Medical School. Unfortunately, he had had a non-flying accident and was disabled from the waist down. Dr. Hyle was in a wheelchair and had to give up surgery. That fall, I brought him over to our sailplane dealer at Sugarbush, Vermont and had the pleasure of giving him an hour soaring flight in our 2-32 high performance sailplane. It was a great thrill for both of us.)

When the 1-7 was ready for production, the market disappeared as a result of depressed economic conditions, so sales were disappointing. Only two gliders were built and sold. The old Franklins were still doing most of the training, and glider buyers said they wanted a high-performance, two-place sailplane rather than a new trainer. This was discouraging to Ernie and Paul, but they were still optimistic about the future of gliding and soaring.

In 1937, there were only a few two-passenger utility gliders but no high-performance sailplanes in the United States and just a few in Europe. Lewin Barringer, General Manager of SSA, felt that high performance, two-place sailplanes were needed in the U.S. to help make the soaring movement grow. His rationale was that such an aircraft would help entice airplane pilots to try the sport, make soaring more of a family sport, and would also provide a way to teach soaring techniques to more glider pilots. Barringer said that if Schweizer built a good two-place, he would encourage the SSA to buy one. Ernie and Paul looked at a number of designs and received input from SSA members before settling on the basic design of the SGS 2-8 (*Figure 10*). The 2-8 design created a great deal of interest. The Airhoppers Gliding Club of Long Island made a down payment for the first ship in the fall of 1937. Its sales price was $1,000.

The 2-8 was considerably larger than anything previously built by the Company. It had a 52 foot wing span with a glide angle ratio of 23 to 1 and a sinking speed of 2.1 feet per second. This performance compared favorably with the day's best European single-place sailplanes. Its construction utilized an aluminum wing and tail, a welded steel tube fuselage, and an aluminum and fabric covering.

The Airhoppers' ship was delivered in the summer of 1938. It had excellent flight characteristics and met the projected performance goals. Unfortunately, one of the Airhoppers' Club members spun the ship in during a training flight and was killed. The accident was attributed to lack of pilot experience. The Airhoppers' ship was rebuilt and was flying again in three months, but, this accident cooled some of the interest in the 2-8.

Barringer talked the SSA into buying a second ship at the increased price of $1,200. This sale helped the credibility of the 2-8 and with potential new business. Schweizer Metal Aircraft hired its first two full-time employees, Paul Nissen and Donald Medrick. Atlee Hauck worked part time until 1939 and remained with the Company until he retired in 1976. Their pay in 1938 was twenty-five cents per hour, which was standard for a small aircraft company.

Barringer planned to use the ship to introduce key individuals to soaring and also to attempt to set some world two-place records. The ship was delivered to the SSA in July, 1939, at the National Soaring Contest in Elmira. During the conest, Paul observed active interest in the 2-8, which he felt could lead to additional sales. While finalizing the SSA 2-8 sale, Paul was directed to see Attorney Robert P. McDowell to get the bill of sale notarized for the SSA. Bob said, "Why don't you boys come to Elmira and build sailplanes here?" He also indicated that Elmira Industries could probably provide some financial assistance to a new manufacturing business and thought that some Elmira businessmen would be willing to invest in the Company. He commented that if Elmira were going to remain the "Glider Capital of America," it should have a sailplane manufacturer.

8

9

10

*8. World's first all-metal glider, the SGU 1-6 was a technical advance in 1937—too far ahead of its time. **9.** Another early model, SGU 1-7, still flying in 1967. **10.** Two-place trainer, the SGS 2-8, helped launch the Schweizers as a commercial company.*

3

THE ORGANIZATION OF SCHWEIZER AIRCRAFT CORP. 1940–1941

In December 1939, Schweizer Metal Aircraft Company relocated in Elmira and was incorporated as Schweizer Aircraft Corp. (SAC). The new corporation had a capitalization of $20,000 made up of 4000 shares of voting stock at $5.00 per share. Ernie and Paul received 53% of the stock for the assets of Schweizer Metal Aircraft Co. This included equipment, inventory, work in process and sailplane designs. The new location was the second story warehouse (12,000 sq. ft.) of the Elmira Knitting Mills in Elmira Heights (*Figure 11*). Elmira Industries (the forerunner of today's Southern Tier Economic Growth) located the Elmira Heights building and agreed to cover the rent for two years. In return for this commitment, they received the cash equivalent ($4,650) in stock which was 23% of total stock outstanding. Attorney Robert P. McDowell took the lead in raising additional funds for the new company by selling stock to twenty-five Elmira businessmen and friends of the Schweizers for a total of $4,710. In 1989 dollars, this gave the new company an amount equal to approximately $25,000 with which to work.

At the Schweizer Corporate Organizational Meeting on January 15, 1940, Ernest, the oldest, was elected President and Secretary. Paul was elected Vice President and Treasurer. It was understood that they would both share the overall responsibility of running the Company. In addition to Ernest and Paul, the following directors were elected: attorney Robert P. McDowell; attorney Harry M. Moseson, who represented Elmira Industries; and William McGrath, a manufacturing executive. Mr. McGrath was Vice President and General Manager of the Eclipse Division of the Bendix Corporation located in Elmira Heights (now a division of the Facet Corporation). (See Appendix 11.)

All Schweizer gliders built up to 1938, including the second SGS 2-8, were licensed in the experimental category by the Civil Aeronautics Administration (CAA). The local CAA representatives said they would resist licensing any more 2-8 sailplanes, since it could carry a passenger until the Company obtained a Approved Type Certificate (ATC) for the model. The ATC was also desirable because buyers would have more confidence in the product, and the aircraft could then be used commercially for selling rides and for instruction.

The certification project was initiated in the fall of 1939. This created a serious technical hurdle for the four-man Schweizer Company. To meet the requirements, the Company had to prove and document that the sailplane structure and control system were structurally sound if built to specifications—and that the ship had safe flight characteristics if flown within the defined limits. With a herculean effort by Ernie and Paul, the ATC was achieved in the spring of 1940. The first certified 2-8 sailplane was sold to the Bell Aircraft Glider Club of Buffalo, New York. The time-consuming certification project and nine months with no sales created serious financial difficulties for SAC.

Ship No. 4 was ordered by Joe Steinhauser with a small down payment. The Elmira Bank & Trust Company of Elmira Heights (now Marine Midland) advanced SAC $1,000 for working capital. The glider was completed in June, but Joe was unable to pay the balance of the money owed. This compounded SAC's financial problems. The ship was put on display and used as a demonstrator during the National Contest at Harris Hill in early July, 1940. Bob Stanley, Chief Test Pilot of Bell Aircraft Corporation and also a leading soaring pilot, did not have a ship to fly in the contest, so Bob was offered 2-8 No. 4 to make a contest flight. Ernie and Paul flipped a coin to decide who would go with Bob, and Ernie won. They took off at noon and landed six and a half hours later on the outskirts of Washington, DC. As Bob approached Washington, he thought he would try to land on the White House lawn, but was too low in altitude to make it. (One could not even consider such a feat today with the tight security.) This flight established a new American two-place distance record of 219 miles. (In 1937, Bob was a Navy squadron commander assigned the responsibility to search for Amelia Earhart in the South Pacific. Bob was later the first American to fly a jet airplane when he flew Bell's prototype in 1942.)

After the contest, ship No. 4 was loaned to Lewin Barringer. He took the 2-8 glider to Sun Valley, Idaho and set a world's two-place altitude record of 14,960 feet. This record-setting soaring expedition was funded by the Union Pacific Railroad which owned the Sun Valley Resort and wanted national publicity. U. S. statesman, W. Averell Harriman, son of the railroad founder, was interested in soaring and arranged for the funding of the expedition. When the 2-8 glider was returned to Elmira in early August, Steinhauser finally had enough money to buy the "Record Breaker." The records helped the SGS 2-8 earn a good reputation and create additional sales. No. 5 was ordered by Ed Knight and No. 6 by seventeen year-old Richard Johnson, who later became a World Champion pilot and today is considered the "Dean" of U.S. soaring pilots. During 1940, SAC's employment grew from 4 to 6 employees. Mr. D. G. Anderson, President and co-founder of Hardinge Brothers of Elmira, became a director of SAC replacing Mr. McGrath who resigned because of illness. (See Appendix 9)

In 1941, the Congress and the military were starting to ask questions about gliders. Adolf Hitler was reported to have used 200,000 glider pilots when he launched the attack on Poland, and during the 1940 invasion of Belgium, Germany had used large gliders towed by airplanes to transport soldiers and artillery. The U.S. military had no glider pilots or cargo gliders. At the request of the Army Air Corps, SAC and Elmira Soaring Corp. (now Harris Hill Soaring Corporation) arranged a glider flight demonstration for a group of Congressmen in order to show gliders in tow and to demonstrate that they were quiet and could land in a short distance on a rough field.

In January, a second 2-8 was ordered by Steinhauser. His

glider school in Chicago was booming as a result of the sudden government interest in gliders. During the following month, three 2-8 kits (gliders 75% complete) were ordered by the National Youth Association, an aviation ground and flight school financed by the State of Michigan and stimulated into action by the war clouds in Europe.

A continual shortage of working capital required SAC to ask the Elmira Heights branch bank for an advance on each firm glider order received. When the bank reneged on an advance for the three kits, Paul talked to our Attorney, Bob McDowell. Bob did some behind the scenes work to arrange for Paul to meet with Fred J. Swan, President of the Chemung Canal Trust Company. Mr. Swan agreed to finance the kits if his organization could have all of SAC's banking business. We agreed and the Chemung Canal became SAC's bank. Mr. Swan also gave Paul a fatherly talk about the importance of making a profit.

Commanding General "Hap" Arnold of the Army Air Corps asked Colonel Fred Dent to organize a military glider program (*Figure 12*). In April of 1941, Dent visited SAC and the Elmira Soaring Corporation at Harris Hill, which had just organized a glider training school. Dent arranged for two groups of ten Air Corps pilots to come to Elmira for flight training. The first group arrived in May and the second group in June, and it wasn't long before the pilots discovered the local girls and vice-versa. Romances bloomed and even a few marriages took place. The majority of these officers became the leaders of the huge World War II military glider program.

Dent ordered three 2-8 gliders to be delivered as soon as possible, and in May the Navy ordered two 2-8 gliders for a secret program (*Figure 13*). The Company had expanded from six employees to fifteen in May, and with the sudden influx of orders, things were in a state of bedlam at SAC.

In March of my senior year at Syracuse University, I signed up to join the Army Air Corps and was scheduled to start pilot training in June. During graduation week I took my final physical exam and was rejected because of a pilonidal cyst discovered on my spine. The military doctors were concerned that a cyst of this type might become infected in combat conditions. Although the problem could have been corrected by surgery, the University and my family doctor advised against it because of the high rate of post-operative infection. (In 1941, sulfa drugs, penicillin and other antibiotics were still not available.) When Ernie and Paul heard about my problem, they called and suggested that I join SAC, which I did during the second week of June.

Until May of that year, SAC had been struggling for orders, and then, almost overnight, we had more than we could handle. Military orders were now on hand for five 2-8's (3 Air Corps and 2 Navy) to be delivered as soon as possible. There was a strong indication that the military would take as many gliders as we could deliver during the next year. Our production rate was approximately one ship every six weeks during the first five months of the year, and we established a goal to increase production to one ship per week by year end. This meant that more people, more equipment, expanded floor area and improved production methods were required.

Until this time, Ernie and Paul had spent part of their time working in the shop, but now they were busy with engineering, sales, financial and administrative matters. They wanted me to help organize the shop and to develop a production control system. This presented a very interesting challenge. I knew how we built gliders on a one-ship basis in Peekskill, and I had a good background in math and science, but I had no training or experience in industrial management. When I arrived at SAC, we decided the best way for me to get into the job was to spend time working in the shop. This approach gave me an opportunity to become familiar with the product and at the same time to learn first hand about current production methods and problem areas. It also gave me the opportunity to get to know the employees personally. I started immediately to read books and periodicals on industrial management and to visit other plants whenever there was an opportunity. Later I also took college extension courses in industrial engineering.

I concentrated my initial efforts in Final Assembly because parts and hardware shortages and manufacturing problems usually surfaced in this area. I soon became the general troubleshooter for the shop and then production manager. As a result, I turned my Final Assembly responsibilities over to Donald Quigley, an ambitious and effective leader in that area. (Don spent the next 43 years at SAC and eventually became a vice-president.) Because of our lack of experience, we made many mistakes, yet overall we made a great deal of progress as well. During the last six months of 1941, fifteen gliders were delivered, and by year end, we met our production goal of one ship per week. Employment grew to 65 people.

A number of important events took place during this period which helped to increase our output. Paul worked out an arrangement with the Knitting Mill to increase our floor area from 12,000 to 24,000 sq. ft. SAC took over the balance of the second floor as well as the basement of the warehouse. A ramp was constructed from the second floor to ground level so large assemblies like wings could be carried up or down. Before building the ramp, sailplanes were lifted or let down by ropes. The ramp from the basement to ground level was modified so a trailer with a glider on it could be towed in and out. Gliders were assembled in the basement, then put on a trailer and transported to Harris Hill where they were test flown. Trailer production became an important component of SAC's business because every military glider order included a trailer.

During this period, we built our first dope and paint spray booth in the basement. Previously, all dope and paint had been manually applied with a brush. We hired Donald Dunton away from Piper Aircraft so SAC could learn Piper's aircraft finishing technology. The preservation and appearance of our products were greatly improved with our new paint technique.

A shortage of aircraft welders in the Elmira area created a serious production problem. SAC's average shop rate in 1941, thirty five cents per hour, was similar to Piper Aircraft's in Lock Haven, Pennsylvania. To attract certified welders, we placed an ad in the Lock Haven newspaper offering Piper welders thirty eight cents per hour and a 48 hour work week. With these enticements, we were able to hire a sufficient number of welders. (Thirty-five cents an hour was an acceptable wage since a gallon of gas cost eleven cents and a nickel would buy a Hershey bar, an ice cream cone or a large coke.)

During July, 1941, while we were madly trying to figure out how to expand glider production, the Curtiss Wright Corporation of Buffalo sent a team of representatives to SAC to evaluate our manufacturing capabilities. They liked what they saw and offered us an opportunity to build the rudder and fin assemblies of the P-40 pursuit airplane. We turned them down because of our production overload, but we suggested that they consider Mercury Aircraft Corp. of Hammondsport, New York. Mercury was comprised of the people and equipment that remained after the Glenn Curtiss Company moved to Buffalo during World War I. Although they were an aircraft company in name only and had no aircraft business, they took the P 40 job, expanded their facilities and became one of Curtiss Wright's largest subcontract suppliers during WWII.

U.S. military leaders wanted troop transport gliders when they saw the contributions made by the German gliders in Crete and Belgium. During the summer of 1941, Wright Field's Air Corps development headquarters requested design studies of military gliders. Ernie became deeply involved, and as a result, two engineers and two draftsmen were added to the SAC staff to assist him with this project. (One engineer was Donald B. Doolittle, a recent graduate from the University of Michigan. He later became the President of All American Engineering Corp., an important SAC customer in the 1960's. After retirement, Don designed the Cyclocrane and became the President of D.C. Associates, manufacturer of the vehicle. This is a special-purpose, heavy-lift airship which SAC helped build in 1983.)

The Air Corps' first thought was to use gliders to sneak troops across enemy lines at night. At Wright Field they wrote specifications and requested preliminary design proposals from SAC and other aircraft manufacturers for eight-passenger and fifteen-passenger gliders. Specifications called for a specific gross weight and a 38 mph stall speed with no flaps. This resulted in gliders with very light wing loading that would fly very slow and float. Our first design, the eight place SGC 8-10, had a 94 foot wing span. The second design, the fifteen place SGC 15-11, had a 115 foot span. When the design studies were complete, it was concluded that the specifications were impractical. The glider would be a monster to handle in even light winds and in turbulence on the ground as well as while airborne. In addition, the military also had some second thoughts about using gliders for sneak attacks because of the rapid development in radar technology.

Wright Field had also written specifications for a higher speed troop transport glider to move soldiers into combat areas.

This appeared to be a more practical way to use gliders in warfare. Waco Aircraft Company of Troy, Ohio took the lead on this program and developed the fifteen place CG-4A glider. During the next three years an unbelievable number—over 10,000—of this model were built by seven different companies. They were used extensively by the Allied Forces in 1943 and 1944 for the invasion of Sicily, Normandy, Holland and Burma. The AAF wanted a minimum of 6,000 cargo glider pilots trained by 1943, so SAC was under great pressure to increase production of the TG-2 training glider.

In the midst of the SAC cargo glider studies, the Air Corps informed Paul of a new policy: "Strategic material, particularly aluminum, should not be used in the construction of training aircraft." The TG-2 had aluminum wings, tail and fuselage fairings. However, the military did allow us to keep the TG-2 in production until August, 1942. Then a new replacement glider had to be in production.

Ernie and staff went right to work on a new two-place trainer which was designated the SGS 2-12 or Air Corps TG-3 (*Figure 14*). This glider was designed in accordance with the new strategic material policy. It had a low-wing configuration with the rear cockpit more forward than that in the TG-2. This put the instructor near the center of gravity and vastly improved the rear-seat visibility. The wings and tail surfaces were all wood. The fuselage was a welded steel tube structure with a wood and steel fairing with fabric covering.

In November, 1941 SAC received an Air Corps order to build two prototypes and a static test article of the TG-3 which was to be used for structural testing. On Saturday, December 6th, Paul and I were in New York City making arrangements to purchase aircraft quality spruce. Ernie was at Wright Field discussing the details of the TG-3 design. While driving home on Sunday, we heard of the Japanese attack on Pearl Harbor. At noon on Monday, we stopped work to listen to President Roosevelt's radio address to Congress. The U.S. had declared war on Japan and Germany. Roosevelt said, December 7th was "a date that will live in infamy." Our directions were firm and clear. Accelerate the TG-2 trainer and have the TG-3 in full production by September, 1942.

Although the TG-2 production rate reached its maximum at the end of 1941 at one ship per week, we still had 35 gliders yet to deliver. We knew that because of the strategic material shortages, no more Air Corps or Navy contracts would be issued for the TG-2. This was especially disappointing because we had worked so hard to get production in high gear, and now had to terminate the project. The last TG-2, Serial No. 57, was completed in August (*Figure 15*).

11

12

***11.** First home of the Schweizer Aircraft Corporation (SAC), the second story of an Elmira, New York, warehouse; ramps were for moving large component assemblies.* ***12.** In 1941, with war approaching, Col. Fred Dent, front, and H.H. (Hap) Arnold, Commanding General of the U.S. Army Air Corps, inspected the all-metal SGS 2-8.*

13

14

15

***13.** The first SAC glider delivered to the U.S. Navy in 1941. **14.** Wood, a non-strategic material, made a comeback in the 2-12/TG-3, a trainer design for the Army Air Corps. **15.** A fleet of trainers in California, 1942.*

4

THE WORLD WAR II PERIOD 1942–1945

The U.S. was now at war with Japan and Germany. Our military leaders realized that a giant air armada was required to win the war. President Roosevelt and George C. Marshall, Commanding General of the U.S. Armed Forces, could see that the Army Air Corps needed more independence from the ground Army leaders to accomplish the new mission. They changed the Air Corps name to Army Air Forces (AAF) and made Henry "Hap" Arnold the Commanding General.

Shortly after the Pearl Harbor raid, we were contacted by the FBI and told to be on the alert for certain individuals involved in the U.S. soaring movement who were suspected of being German spies. There was good reason for this concern because some members of the German Embassy staff in Washington, D.C. had attended and/or participated in the National Soaring Contest in Elmira from 1937 to 1940.

Late in December the AAF decided to purchase at fair market value all licensed gliders in the U.S. and use them for their flight training program. This turned out to be a bonanza for those people who fixed up old gliders and sold them to Air Corps' representatives who had little knowledge about the value of gliders. The AAF's acquisition put an end to pleasure sailplane flying until after the war.

The Government immediately set up war time Civil Defense regulations to guard against sabotage and invasion as well as to accelerate production of war materials. A national priority system was established so that strategic material and supplies required for the war effort were given first consideration. Therefore, many commercial manufacturers converted to military production because material was not available. For example, Steinway Piano and a number of furniture manufacturers were given contracts to build the all-wood CG-4A cargo glider. Auto companies stopped their commercial production and converted to building jeeps, tanks, airplanes, etc. Ford built the Consolidated B-24 Bomber, and General Motors built the Grumman Avenger Torpedo Bomber.

In January, 1942 the U.S. War Department took over supervision of all manufacturing plants involved in military production. An Army Captain was assigned to SAC and to three or four other plants in the area. As the officer in charge, his main concerns were plant security, contract delivery schedules, military deferments and manufacturing material supply problems. The Air Corps also had quality control representatives who visited SAC to inspect and buy-out finished products such as gliders. For the TG-2, CAA inspectors were also involved because the Air Corps contracted to buy CAA certified gliders. Unfortunately, the Government regulations did not specify whether the Air Corps or the CAA had the final say. The politics of this situation often created production problems for us because each inspector wanted the final word, and they often tried to wait each other out. On a number of occasions, I picked up the Air Corps inspector at his hotel late at night just so he could complete his acceptance check, and hence, have the last word.

Because SAC was building military aircraft, a plant-wide security program was required which included around the clock guards. A background check was made on all employees and everyone had to wear identification badges. Our old building had no fence around it and had many doors, so it was nearly impossible to guard properly. I am sure the enemy could have sabotaged us at any time. This new requirement created serious problems for SAC for two reasons: We did not have sufficient staff to enforce the new security regulations, and this expense had not been included in our product cost. The rapid wartime inflation made it very difficult for us to keep our product costs in line with the negotiated prices.

In February, 1942, the static test model of the TG-3 was completed and taken to Wright Field, the AAF proving ground, where it underwent severe static structural load tests. Up to this time, it was the only glider to go through the tests without a failure. This was a credit to Ernie and his engineering staff. The military was impressed by the design and the state-of-the-art wood wing construction. The wing had just one spar with a stressed skin, formed plywood leading edge which formed a structural D tube. As a result of the successful static test results, the AAF ordered 75 ships at our bid price of $3900.

The plant was growing and additional management staff was needed. During the first three months of 1942, our employment increased from 65 to 90. In March of 1942, Eugene S. Bardwell was hired as Personnel Manager. Bardwell was a Methodist Minister and a former newspaper reporter for the *Syracuse Herald*. He had a great sense of humor and a new joke every day. He had been the registrar of the Elmira Aviation Ground School located on the first floor of the Knitting Mill warehouse. His past relationship with SAC proved beneficial because he knew most of our employees. He had directed many of them from the ground school to SAC. One of Bardwell's first jobs was to bring our employee records up to date. Until this time, SAC management had been more interested in building gliders than in keeping good employee records.

In May, the TG-3 prototype was flown for the first time by our test pilot, Emil Lehecka. After a thorough flight test program at SAC, the prototype was then taken to Wright Field and flown by the AAF test pilots. The design was approved for production with a few modifications and renamed the TG-3A.

The Air Corps wanted deliveries at a rate of one per day as soon as possible, so we were tooling and planning accordingly. It was obvious to us and to the military officer in charge of SAC that we needed more floor space, but we also concluded that it was unwise to invest more money in the old factory away from the airport. Paul was able to convince the AAF representatives at Wright Field that SAC had a facility problem. A military production team visited our plant and advised the Defense Plant Corporation in Washington of our need. The Defense

Plant Corporation approved the request for a new plant to be built adjacent to the Chemung County Airport in Big Flats. They would own the plant, and SAC would lease it from the Government agency. This was the method used to build and finance most defense plants during WWII.

SAC acted as their agent to find the plot of land and to line up an architect. The Defense Plant Corporation approved the land purchase, drawings and the construction contract. In September, 1942 we went to work building a new plant scheduled to be completed in January, 1943. The contract price to build the plant was $172,564, which amounted to $5.55 per square foot. Robert Bickford was the architect and Welliver Construction Company was the builder (*Figure 16*).

The plant site was a 29.1 acre plot on the east side of the airport. (See Appendix 6) The land was purchased from farmer Steven Kohan at $100 per acre. Kahon had planted Christmas trees on three acres, so he wanted $20 more an acre for this area. The total cost of the land was $2970. The Sunday before construction was scheduled to begin, Paul, Ernie and I went to look over the plant site. There had been a severe thunderstorm on the preceding Saturday night, and we noticed that airport drainage water had flowed over part of the proposed plant site. Fortunately, we made the decision that day to have the architect revise the plot plan and lift the complete plant floor one foot. (In 1975, we had a flood that resulted in 4 inches of water in our plant. If we had not visited the site on that Sunday afternoon, there would have been 16 inches of water in 1975.)

When it was announced that SAC was building a new 31,000 square foot plant at the Chemung County Airport in Big Flats, we heard criticism from employees and from Elmira businessmen. They thought the site was too far from town and that it would be hard to attract employees and reliable business services. Big Flats and neighboring Horseheads were very small villages at that time with nothing but farm land between them. In 1940, 1841 people lived in the whole township of Big Flats where the SAC site was located, today the population has more than tripled.

As part of a tremendous Air Force build up, the AAF wanted 6,000 trained glider pilots by the end of 1943. This required five civilian-operated glider training bases which were to be supervised by the AAF: in California, Texas, Arizona, Arkansas and Elmira, New York. The local operation was run by the Elmira Area Soaring Corp. (now Harris Hill Soaring Corp.). In the winter of 1942, the flight operations were moved to Mobile, Alabama to avoid the winter weather, but the organization was still managed by Elmira personnel. Edward A. Mooers, President of the Hilliard Corp. of Elmira and later a Director of SAC, was the C.E.O. of the Elmira Area Soaring Corp. throughout WWII.

Once the bases were established with instructors and ground personnel, the AAF-owned gliders were distributed. This put more pressure on SAC because the AAF training command started sending students before there were sufficient gliders to accommodate their training program requirements.

Piper Aircraft suggested to the AAF that trainees could go aloft in light planes, such as the J3 Cub, cut their engines and fly their aircraft as gliders. However, AAF felt it was important for students to receive aero-tow experience and did not accept Piper's proposal. The three U.S. training glider manufacturers (Corcoran Aircraft's TG-lA, Laister Kauffmann's TG-4A and SAC's TG-3A) were under great pressure to accelerate production. The AAF liked our glider, and, in desperation for more aircraft, they gave Air Gliders, Inc. of Barberton, Ohio a cost plus contract to build 50 Schweizer TG-3A gliders—even though Air Gliders had no facility and no prior manufacturing experience. The AAF could do this because it paid for the development of the TG-3A design. SAC received payments for production support service to Air Gliders and $150 royalty for each glider delivered. We were not happy with the AAF action because we felt that by the time Air Gliders was finally in production, SAC could have produced all of the TG-3A gliders required.

After Piper's light plane proposal was turned down, Aeronca Aircraft decided to modify their two-place training airplane (less engine) into a three-place training glider. Their prototype, which they built at their own expense, was not a good training glider. But because it could be available in large quantities in a short time, the AAF bought the concept. In the fall of 1942, the AAF ordered 250 airplane/glider conversions from each of the following light airplane manufacturers: Piper, Aeronca Aircraft Corp. and Taylorcraft Aviation Corp.

In November, 1942, our TG-3A contract was increased from 75 to 113 gliders, all to be delivered by July, 1943. By year end 1942, 22 gliders had been delivered, which left a balance of 91 to be built during the first seven months of 1943. We had completed the tooling for the detail parts and assemblies that were required for SAC to produce aircraft at a rate of one per day, but more floor space was needed to accelerate the TG-3A program. Unfortunately, the new plant at the airport was a month behind schedule and would not be available until the last week in February.

By year end 1942, SAC's employment had increased from 65 to 154 workers. A number of key employees who joined the Company that year played important roles in the long-range development of SAC. For example, Ernest Whidden, woodworker, later became General Fabrication Superintendent; Paul L. Pullen, metal parts fabricator, later became General Factory Superintendent and Vice President; Nicholas Haich, accountant, later became Treasurer and Eileen Weed, Secretary, later became Mrs. Ernest Schweizer.

About 25 women joined SAC's work force in 1942. Some left office or clerking jobs for more money, while others went to work to help the war effort, but because of the shortage of men, the majority saw an opportunity for factory work for the first time. Our wood rib department was staffed by about twelve women and one lead man. (We still left the supervision up to a man—how times have changed!) Most of the women ranged in age from 30 to 50 years old, and we considered them old so we nicknamed the department "the hen house". Their job was to glue and tack wing and tail rib parts together, a delicate job which they could do better than men could.

Vera Brown came to me one day and said she wanted to transfer to the covering department because she was allergic to the glue used in the rib department. She also said that her doctor wanted to know what chemicals were in the glue. I told her it was urea resin and spelled it out so she could write it down. Her husband, Charlie, who was a millwright, came over to me later and asked what urea resin was. I told him, "It's horse p---" (the commonly used word for urine). Vera worked for SAC for the next twenty years, and whenever I saw her, we shared a private laugh.

In January, 1943 seven TG-3A training gliders were delivered. Production was accelerating but was handicapped by a lack of space and poor working conditions in the Elmira Heights factory. The heating system was inadequate, and we lacked the humidity control essential for building wooden aircraft. Wood gluing operations were often held up because room temperatures were below the minimum requirement. Wood parts in production often developed unacceptable end checks or cracks because the dry hot air absorbed moisture from the wood. In addition, the plant lacked proper lighting, power connections, storage space and a nearby flight test facility. These conditions would be corrected when SAC moved to the new plant.

We moved into our new facility at the end of February. First we moved the large assembly fixtures and equipment. To keep production loss at a minimum, the bulk of the move was completed during the last weekend in February. Our employees were proud of the new plant, and they cooperated in every way possible to make the move a smooth transition.

The additional space and humidity-controlled wood shop really paid off (*Figure 17*). Employees were enthusiastic about their new facility and eager to get the work out. SAC built 12 TG-3A gliders in March (*Figure 18*). The man-hours required to produce a glider dropped from over 2000 to 1400. The Company had been losing money, but we expected to make it up on the anticipated follow-on order for 100 TG 3A's. With the production rate increased, we were now sure we could complete the contract on schedule in July. Paul informed Wright Field contract personnel that four month's lead time was required for a follow-on order to keep production going without interruption.

On May 10, the AAF announced that it had sufficient quantities of training gliders, and SAC should prepare to switch its production to other military projects. After recovering from the shock, we started immediately to look for new AAF projects.

The TG-3A production increased to 18 per month in June, and the contract was completed on schedule in July. The last TG-3A, serial No. 114, was built in August as a Company demonstrator. When the final cost accounting for the TG-3A contract was completed, SAC determined it had lost $26,500 on the project. We knew we were losing money. Unofficially, the AAF officers told us they would take care of the loss with the follow-on order.

Because no follow-on contract was awarded, Paul and our treasurer, Nick Haich, filed a recovery claim for $26,500 ($240 per glider) with the AAF. The claim was based upon the fact that SAC had met the contract schedule in spite of the following conditions: (1) SAC had incorporated the increased work scope verbally requested by AAF representatives, without proper documentation, in order to meet production schedules; (2) costly production delays had been caused by conditions beyond SAC's control; and (3) actual wage inflation had exceeded the calculated government projection in spite of wage and price control.

No recovery was received even though many AAF officers who worked with us gave SAC high marks for our TG 3A contract performance. Air Gliders, Inc. had a cost-plus contract and recovered all of their costs, close to a million dollars, even though they delivered only one glider to the AAF. SAC made the military officers involved look good, but when the chips were down, military regulations prevailed. We had been naive, but we learned a very important lesson.

While the TG-3A production was winding down, I had some more thoughts about my personal military responsibilities. I went to Rochester to talk to the Navy about a commission. They said with my pilonidal cyst, I would only qualify for limited service duty, and according to my classification, I was frozen in my job. I also talked to the AAF captain in charge of our plant, and he said: "You and your two brothers are more valuable in Elmira than in uniform." With that, I was ready to accept the next SAC challenge.

Our employment, which had peaked at 221 in March, dropped to 85 employees in August. With the help of the AAF, other work was lined up, and SAC became involved with tooling and production development on a number of new programs. The following projects were put in work at SAC during the last five months of 1943: 1. *U.S. Navy TDR-l Secret Expendable Torpedo Bomber*

American Aviation Corp. of Jamestown, New York, had received a contract to build an expendable torpedo bomber for the Navy called the TDR-l (*Figure 19*). This aircraft was designed by the Navy to be flown with a pilot or as a drone when controlled by radio from a mother ship nearby. SAC was awarded a cost-plus, fixed-fee contract to build approximately 20% of the airplane. Our job was to tool and build the wing center sections which incorporated the engine mount, the cockpit canopy, and miscellaneous detail parts. An order was received in July, 1943 for 50 sets of assemblies to be delivered during the following 18 months. The Navy did not allow any information to be released to the press on this aircraft program. The employees at Jamestown and Elmira knew they were building a secret military airplane, but only the individuals with a secret clearance, including the three Schweizers, were aware of the intended mission.

AAF C-46 Transport Aircraft

SAC was awarded a cost-plus, fixed-fee contract in September to tool and build 700 C-46 fuselage under wing assemblies. The C-46 was a cargo and troop transport aircraft designed and built by Curtiss Wright Corp. of Buffalo, New York (*Figure 20*). Tooling was started immediately and assemblies were scheduled for delivery starting in January, 1944 and continuing during the next 18 months.

AAF Glider Air Pick-up System

The All American Engineering Corp. of Wilmington, Delaware, developed a glider pick-up system which enabled a troop transport glider to be towed aloft from a short field by a C-47 (DC3) aircraft as it flew over the glider at a low altitude (*Figure 21*). During the fall of 1943, SAC received an order to tool and produce kits of parts and hardware required to install the All American winch system in the C-47 airplane.

AAF P-47 Fighter Bomber

In November, SAC bid and was awarded a fixed-price contract to build a large quantity of welded assemblies for the P-47. This aircraft was designed and built by Republic Aircraft Corp. of

Farmingdale, New York. The P-47 was one of the leading American fighters in the European theater.

These new subcontract programs necessitated additional capital for equipment as well as working capital to finance the start-up costs. The AAF glider business provided the opportunity for SAC to show the government that our Company could produce a quality military product on schedule under adverse conditions. This reputation helped Bob McDowell and Paul convince the U.S. Smaller War Plants Corp. to grant SAC the necessary loans for the new work. The Smaller War Plants Corp. had been established to provide the funds for facilities, equipment, and working capital that small businesses required to manufacture for the war effort. The Smaller War Plants Corp. first advanced SAC $30,000 to buy equipment. They actually owned this equipment, and we leased it from them. They also provided a 90% quarantee to Chemung Canal Trust Co. so that SAC could acquire a $50,000 working capital loan.

This new subcontract work gave SAC the opportunity to take a major step forward in metal-aircraft construction technology. Some of the equipment added at that time included: a 300 ton hydro press with a rubber pad, aluminum processing set up, 12 foot swing arm drill-router, sheet metal fabricating machines, machine shop equipment and assembly hand tools, such as 50 riveting guns. The home-made drop hammer in our barn in Peekskill was retired and replaced with a small rope drop hammer.

The transition from a one-product sailplane manufacturer to an aircraft job shop caused a complicated and difficult management problem. We had laid off 135 employees, and, although we were trying to keep our staff of key people together, at times we did not have enough work to keep everyone busy. After employment bottomed out at 88 in August, we grew to 113 by year end. The subcontract work enabled us to recover our losses from the TG-3A program, and SAC ended the year with a profit of $9,500 in 1943. Our hourly cost, including labor and overhead, was under $2.00 per hour, so the profit amounted to a fair amount of money.

Normally the Schweizer brothers would get together to talk over problems once a day, usually in Ernie's office. During the summer of 1943, I noticed that the meetings were switched to my office, and Ernie always sat in the same chair. One day I sat in that chair and noticed that it lined up with Eileen Weed's desk. I realized there was some chemistry in process between Ernie and Eileen. On December 11, 1943 they were married at the Millport Methodist Church. Our Personnel Manager, and ex-minister, Gene Bardwell wanted the job of marrying them, but he lost out to Eileen's minister.

By 1944 the U.S. had fully converted to a war-time economy, and nearly everyone was cooperating with the war effort. Even politicians from opposite parties forgot their differences. In an effort to keep inflation from skyrocketing, the government had frozen wages, prices and rent. Congress had also passed a surplus profits tax in an attempt to control war-time profiteering.

The urgent military requirement for war materials and supplies caused many shortages on the home front, so a national rationing system was established and successfully administered by local volunteer boards in each county. Rationed items included: meat, butter, sugar, coffee, canned goods, shoes, oils and gasoline. Citizens were issued monthly ration books with stamps for each item. If an individual had a legitimate need for more of one item, such as gas for a car pool, he could apply to the board for additional stamps.

When my girl friend, Peggy (Margaret Gayle Hardy), and I went to the movies or dinner, we normally rode the bus or our bicycles to save gas. Peggy, a 1941 graduate of Connecticut College for Women, was a reporter for the *Elmira Star Gazette.* She started on the newspaper at the social desk, and by 1944 she had progressed to a reporter with a Sunday column.

On Saturday, the 29th of January, 1944 my two older brothers and I left the plant an hour early for my wedding. I was married to Peggy Hardy at 4:00 p.m. The ceremony was held at the home of her mother in Elmira, with only immediate family members present. Bardwell was again disappointed because he did not get the call.

Early in January, American Aviation of Jamestown, New York had notified us that their first TDR-1 (secret expendable torpedo bomber) had an in-flight problem, and they had lost the ship and test pilot. This was kept confidential; the Navy did not allow any radio or newspaper reports of the crash. I was handling the TDR-1 coordination with American Aviation and was told, late in the day, to be at Jamestown for an important meeting at 8:00 a.m. the next day. The only way I could get there on time was to drive 220 miles on a narrow, winding, rough road. I took a night shift employee, Leo Bernat, with me to drive so I could sleep in the car. (Leo was drafted the following month, joined the infantry and was killed in action in Germany on December 21, 1944.) Around midnight, we stopped for a coffee break in an old restaurant at a small town called Bolivar. I went to the men's room, which was at the end of a long hallway. The Bolivar air raid siren went off while I was in the men's room, and all the lights in the restaurant and in the town were turned off. As I tried to find my way back to the restaurant, I tripped over a mop pail filled with water. I fell, got all wet, ripped my pants, and hurt my leg. I had no extra clothes with me; so when the lights went on a half hour later, I had no choice but to continue the trip dressed as I was. When I arrived at the 8:00 a.m. meeting, my pants were wrinkled and torn, and I was limping. The subcontract manager took one look at me and said, "Bill, you look like you had a rough night."

All the key subcontractors were present at the meeting. The Navy informed us that their preliminary investigation indicated that the crash was the result of poor workmanship or defective material. They ordered all assemblies, parts, and materials to be reinspected. SAC had delivered about ten sets of airplane parts, and some were now in American Aviation's production line. It was agreed that anything on the line would be reinspected by American Aviation, and all other items would be returned to SAC. This became a serious problem because our Navy inspector at SAC had limited aircraft knowledge, and now he was scared of his own shadow. After we reinspected a part and found it met specifications, he would sometimes find microscopic reasons why he could not accept the part. TDR-l production at subcontractors' plants and at Jamestown was tied up in knots. Fortunately for SAC, our other work was going well, especially our largest project, the C-46 Curtiss underwing fuselage assembly.

By the end of March, the TDR-l project was moving again; and American Aviation had delivered four or five aircraft. However, on April 4, 1944, the Navy terminated the program without any advance notice. Although no public statement was made by the Navy, we were told that the rapid development of shipboard radar (which was then able to compensate for the rocking of the ships) had made the expendable TDR-l aircraft obsolete. The TDR-l had also become impractical for the torpedo bombing mission because it lacked speed and maneuverability as compared to the suicidal Japanese Kamikaze torpedo bomber.

Later we learned that our first glider delivered to the Navy in June, 1941 had played an important role in the development of the air-to-air flight control system used in the TDR-l mission. The glider was towed aloft by an airplane. A second pilot in the tow-plane had a radio which would operate the glider's controls. He actually flew the glider while it was in tow and also after it was released. The glider pilot only monitored the controls to prove out the radio system. Later, in an effort to simulate an actual mission, the Navy made tows and landings without a pilot in the glider.

The Normandy invasion by the Allied Forces took place on June 6, 1944. Of the more than 11,000 aircraft that participated in the invasion, over 1000 were cargo gliders that carried troops, jeeps, light artillery and small tanks. These gliders continued to play an important role in the war as the Allied Forces swept across France into Germany. Many of their pilots had received their basic training in Schweizer gliders.

Helicopters were not used in the European Theatre. They were just in the development stage and were not available to the military in quantity until late in 1944. Only five years earlier, in September, 1939, Igor Sikorsky made the first successful controlled helicopter flight in a very crude machine called the VS-300. Sikorsky successes with helicopters followed quickly, and by 1943 the U.S. military was actively interested in Sikorsky's whirlybirds. With a contract from the AAF, the XR-4 experimental aircraft was placed in production at Sikorsky's facility at Bridgeport, Connecticut. Two improved versions of the R-4 were simultaneously developed and became the R-5 and R-6.

In the spring of 1944, the AAF gave Sikorsky a letter-of-intent to purchase 1000 of the R-6 helicopters even though the model was still in the design stage (*Figure* 22). This was a two-passenger observation ship powered by a 245 hp Franklin Engine built by Aircooled Motors of Syracuse, New York. In June,

1944 SAC received an order from Aircooled to build the engine housing and external cooling system. This was SAC's first introduction to helicopter production.

The first recorded mercy mission by a helicopter occurred in January, 1944. In a snowstorm, the Coast Guard flew blood plasma to 100 crewmen burned in an explosion aboard a U.S. destroyer a few miles out of New York Harbor. The military services immediately became interested in having a fleet of helicopters.

The SGU 1-19, a single-place training glider built from nonstrategic material, was designed by Ernie and his staff as a fill-in engineering job during 1944 (*Figure* 23). The objective was to have a low-cost trainer ready as the war clouds dissipated for the postwar glider market. In the fall, with a minimum of tooling, a "quick and dirty" prototype of the SGU 1-19 was built. It flew well, and we were glad to have a ship available to fly for pleasure.

On the 19th of November, Peg and I had a son, William Stuart Schweizer. Peg's grandmother was concerned that we were going to have a "premature baby." The day Stu was born, I called her and said, "We had a boy, and it has been nine months and 19 days since our wedding." She replied, "What did you do the first 19 days?" Doctor Scott Howland kept Peg in her hospital bed for nine days after Stu was born. This was standard practice at that time. When she finally got out of bed, she practically had to learn to walk again. Peg's private room at the Arnot Ogden Memorial Hospital cost a total of $68.75. Dr. Howland, Elmira's first obstetrician, charged a total of $50.00.

During 1944, SAC performed subcontract manufacturing work for five companies, with the C-46 Curtiss project amounting to 60% of our business. It was a general education for us to learn how to follow and understand the drawings and quality specifications of each company, but we picked up new ideas that helped us improve our manufacturing know-how and management control systems. SAC had a profitable year, which allowed the Company to improve our shop and office equipment and our inventory of supplies. SAC's average employment for the year was 116 people.

The war was now going well for the Allied Forces and as early as January, 1945 Washington started to cut back some military programs. The U.S. aviation industry began to plan products for the postwar market, and SAC followed suit. The Company hired Frank Hurtt, a personal friend of the Schweizers, who had advertising and commercial art experience in New York City before the war. Frank worked with Paul to develop a marketing program to promote both SAC and our postwar gliders. Frank had been a member of the Hudson Valley Club, owners of the first SGU 1-7 glider. During the war, he was a glider instructor at the AAF Mobile, Alabama base and later taught power flying there.

Frank proposed a series of Schweizer ads in *Aero Digest,* the leading aviation magazine at that time. The magazine's representatives visited the Company to discuss the proposed ads and were given a tour of our shop. They were intrigued by the rotating assembly jigs we used to build the C-46 Curtiss project. The jigs used when the unit was built at the Curtiss plant were stationary which presented many difficulties for the assemblers. We explained that in order to improve workmanship and production efficiency, the assembly jigs were designed to rotate. This allowed the worker to perform his work conveniently with no climbing or crawling under the assembly (*Figure 24*). *Aero Digest* was interested in publishing an article on this subject. We thought this would be a good and inexpensive way to promote SAC, so I wrote an article with the help of my "reporter wife." It was published in February, 1945.

On January 7th, Ernie and Eileen had a daughter, Susan Eileen Schweizer. (The race was on, but we both ended up with four children.) Ernie, the proud father, opened the Coke refrigerator for the employees. Then, Coke came in a bottle and cost 5 cents. In March of 1945, SAC won the competitive bid to build the two rudders for the AAF C-82 Fairchild Flying Boxcar. The project was expected to continue in production during the postwar period so the aircraft would be available for the U. S. Army of Occupation in Europe and Japan. We were, therefore, very pleased to win this job.

The C-82 was a cargo airplane with a rear loading ramp door large enough to accommodate a pick-up truck. It was also an ideal ship for paratroopers; with a rear door exit, the prop blast was minimal, and the high tail precluded chute fouling.

On April 12, 1945 Franklin D. Roosevelt died, and Harry S.

Truman became the President of the United States. Victory in Europe (VE Day) occurred on May 7, 1945. The first atomic bomb was dropped on Hiroshima on August 6, 1945 and the second on Nagasaki on August 9, 1945. On August 14th (VJ Day), Japan surrendered. On August 24th, all AAF subcontract work was cancelled, with the exception of the Fairchild C-82 rudder project. Schweizer was forced to lay off 51 of its 149 employees.

When the mass contract cancellation took place, SAC was in a healthy financial position. In theory, when a contract is cancelled, the government pays for the inventory of raw material and parts on hand that would have been required to meet the contract schedule. We were aware, however, that inventory payments in contract cancellations were usually a judgment call. Therefore, when the war started to change in favor of the Allies, we worked to keep our inventory at a minimum. Our foresight paid off, and SAC received a fair settlement which resulted in additional profit.

The extremely high war-time corporation tax rate prevented the Company from keeping a reasonable amount of profit. Therefore, during the last four months of the year, we decided to invest our year-to-date profit in product development and marketing. This would allow SAC to get off to a good start in 1946. The Company's objective was to return to the glider business and to develop a product line of sailplanes. Our first project was a single-place trainer, the SGU 1-19, which was already in work. Two other projects were on the drawing board: a two-place, advanced trainer which was an up-dated version of the Army SGS 2-8 and a high-performance, single-place competitive sailplane.

When the war ended, the light-plane manufacturers looked for a peace-time bonanza in sales, which was confirmed by an industry-financed survey. In the fall of 1945, the industry could not meet demand. Piper Aircraft was building 15 Cubs per day.

SAC was overwhelmed with the same grand illusion. The Air Age was here, and Schweizer was preparing for the explosion of the gliding and soaring movement. In November, 1945 SAC hired three ex-Air Force pilots to work with Paul to set up a sales department. One of the pilots was Larry Creighton, a well-known Elmiran. At that time, light planes like the Piper Cub, Aeronca, and Taylorcraft had a sales price between 2000 and 2500 dollars. We felt that in order to make the SGU 1-19 competitive, it should sell for about 50% of the light plane price.

We had a good start on the 1-19 production development when our military contracts were cancelled in August, 1945. The FAA certification was already underway and was completed in November, 1945. The general plan was to have the single-place trainer ready for the market by January, 1946. Our sales forecast called for 440 ships to be sold in 1946. (This now seems like a very optimistic projection.)

In order to achieve the sales goal, the 1-19 glider had to be thoroughly tooled so it would go together like an erector set with a minimum of hand labor. To achieve the desired price, we calculated that a minimum of 400 gliders had to be built and sold. The sales price would be based on the projected man-hours after the first 100 units were built. Assuming a production rate of two ships a day, we established a production estimate of 230 man-hours per ship as the shop goal. The price breakdown for the 1-19 was as follows:

Labor rate of .90 cents per hour x 230 hours =	$207
Overhead and administration cost estimated at 150% of manufacturing labor cost	$311
Material cost plus handling & storage	$232
Total Cost	$750
Profit 12.5%	$ 94
Sales price to dealer	$844
Dealer's Commission 25%	$281
Sales price to customer	$1125

According to our production estimate, 58 workers were required to build two ships per day. SAC had about 30 workers on the SGU 1-19 tooling and production development. These individuals would be switched to production, and the Personnel Department was scheduled to recall about 25 people during January, 1946. By year's end, the Sales Department had about 20 good domestic dealer prospects and a number of foreign sales leads. This was encouraging, but we started to have some new concerns. Our salesmen found out quickly that the airplane fixed-base operators (FBO) wanted a low-cost, two-place glider which would allow them to give dual instruction and rides using aero tow. Early in December, Ernie dropped the project of updating the military TG-2 glider and went to work on a low-cost, two-place sailplane, the SGU 2-22 (*Figure 25*).

16

17

18

16. The new Schweizer plant at the Chemung County Airport, near Elmira, N.Y., March 1943. *17. TG-3 trainer wing assembly in the humidity-controlled wood shop.* ***18.*** Final assembly of TG-3 trainers.

19 

20 

21 

19. *U.S. Navy TDR-1 expendable torpedo bomber by Republic Aviation, 20% Schweizer-built.* Warren B. Skelton ***20.*** *Curtiss Wright C-46 with SAC fuselage and underwing assemblies.* Smithsonian Institution ***21.*** *Testing a USAF glider pick-up system.* Loomis National Soaring Museum.

22

23

22. Sikorsky R-6 observation helicopter with SAC components, first to go into military production, 1944. Sergi Sikorsky Collection *23. The SGU 1-19, the first SAC glider after World War II built on non-strategic materials.*

23A

24

***23A.** C-46 underwing component and **24.** innovative Schweizer-designed rotating assembly for manufacturing.* Aero Digest

25

26

25. *The SGU 2-22 training glider; 258 were built, mostly in the 1950s.* **26.** *Attempts to motorize the SGU 1-19 fell short of expectations; the project was dropped as the available 16hp engine was not powerful enough.*

5

THE POST WORLD WAR II ERA 1946–1949

In January, the single-place SGU 1-19 was FAA certified, tooled, and production was underway, and the SGU 2-22 prototype, a low-cost, two-place trainer was put in work. In answer to the Sales Department's request, the Company set a goal to certify the 2-22 and have it tooled for production by May. In some cases, to expedite the project, the design was finalized while the prototype was being built. It was a real Company fire drill, and everyone pitched in to make it happen. The 1-19 was put into production first because it was developed as a fill-in job during the war and built from non-strategic materials.

Ten 1-19 gliders were produced in January-and the production schedule called for 20 in February, 30 in March, 40 in April and then for production to remain steady at a rate of two gliders per day. By January, our glider salesmen had ten firm orders and about ten good sales prospects for the 1-19. However, our salesmen were somewhat discouraged because they were convinced that large-volume sales would not develop until they had a two-place glider to sell with the 1-19. The Schweizer brothers realized the importance of getting the two-place in production but were not ready to accept the Sales Department's gloomy conclusion. We felt the spring weather along with more glider demonstrations would help stimulate sales. Demonstrations along with direct selling were now required.

Most of our sales prospects were located at airports, and all of our salesmen were pilots, so SAC purchased an airplane. An AAF surplus BT-13 was purchased for $975, a fraction of the original cost. The company aircraft allowed sales personnel to make more calls per day, so their traveling cost was reduced.

As a result of WWII glider training experience, aero tow and dual instruction were now becoming the accepted methods of launching gliders and training students. During the prewar period, two principal methods were used to launch gliders: motor-driven winch or auto tow. SAC knew the change from single-place to dual instruction was coming, but we did not think it would happen so fast.

The clubs were slow to reorganize after the war because most members or potential members had new family responsibilities and additional expenses. Therefore, our principal prospects were the airport FBOs who wanted to aero tow two-place gliders. SAC looked into ways to simplify the launching of gliders and to make them more acceptable to airports.

During this postwar period, there were numerous European war refugees traveling around the U.S. looking for a home. A number of these were scientists who were involved in gliding before the war and who came to Elmira because they were familiar with Schweizer sailplanes. When we talked to them about new methods to launch gliders, they generally suggested motor gliders or a portable rocket. One scientist tried to sell his glider design to us, then his helicopter, but without success. Then as he was leaving, he said he also had the cure for the common cold but assumed we did not want to get into the drug business.

On an experimental basis, Ernie converted a 1-19 to a self-launching motor glider. A 16hp Andover Motors engine, which was the auxiliary powerplant used on the B-29 bomber, was mounted over the wing center section and fitted with a pusher propeller (*Figure 26*). It was an interesting experimental vehicle but had little commercial value. The motor glider was underpowered, and there were no satisfactory 20 to 25hp engines available.

SAC also made the 1-19 glider available in kit form for the home builder and aviation schools. However, only a small quantity of kits were sold. The results of this project did not justify the time and effort required to develop the instruction manual nor the cost associated with marketing the kit.

Our glider sales program suffered a further setback when the AAF released over 1000 WWII two-place training gliders for public sale at about 20% of their original cost. The sales price ranged from $350 to $500 per glider compared to $1500 for a new 2-22 (*Figure 25*). SAC produced twenty 1-19 gliders in February. Production was reduced to ten gliders in March and then was stopped in April because there were more than twenty complete ships in inventory.

The new prototype 2-22 made its first flight on the 8th of February. It flew well, and our salesmen thought it was just what the airport FBOs wanted. Unfortunately, it took about three months to certify and complete production tooling. SAC was running out of funds for product development and was faced with the standard manufacturer's dilemma: How much tooling could we do on the 2-22 project and still achieve a competitive price? Due to financial pressure, SAC decided not to tool the 2-22 as thoroughly as we did the 1-19.

To help create interest in the new prototype 2-22, SAC's Frank Hurtt and Richard Powell made a record duration flight of 10 hours and 9 minutes on the Harris Hill ridge. Although the 2-22 was designed to sell for just under $1500, it proved to be hard to sell to the airport FBOs in competition with the bargain-priced AAF surplus trainers.

The Schweizer brothers finally accepted the fact that there would be a small market for new gliders until the surplus ships were absorbed. In spite of financial problems, however, SAC decided to complete the production development of the 2-22. We had faith in the ship and believed a future market for it would develop. The FAA Certification was completed in May, and there were three firm orders for the new ship with a few very good prospects. A realistic production program that would at least break even called for producing and selling one 2-22 per week. Unfortunately, the market was much smaller than that.

The Soaring Society of America (SSA) was inactive during WWII but was reorganized in the spring of 1946. Ernie and Paul were elected directors of the SSA. This was important public relations activity for the Company. After the war, there were many ex-servicemen and women who wanted to learn to fly gliders but did not have the funds to take lessons. The Society was instrumental in getting the G. I. Training Bill to include glider training. To take advantage of this, SAC organized a glider school, which opened for business May 17, 1946. The three pilot salesmen taught at the glider school and continued to work on glider sale leads at the same time.

With the bargain-priced military gliders flooding the market, the sailplane manufacturing business outlook seemed bleak at SAC for the next year or two. Our bread-and-butter business became the manufacture of the rudders and ailerons for the Fairchild C-82. The Flying Boxcar actually turned out to be one of the very few military aircraft projects not cancelled after VJ Day. SAC was extremely fortunate to have this job continued. Most of our subcontract competitors went out of business or converted to non-aircraft production. The C-82 work at SAC required about 35 shop employees. With the low volume 2-22 glider production, aircraft service and repair, as well as the glider school, the total SAC organization was reduced to 71 employees in May.

My second son, Paul Hardy Schweizer, was born on May 3, 1946. Three weeks later, on May 28, the Chemung River flooded. It was the worst flood in the history of this region. There were two to six feet of water in downtown Elmira. Peg and I lived at 405 Hoffman St., two blocks north of Church St., and water came within 200 feet of our home. Ernie lived on Hampton Road, on the southside of Elmira, and he was flooded out of his home. We had no water problem at SAC. Piper Aircraft at Lock Haven was devastated with eight feet of water in the main assembly plant.

That spring I became concerned about SAC's ability to support three executive salaries. The sailplane business was flat, and aircraft subcontracting opportunities were very scarce. I thought, in fairness to my brothers, it might be a good time for me to look around for another position. I was 28 years old and wanted a career in aviation. I realized that some diversified aircraft experience and additional formal education in industrial engineering and management would be beneficial to me, and, I hoped, to SAC in the long range. This could not be accomplished in Elmira, so I decided to start looking around.

Commonwealth Aircraft Corp of Valley Stream, Long

Island, New York, manufacturer of the Navy J2F WWII air/sea rescue amphibian, was getting back into commercial aircraft production. This company had purchased the design rights for a small twin-engine, all-wood amphibian called the "Trimmer." They were looking for someone with experience in building molded plywood, stressed skin aircraft structures. An FAA inspector who had serviced SAC during the TG-3A production and was impressed by our operation and recommended me for the job. Commonwealth knew our business at SAC was very low. They contacted me in April and offered me a job, which I turned down. A month later they came back again with a better job proposal. They offered me the position of assistant factory manager in charge of the Trimmer Amphibian manufacturing operation.

This opportunity created a very difficult decision for me because of my loyalty to SAC and to my brothers. I enjoyed my work at SAC, and my brothers and I worked well together. Although I was a member of SAC's management, I did not have stock ownership because my brothers started the Company while I was in college. After a long soul-searching talk with my brothers, I decided this was the time for me to get some varied aircraft experience with another company, so I accepted the Commonwealth offer.

I joined Commonwealth Aircraft Corp on June 15, 1946 as assistant to the factory manager. After receiving an introduction to the company's systems at the main Valley Stream plant on July 15th, I was appointed assistant factory manager in charge of the Port Washington plant where the Trimmer amphibian was being manufactured.

In the July 19 issue of the *Elmira Star Gazette,* a story caused great concern among SAC's employees and management. The Aviation Committee of the County Board of Supervisors had decided to recommend that the Board file an application with the government to turn over the government-owned building occupied by SAC to the county free of charge. The Aviation Committee wanted to use the facility as the county's air terminal.

Ernie and Paul met with the employees and explained that this was only the idea of three or four supervisors on the Aviation Committee and that the Board was composed of 23 supervisors. They also said that SAC was negotiating with the government to buy the facility, but if worst came to worst and the proposal did receive approval, it would take many months to consummate. SAC would have ample time to secure new quarters. Leslie D. Clute, a leading Elmira citizen and businessman, was asked by Attorney Bob McDowell to assist SAC with this problem. With Mr. Clute's help and assistance from SAC Directors and the Chamber of Commerce, Ernie and Paul were able to convince the County Supervisors that the Aviation Committee's proposal was not in the best interest of the community. In August, Mr. Clute was elected a director of SAC. (See Appendix 11)

In September, Piper Aircraft gave SAC an order to build the tail surfaces for their new prototype all-aluminum, four-place Sky Sedan. They also wanted a quotation on 1000 and 5000 sets of production tail surfaces. Piper's combined production of the two-place trainer and the three-place Cruiser totalled 30 airplanes a day. Employment had increased from a war-time average of 400 to 2600. Piper had no room for the Sky Sedan production and planned to subcontract the project. In the late fall, however, the aircraft demand was starting to decrease and the Sky Sedan project was put on hold.

In November, Fairchild's C-82 schedule was reduced by 50%, and SAC employment dropped to 65 employees. It became clear that SAC must start looking for commercial products.

The 2-22 glider was a bright spot. The current demand was only about one or two gliders per month, but there were good indications of a growing long-range market for the ship. My brothers felt that a high-performance, single-place sailplane was needed to help support the 2-22 and contribute to the growth of the soaring movement. Ernie, with Paul's input, came up with a preliminary design for the high-performance SGS 1-21. The business plan called for management to come up with 20 orders complete with a down payment to help finance the development.

My job at Commonwealth Aircraft Corp. was an interesting learning experience. However, I was under a great deal of pressure because my bosses' goals were unrealistic. They were trying to satisfy the unreasonable demands of our sales department. The light airplane industry was booming and manufacturers could not meet the demand.

Commonwealth was building three different airplanes: a Navy air/sea rescue amphibian, the Skyranger, a deluxe high performance two-place plane (production rate 5 per day) and the Trimmer Amphibian, which was my project. Commonwealth purchased the Trimmer design and a flying prototype from the designer, Gilbert Trimmer. This small, all-wood, twin-engine amphibian was designed to sell for $6,000. Commonwealth had experience during WWII building an all-metal Navy JF "Duck" air/sea rescue amphibian aircraft. They planned to go head-to-head with the new all-metal Seabee amphibian built by Republic Aviation Corp. Republic, a war-time producer of fighter aircraft, had invested millions in the Seabee program as their major post-war commercial airplane project. It was designed to be built with automotive production methods, and the sales price was an unbelievable $3,995. Both companies had orders and deposits for a large quantity of amphibians. The general feeling was that they could sell all they could build.

In mid-July, when I took over the management of the Port Washington division, a new Trimmer prototype with the necessary changes to meet FAA certification was under construction. The production planning and tooling was aimed at aircraft deliveries starting in October.

As I became familiar with the airplane's design, I became concerned whether the Trimmer could be built and sold profitably for $6,000. I found out later that Commonwealth had accepted Gil Trimmer's sales price for the aircraft without making their own detailed cost analysis. I made my own ballpark estimate, and it looked like the price should be at least $10,000.

I had my methods engineering group make an accurate bill-of-material and a detailed man-hour estimate for all parts and assemblies required to build the Trimmer Amphibian. The manufacturing data and estimates were completed early in September. When I applied the company's standard cost information plus dealer's commission to the material cost and labor estimate, it showed the Trimmer's sales price should be $11,500. I rechecked the figures carefully before I showed it to my boss, who was vice president in charge of manufacturing.

At first, he did not believe the figures. Then, I prepared a confidential report with charts, learning curves, graphs, etc. After a careful study, he agreed that my figures were logical and he became concerned. We were spending large dollars preparing the design for production. The new prototype for FAA certification was flying, and the expensive manufacturing tooling program was almost complete. We had purchased the engines and raw materials for 50 airplanes.

My boss and I both realized that if the program was not going to be profitable, it would reflect on both of us. A meeting was arranged with the president of the company, and we showed him our findings. The question was: Would the Trimmer Amphibian sell at a price of $11,000 to $12,000? (In 1988 dollars, this would be a $180,000 airplane.) In late October, the aircraft industry sales were starting to soften and the president stopped the Trimmer project. I closed up the Port Washington plant and was paid until the end of the year. I had two months to find a job. By year end, the light plane industry plunged into a depression.

Over thirty-two thousand commercial light planes had been built since VJ Day in August, 1945. By February, 1947 the complete light plane industry was at a standstill. Even Piper Aircraft was in the hands of its New York City bank, Manufacturers Trust Co.

Business analysts said the industry depression was caused by the manufacturers' false notion of the size of the market. There was a very large shortage of airplanes after the war, and many buyers who wanted just one aircraft placed orders with two or three concerns and then took the first one available. In addition, many people who wanted an airplane found out they could not afford one.

In 1947, the Army Air Forces became a separate military service independent from the U.S. Army and was named the United States Air Force (USAF).

That year, Chuck Yeager, a USAF Captain, made the first supersonic flight in a Bell Aircraft rocket plane, the X-1. Meanwhile, Ernie and Paul had their problems at SAC. Glider sales were even slower than the 1946 level because Army surplus gliders were still available at a very low price. SAC decided to disband the glider dealer organization and sell directly to the customer. Unfortunately, the lower price did not significantly improve sales. At the same time, new subcontract business was at a virtual standstill because military aircraft builders had a huge surplus of facilities and available manpower. Therefore, for survival SAC had to acquire some non-aircraft business.

Larry Creighton, one of SAC's glider salesmen, left the Company in the summer of 1946 to run his family-owned milk distribution business in the Elmira area. He was aware of SAC's desire to diversify and suggested the Company consider building aluminum milk cases. He pointed out that Thatcher Glass Manufacturing Corp., a leading producer of milk bottles, had its main office in Elmira and might also be interested in the aluminum cases.

Larry explained that when the war ended the milk bottle industry switched from round to square bottles to make their product more efficient from a space standpoint. Wooden milk cases, which held 12 bottles, were still the standard in the industry, even though they were heavy and unsanitary.

The Schweizers liked the suggestion and built some experimental cases. They were used in Larry's operation and also reviewed by key individuals in the dairy industry including some Thatcher Glass executives. With some modifications, Larry felt aluminum cases would be enthusiastically received.

Larry decided to form a company which would buy cases from SAC and distribute them on a national basis. He and two Thatcher Glass executives and a local dairy equipment distributor formed a company called Glider Metal Products, Inc. SAC received an order with a down payment from them in February for six freight car loads of aluminum milk cases (17,600) at two dollars per case.

We had high hopes for the new product, but sales did not develop as expected. All of the milk cases were eventually sold by Glider Products, but SAC did not receive a reorder. Larry and his partners felt they got into the business about a year too late. It was a selling job to get dairies to convert from wooden to aluminum cases in spite of their advantages. In retrospect, Glider Products was actually ahead of its time because aluminum milk cases were to become the standard in the industry in the 1950's and 1960's before the advent of plastic.

SAC also investigated a number of other commercial products such as beer containers, bread baskets and other lightweight, aluminum containers but did not develop any volume orders. After years of building high quality aircraft products, the Company found itself at a slight competitive disadvantage. It was hard to shift gears and produce low-cost, slam-bang commercial products.

Even though in 1947 there was a good supply of training gliders available for the soaring movement, there were very few high-performance, single-place contest sailplanes. Those available were largely pre WWII European designs or homebuilts. Ernie and Paul felt there should be a market for a contest-type sailplane. The Company already had a preliminary design for a ship of this type, the SGS 1-21. However, that project had been set aside because the Sales Department had wanted a two-place trainer immediately. Therefore, the 2-22 had taken precedence. The design of the 1-21 was put back on the drawing board in the fall of 1947. The Company also released the preliminary design and specification of the 1-21 to the soaring public and announced that if there was sufficient interest, SAC would build the ship. The Company's business plan called for 20 firm orders before sailplane production would start.

However, when the design phase was complete in January, 1947 there were only two firm orders. The first order came from Dick Comey, the General Manager of the Soaring Society of America (SSA). He wanted his 1-21 ready to fly in the National Soaring Contest in July at Wichita Falls, Texas. Comey's request presented a difficult decision for the Schweizers. Here was an opportunity to show off the 1-21 at the nationals and to have a top, competitive pilot fly it. If it performed well, SAC felt it would be of great value to the Company. The Schweizers concluded that it was hard to sell a "paper airplane," a design that had not been built and flown. Therefore, they made the decision to build two prototypes with minimum tooling.

With a Herculean effort from SAC personnel, Comey's ship was completed a week before the contest. This left him little time for testing and practice flying. The ship flew well and exceeded its estimated performance, and Comey won the championship. In doing so, he set a new distance record of 303 miles, flew 1748 miles during 11 contest flights, and spent 50 hours in the air.

The 1-21 was a step ahead of the other contest ships available in the country at that time (*Figure 27*). Ten years later Stan Smith won the National Championship with the same ship. The

1-21 had an all-aluminum structure with a streamlined monocoque fuselage. The ship also had two new features: spoilers on the top and bottom of the wing, which could be locked in four positions, and wing water ballast tanks with dump valves, which permitted a 260 lb load of water for high speed cruising on days when the air currents were strong.

The 1-21 was designed to sell at three to four thousand dollars. After building two ships, however, a cost analysis showed it would cost five to six thousand dollars to build it on a production basis. In spite of the 1-21's acceptance, the cost was more than people were ready to pay for a sailplane. An analysis of the 1-21 design showed the ship could be simplified without hindering its performance. An outgrowth of this ship was the SGU 1-23, of which 74 were built over the next 15 years (*Figure 28*).

Meanwhile, Paul and attorney McDowell continued to negotiate with the government to buy the Big Flats building and equipment. Late in 1947, SAC was finally allowed to purchase the plant from the War Assets Administration for $110,500 on a ten-year mortgage with a 20% down payment. The government-owned equipment was purchased for $22,517 with a five-year mortgage and a 20% down payment. The cost of the building, land and equipment amounted to approximately 40% of its original cost. Because the mortgage payments were less than the monthly rent payments to the government, SAC was actually able to reduce its operating costs and, at the same time, acquire an asset.

As soon as I closed up the Commonwealth Port Washington plant, I was busy job hunting. A week or two later, an interesting opportunity developed. The executive vice president of Edo Aircraft Corp., the leading aircraft float builders, told my former boss they were looking for someone to head up their production engineering section. My ex-boss recommended me for the job. After a series of interviews, I understood that I was the number one candidate. My Commonwealth salary ended on December 31th, and I was anxious to get started at Edo.

In the meantime, I heard that Long Island Agricultural and Technical Institute at Farmingdale was looking for someone to do liaison work with the Long Island aircraft industry. Long

Island A & T, a division of the New York State University system, was originally a two-year agricultural college. After WWII, the college set up a technical division to serve Long Island industry. The director of the new technical division wanted a liaison person on his staff to keep in touch with the aircraft industry and determine how the institute could be of service.

I interviewed for the job and the director seemed interested in me. He was not sure if liaison work with the aircraft industry would be a full-time job in the beginning. When he found out I could teach basic college physics, he offered me both the liaison job and the physics position on a fifty-fifty arrangement starting in January.

I checked back with Edo, and they gave me encouragement but there was no firm job offer. I decided to accept the Long Island A & T offer, since it had some appealing fringe benefits. They encouraged their staff to do graduate work and permitted time off for this purpose as long as it did not interfere with job performance. I was also somewhat tired of the industrial rat race and needed some time off from it. Two or three days after I accepted the teaching job, the Edo job came through. I stuck with my first decision, and I believe it turned out well for me.

I started my new job in January and began teaching two classes of physics in February. I applied and was accepted at the Graduate School of Business at New York University. This was a top notch business school that operated from 3 p.m. to 10 p.m. for junior executives in the New York City area. I started in the spring term of 1947 with a major in industrial management. In addition to graduate courses in business management, my program included all of the basic industrial engineering subjects required for that degree. Besides my undergraduate Bachelor of Science degree, when I completed the program, I would have the equivalent of an undergraduate industrial engineering degree as well. I continued two evenings a week and completed my Masters program in December, 1950.

The liaison work with the Long Island aircraft industry opened many doors for me, and many of the contacts were helpful to me in later years. I was also able to do some liaison and investigative work for SAC. My brother Paul was not married, and he would come to Long Island to spend Christmas with us. This gave us an opportunity to catch up on family matters and to exchange business information. I normally spent a week or two in Elmira each summer, and we talked over mutual problems.

Just when Ernie and Paul thought everything was running smoother at SAC, they experienced another serious setback. Since WWII, SAC had been building the rudders and elevators for the Fairchild C-82, the Flying Boxcar. This was profitable work, and Fairchild was pleased with SAC's performance. After the postwar glider sales problem, SAC had kept its development and promotional expenses in line with what the business could afford. Since Fairchild was SAC's largest customer, their economic well-being was very important to us. In November of 1947, the USAF stretched out the C-82's airplane schedule. Fairchild pulled back all airframe subcontracts except for the work at SAC. The scheduled rate was reduced 40%, and SAC would complete its orders by June, 1948 with no promise of a follow-on contract. This resulted in a layoff of twelve people, and the Company ended the year with 55 employees.

In spite of the problems ahead, SAC paid its first Christmas Bonus of $2,639 (15% of profit before taxes), which averaged $51.76 per individual. The employees worked hard during the year without wage increases to help the Company compete for new work which was profitable. The bonus was a surprise payment made to all employees the day before Christmas. It amounted to approximately a week's pay and was greatly appreciated.

In January, 1948, at a Farmingdale TV store, I watched President Harry S. Truman give his state of the union address. Television had started to replace radio with live coverage of important political events. The demand for television sets was enormous, and manufacturers could not meet the demand. TV stores placed sets in their windows, and crowds gathered on the sidewalks to watch programs. There were about 10,000 sets in the United States in December, 1945, and five years later there were over six million. Peg and I held off buying a TV set until 1949 because we did not quite accept TV, and it was expensive. Meanwhile our kids became very friendly with neighbors who did have TV sets.

The post-war environment was creating rapid social, technological and economic changes. Society had many new demands for expendable income, which directly affected commercial glider and airplane sales. Employees were demanding increases in wages and fringe benefits. SAC's average wage in January, 1948 was $1.10 per hour, which reflected a 20% increase over a two-year period. Employees were starting to expect hospital insurance, life insurance, paid holidays, paid annual vacation, etc. SAC had just established an annual vacation plan, which was a major new operating cost. The plan granted one week vacation for one year's service and progressed to two weeks for five years service. SAC employees were paid in cash as required by law because there were no banks or check cashing services in the vicinity. In 1948, there were no polio shots, credit cards, coin vending soft drink machines or small computers. Chips meant a piece of wood, hardware meant nuts and bolts, and software was not a word found in the dictionary.

The U.S. Air Force continued a modest postwar cargo glider development program after the war. Although the value of the cargo glider was in question, most military leaders agreed that a great deal had been learned about cargo glider operations during WWII and that such a vehicle should be re-evaluated. As a result of that decision, the cargo glider section was reinstated at Wright Field and manned by officers who had gained glider experience during WWII. Major Floyd Sweet, an active soaring pilot formerly from Elmira, was named the Project Engineer of the Wright Field assault transport section. His first job was to define the cargo glider's function in modern warfare. The next step was for the engineers to write design specifications for the proposed ship. They planned two gliders, a twenty and a fifty-passenger model, which they proposed to build, test and evaluate. The twenty-passenger glider was put in work first and identified as the CG-18. It was basically a replacement for the all-wood WWII CG-4A glider. The specifications called for all-metal construction, a rear loading ramp, and the capability of being towed at over 200 MPH.

Chase Aircraft Co., Inc. of West Trenton, New Jersey was a small military aircraft modification company headed by an aggressive Russian, Mike Stroukoff. When he learned about the AAF cargo glider proposal, he hired a few top-notch engineers with experience in the cargo glider field. As part of their quotation, they developed a functional preliminary design to the specifications. Wright Field liked their ideas. Chase's competitors were four or five large aircraft companies with little experience in the field and high hourly cost structures. This gave Chase a distinct advantage; as a result, it received an order to design and build seven CG-18 gliders.

Chase lacked adequate manufacturing facilities, so the company required assistance from aircraft subcontractors. Major Sweet was a good friend of the Schweizers and was familiar with the Company's experience and capabilities, so he suggested that Stroukoff consider SAC. Chase personnel looked over our Company and liked what they saw. SAC was, therefore, given an opportunity to quote on the tooling and construction of seven sets of tail surfaces for the CG-18. SAC won the competition and received this order in December of 1947. With the Fairchild C-82 due to phase out in June, 1948, this new business was a lifesaver for our Company.

The glider business at SAC was at a standstill except for the continued interest from contest pilots for a high performance sailplane. In January, SAC decided to build one prototype of a simplified design that had been under study during the previous six months. The ship was called the SGS 1-23. The goal was to have the ship ready for the national contest to be held in July, 1948 in Elmira. SAC received a firm order for the prototype from Bill Frutchy, an ex-AAF pilot from Elmira. The ship made a good showing, but Frutchy did not have sufficient contest experience to win the competition.

Although our glider business was depressed, we were still optimistic about the future of this product line. We spent a significant amount of time and effort promoting our glider school program, and with the help of the GI Bill, the school continued to be profitable for SAC.

SAC was desperate for additional business and was continually bidding on non-aircraft military supply equipment open to public bid. Normally, there were numerous bidders and the competition was fierce. Whenever SAC won a bid, the first question asked was: "What did we leave out of the estimate?" In the summer of 1948, SAC bid on 2850 dollies to be used for transporting auxiliary power units. The Company's bid was $60,000 or $21.05 per unit. The material cost was $10.50 which left $10.55 for labor to manufacture, package and ship each unit.

After the award, SAC Treasurer, Nick Haich, looked over the bid and noticed that the contingency and profit of 15% had been left out of the bid. The factory personnel made the parts and the office staff, including Personnel Director Eugene S. Bardwell and the Schweizer boys pitched in to assemble and package the dollies to avoid a loss on the job.

The first Chase CG-18 glider flew in June, 1948. The test pilot experienced operational problems in high speed tows of over 200 mph and in making landings on short fields. The AAF and Chase both agreed they should consider converting the glider to an airplane. On an experimental basis, two engines, with nacelles from another military airplane, were mounted under each wing. The ship became the C-122 and was first flown in late September. After the first flight, the Chase test pilot told Stroukoff that the airplane needed a new horizontal tail with more dihedral and span. Stroukoff, the excitable Russian, did not agree and fired the test pilot. Subsequently, the AAF pilot flew the airplane and agreed with the Chase pilot. As a result, the AAF told Stroukoff to change the tail, or they would cancel the contract. Stroukoff called Ernie early in October and said he needed a new tail for the C-122 with more span and 10 degree dihedral. This resulted in a major design change and required a considerable amount of new tooling. SAC worked around the clock, and six weeks later delivered the new tail to Chase. The new tail improved the flight characteristics of the C-122 and made it an acceptable airplane. This SAC fire drill saved the job for Chase as well as for Schweizer.

In the meantime, things were working out well for me at the State University. I enjoyed teaching basic college physics. Because of my keen interest in aerodynamics, I gave my students a little extra on the theory of why and how airplanes fly. My graduate school work plus family responsibilities kept me busy. Because of my practical experience, I found the industrial engineering courses especially enjoyable and worthwhile. Fortunately, Peg and I worked well together, and we enjoyed our family life. My liaison work with the Long Island aircraft industry was very interesting and quite a learning experience for me. I was also pleased that, in a small way, my knowledge about the Long Island aircraft industry was helpful to my brothers at SAC.

On February 14, 1948, our third son, John, was born. My

mother-in-law commented, "For a production control expert, three sons in four years does not look very good." On March 21, 1948, Ernie and Eileen had their first son, Leslie Ernest Schweizer.

In January, 1949 there was an opening on the SAC board because Douglas G. Anderson, President of Hardinge, had resigned due to other business pressures. The Directors looked for a replacement who might be helpful to the Schweizer brothers in developing a plan to obtain new business. Alexander G. Long, Vice President in charge of Manufacturing at American LaFrance Foamite Corp., appeared to be an excellent candidate and agreed to serve. (See Appendix 9.)

At the February Directors' Meeting, it was suggested by Mr. Long that SAC management should find some qualified manufacturing representatives who could help direct business opportunities or bids to the Company. A representative of this type normally works on a commission basis and is assigned to a geographic area or to specific companies.

Director Les Clute suggested SAC management talk to his friend George Chamberlain of Buffalo about representing Schweizer. George was a former buyer for Curtiss Wright during WWII, so he knew his way around aircraft purchasing organizations. He represented three or four other concerns who each had different types of product lines and capabilities. They would not be competing for the same work, since none of them had the capability to build airframe assemblies. He was interviewed and hired to represent Schweizer at Curtiss Wright and Bell Aircraft in the Buffalo area.

In 1949 the production of the Chase Aircraft control surfaces constituted the major part of SAC's work. In July, Chase received an order to build fourteen C-122 cargo airplanes. This was the CG-18 cargo glider design that had been converted to an airplane. In turn Schweizer received a contract from Chase to build the C-122 control surfaces. With this new order SAC's Chase business volume would continue at the same level until the fall of 1950. This project required about 20 direct shop workers. During the year, a number of small jobs were also acquired from other companies including Link Aviation and Curtiss Wright Rocket Division. However, more production was needed to make the Company profitable.

In spite of the fact that SAC needed work, the production of the high performance SGS 1-23 developed in 1948 was on hold because management estimated that ten firm orders were needed to make the program viable. By January, 1949 there were five orders and by March, there were nine (*Figure 28*). The Directors then agreed that the sailplane should be produced. The ten ships were completed by year end, but the project was not financially a break-even. This was due to delivery pressure which forced production to start before tooling was completed and resulted in more costly hand work. The sales price of the standard 1-23 was $2200. However, most ships were sold with extra equipment and special options; so the average price was over $2500 which helped to reduce the cost overrun.

To attract a major airline to service the Elmira area, Chemung County had to extend their 4500 foot runway (24/6) to 5200 feet. In order to do this, they needed 12.5 acres of the north end of SAC's 29.1 acre plot of land. SAC was not using the land, and the Directors felt that the Company should cooperate. The rationale was that airport improvements should be a plus for the Company, and if SAC wanted to expand, there was land available to the east. The 12.5 acres were sold to the County in August 1949 for $2200. This was a little over the going price for airport land at that time, $150 per acre.

In August, George Chamberlain acquired some experimental helicopter work for SAC from Bell Helicopter Co. on the new Model 47 helicopter, which three years later played a very important role in the Korean War. Incidentally, this was the whirlybird used in the television show,"M*A*S*H". This introductory work with Bell gave SAC an opportunity to prove itself and was the beginning of a long and successful business relationship with the Bell Helicopter Co.

Progress was made in business development in 1949, and SAC's backlog was increasing. In January, SAC had 40 employees and by year end, 69. The Corporation's gross sales for 1949 were $248,000. In June, 1949 the Company had an operating loss of $9,100 which was reduced to $2,300 by the end of the year.

At Long Island A&T, I was relieved of my half-time physics teaching assignment and asked by the director of the technical division to develop a one-semester course entitled "Introduction to Industrial Management." The course was designed to provide the student with some background of how an industrial organization functioned. It was hoped that this course would help the technical student make a better adjustment to his job in industry. The curriculum included a brief background of the various types of corporate organizations and attempted to provide the student with an understanding of the responsibilities and the relationship of several common industrial functions such as product design, tool design, inspection, quality control, manufacturing methods, production control, material control, time study, purchasing, personnel, industrial relations, general accounting, cost accounting, etc. I felt that the course was well received by the students, and I enjoyed teaching it.

As part of my liaison work with the Long Island aircraft industry, I learned that the personnel departments in a number of plants were interested in finding out what other companies were doing in the areas of job evaluation and merit rating. During WWII, due to government price and wage control, all of the manufacturing companies were required to have some formal system. However, after the war it was optional. I carried out a survey of job evaluation trends in seven Long Island aviation plants. After the companies studied and released the report, it was published in the August 15, 1949 issue of Aviation Week.

As the Schweizer business grew, so too did the Schweizer family. On September 4, 1949, Ernie and Eileen had their third child, a cute little girl, Sally Schweizer. Now they were even with Peg and me. My brother Paul, who was not married, had bought the old Owen farm on Route 17, Big Flats. My father, who had retired from business, moved to Elmira and lived with Paul.

27 

28 

27. The 1-21 carried Dick Comey to the 1947 national soaring championship; ten years later Stanley Smith won it in the very same sailplane. ***28.*** *Paul A. Schweizer flying the SGS 1-23 in 1949. This sailplane stayed in production from 1948 to 1974, and 74 ships were built. With annual design updating, it remained competitive. In 1961, Paul F. Bikle set the world altitude record of 42,303 feet in a 1-21.*

6

THE KOREAN WAR PERIOD 1950–1953

The big news story for the last six months of 1949 was the trial of the former high U.S. State Department official, Alger Hiss. In January, 1950, he was found guilty of passing documents to the admitted spy, Whittaker Chambers. In his effort to defend the nation against possible aggressors, President Truman ordered the construction of the hydrogen bomb, the "super bomb."

In June, Truman ordered the U.S. Air Force and Navy to fight in aid of South Korea. Trouble had been brewing in the Far East since the summer of 1949, and our military had been preparing for war. The USAF had a requirement for an assault aircraft to move troops and large equipment into the battlefield. Chase Aircraft received an USAF contract to build two experimental aircraft: the XCG-20, a 50-passenger glider; and the XC-123, a powered airplane version of the XCG-20. The USAF planned to evaluate both of these aircraft and determine which one could best perform the mission (*Figure 29*).

In January, 1950 SAC received an order from Chase to build a set of tail surfaces for both the XCG-20 and XC-123. The contract called for SAC to build the two sets with minimum tooling and deliver them within eight months. This created another real fire drill at SAC.

The tail surfaces for the two 50 passenger ships were delivered during the third quarter of the year. In addition, the production of the fourteen sets of tail surfaces for the smaller Chase 20-passenger airplane continued at the rate of one set per month. During the first three quarters of 1950, Chase was our largest customer, but by mid-year, the Korean War was underway and other work developed with Bell and the USAF. Therefore, in the fourth quarter, our customer base was far more diversified.

After the 50-passenger transport glider and airplane was flown and evaluated, the USAF concluded that the glider was not suitable for the mission. However, the Air Force was very favorably impressed by the airplane version of the glider, the XC-123, as an assault transport. It had the capability to operate with a full load from an unpaved runway on a relatively small field.

The Chase XC-123 50-passenger assault transport had an interesting history. We watched it develop and change manufacturers twice. SAC became involved with it again in the mid-1950's when the airplane was built by Fairchild Aircraft Corp. Soon after the Korean War started, the USAF decided they needed a large quantity of C-123 transports. Chase Aircraft did not have the facilities or organization to take on this production responsibility. The AAF paid Chase handsomely for their part in the development of the design and then looked for a large aircraft manufacturer to build the C-123.

During WWII, Kasier Industries had developed an outstanding record for building Navy ships and airplanes and still owned the Ford Willow Run Plant in Detroit where the B-24 bomber had been built. Kaiser was awarded a contract in 1951 to build a large quantity of C-123 airplanes. Unfortunately, they had problems getting the airplane in production, and when the war ended in 1953, the Kaiser contract was cancelled before they delivered their first completed C-123. The USAF still had a requirement for a quantity of C-123s, so in 1954, Fairchild Aircraft was awarded a contract to build the assault transport. SAC became a major subcontractor on the project.

As a result of the Korean War aerial combat, tow targets were needed to train fighter pilots in air-to-air target practice. In June of 1950, SAC was awarded a fixed-price contract by the U.S. Navy to build a quantity of 141 Aero X-27A Tow Targets (*Figure 30*). This vehicle was designed for the Navy by Chance

Vought Corp. The target mission was to tow the craft aloft by an airplane, similar to the way a glider was launched. When at the desired altitude, a winch in the aft fuselage section of the tow plane extended the tow line so the target X-27A trailed the tow plane by about a mile. Fighter airplanes then made passes and shot at the target for practice.

Our Company was the low bidder of nine other aircraft companies, nosing out Beech Aircraft by a few dollars per unit. The aircraft industry was hungry for work, and in an effort to win contracts, jobs were bid without a safety factor and often ended up under-priced. That was what happened to SAC on the tow target contract. The SAC bid price per target was about 10% too low. In addition, SAC's bid was submitted in the spring of 1950 just before the Korean War started, and we did not foresee the rapid inflation ahead. By year end, 37 targets had been delivered, and SAC had a $40,000 loss on the project. However, we hoped that the Company would break even on the balance of 104 left to build and that a follow-on contract would develop at the proper price.

Finally by the fall of 1950, George Chamberlain's work at Bell Aircraft began to pay off for Schweizer. Initially we built a section of the Bell Model 47 helicopter's welded fuselage and then gradually took over the complete structure (*Figure 31*). The original Bell schedule was for one ship set of parts per week and then it rapidly increased because the U.S. Army found out that the helicopter was a valuable new tool for liaison and rescue work in Korea (*Figure* 32).

The U.S. Army told Bell Helicopter Company that they would buy as many Model 47 helicopters as Bell could build through 1952. Bell's goal was to increase its production rate to two ships per day. To assist with their acceleration, SAC accepted the job of building the complete cabin assembly.

SAC's backlog of orders grew from $250,000 in September to $600,000 in December, 1950. Employment increased from 75 to 165 during this period. Fortunately, the Bell and Chase work was profitable and absorbed the tow target loss. The Company ended the year with sales of $364,192 and a small profit of $3,997.

Since the end of WWII, SAC had been struggling due to a lack of profitable business. This condition required that Ernie and Paul make many personal sacrifices to keep the Company alive. Then in 1950, they had a new challenge—more business than they could handle. This created a shortage of floor space, equipment and working capital. This situation also highlighted the fact that more sophisticated production and quality control systems were necessary at SAC.

Financing of the business for the increased volume was probably SAC's most serious problem. During the previous five years, there had been practically no growth in the Company's working capital, which comes from profits earned or the sale of stock. Management tried to raise money with a stock offer in 1947 and again in the fall of 1950. Both attempts were unsuccessful because of the Company's poor earnings record and because there was no market for the Schweizer stock. The Chemung Canal Trust Co. reluctantly supported SAC with the essential working capital loans so it could squeak by.

Due to the capital problem, we were forced to purchase mostly used equipment. Ernie was interested in machinery and picked up some real bargains. We often kidded Ernie about how he found these opportunities. We said that when he planned to visit a machinery dealer, he just avoided shaving for a few days and wore his favorite old hat.

Winston Churchill was returned to power in 1951 after being defeated five years earlier. Joe Louis was knocked out by Rocky Marciano. According to Jane's Naval Annual, the Soviet Union planned to increase their submarine fleet to 1,000, which was considered to be far in excess of normal requirements for defense. President Truman relieved General Douglas MacArthur of his Far East command for not supporting the United States and United Nations policies in fighting the Korean War.

With the war in high gear, and being an industrial engineer with practical aircraft manufacturing experience, I had a number of lucrative job opportunities in the Long Island aircraft industry that became more difficult to refuse. My job was going well at Long Island A.&T., and I had just received a promotion. The salary was good for a teaching job because we were part of the new, expanded New York State University system. On the negative side, I had opportunities to do consulting work on Long Island but had to turn them down because there would have been a conflict of interest with my industrial liaison work at the college. However, on my vacation and on some weekends during the previous year, I did consulting work at Helio Aircraft Corp., Norwood, Massachusetts.

Helio Aircraft was founded by an MIT aerodynamicist and a Harvard Business School marketing professor. They developed an aircraft that was capable of landing on and taking off from a football field. Their management lacked practical aircraft manufacturing engineering know-how and needed a consultant to assist them in aircraft production planning, tooling and estimating. This was an interesting assignment and helped me realize I wanted to get back into the aircraft manufacturing business. Peggy and I had three fine young boys and decided we did not want to bring them up in the Long Island area. Stuart, our oldest, was in first grade. Peg, being an up-stater, did not want the boys to acquire a New York City accent.

From time-to-time, my brothers and I talked about my rejoining SAC. In January, 1951, Ernie and Paul, with the approval of the Directors, offered me an opportunity to return to SAC as an equal partner in ownership and management. This appealed to me, and I accepted the offer. To become an equal partner, it was necessary for me to invest all my savings and to take on a long-term loan from a local bank. The three Schweizer brothers each owned approximately 25% of the Company's stock, and the balance was owned by 30 other individuals.

I completed my teaching job on May 15, 1951 and rejoined SAC as Vice President in charge of manufacturing. I had left SAC exactly five years earlier to acquire outside experience and additional industrial engineering and business management education. Upon my return to SAC, I was pleased to receive the full cooperation and friendship of our employees and key personnel—Eugene Bardwell, Nick Haich, Paul Pullen, Ernie Whidden, Don Semski, Don Quigley, Howie Burr, Don Dunton and John Griswold. I also found that conditions in the cafeteria had not changed. No one could tell the difference between the meat loaf and the Spanish rice. Everyone received a large or small portion depending on "Ma" Ballard's mood of the day or whether she liked them.

It was agreed by the three Schweizers that each one would have his area of responsibility in the operation of the Company. All three would work on business development and work as a team on major operating decisions and Company policy items. If two wanted to go in one direction and the third did not, the majority ruled. Once a decision was reached, we displayed a united front.

From our experience as a family organization, we learned that a trio works better than a two-man management team. We also learned that good communications and a healthy respect for each other's rights were extremely important. In my opinion, these two factors, critical to the survival of any family business, gave us a strong management team. With three individuals answering to the name of Schweizer, more territory could be covered in one day. One could be visiting a subcontractor, a second in Washington on military business, and the third home minding the store.

The Tow Target project, which had been in production since June, 1950, was developing into a large Navy project even though it had not yet been put in service in their fighter aircraft training centers. President Truman's new mandate for joint service cooperation required the Navy to offer their 27A Tow Target to the USAF. As a result, the new joint service requirement for the 27A called for an additional 1000 targets.

In January, the Navy negotiated a follow-on order with SAC for 320 targets. The new price was 10% higher than the original contract price. We felt comfortable with it now that production was running smoothly. Deliveries on the new order started in April at a rate of 32 per month. During the negotiations with the Navy, we asked for a recovery of our loss on the first order, but we were turned down.

In June of 1951, the Navy decided to purchase 700 more 27A targets on a competitive bid. SAC's price proposal was based on our actual experience which included some improvements. To our surprise, we were underbid by East Coast Aviation Corp. of White Plains, New York. They bid the exact same price as we had on our original order the year before. We did not know how they came up with their price but knew it was too low. In addition, material and labor costs had inflated significantly since the start of the Korean War. Within a month, East Coast was at our door asking us to be a partner on the project. We turned them down.

In the fall of 1951, Ernie visited the Navy fighter plane base at Patuxent, Maryland because their first shipments of 27A targets were not flying properly. He watched one roll up into a ball of metal on take-off. There were no movable control surfaces or guidance systems in the tow target to keep it flying level while it was being towed. Ernie agreed with the flight personnel at Patuxent that the 27A in its present form was not practical. It was unbelievable that the Navy had launched a major production program without first building some prototype targets and thoroughly testing them. Three months later, the production project was cancelled. It did not affect SAC because we were just finishing our second contract. East Coast, which was behind schedule and in financial trouble, accepted the cancellation gladly. They were paid off by the government for all their direct costs on the project.

On the other hand, military writers reported that the new Bell Model 47 Helicopter was a success and playing a vital part in the rescue and liaison mission in Korea. The amount of work SAC performed on each helicopter was increasing as was the rate of production. By September, SAC was producing two ship sets of parts per day which now included the cabin assembly. George Chamberlain, our Bell representative, received an excellent return since his fee was tied to our volume of Bell business. We found George easy to work with and he performed a number of other liaison functions for our Company. He had confidence in Schweizer and showed it by his willingness to invest 50% of his fee in SAC stock. In November of 1951, he was elected a Director of our Company because we felt he could help SAC with long-range business developments. (See Appendix 11.)

Back in 1948, the USAF had cut Fairchild's C-82 production rate to a trickle, and SAC lost its C-82 airframe subcontract work. We kept in contact with Fairchild, however, and did some small rush jobs for them from time-to-time. Fortunately for Fairchild the USAF provided funds so they could continue to develop and improve their cargo airplane. This led directly from the C-82 to the large and more powerful C-119 transport airplane (*Figure 33*). Suddenly the C-119 was in great demand in 1951 to support the Korean War effort, but only a small quantity had been built. The military wanted additional airplanes as soon as possible for delivery of equipment and supplies to our fighting men in Korea. The USAF increased Fairchild's production quota to 30 aircraft per month starting in November of 1951. Fairchild needed help and asked us to assist. They negotiated a large quantity order for C-119 ailerons and rudders (*Figure 34, 35*). This new Fairchild project worked out well for SAC because our Chase work had been completed and the 27A tow target was scheduled to phase out in January, 1952.

In January, 1951, our shop superintendent, Paul Pullen, observed about ten employees wearing UAW buttons. They continued to wear them for the next month, but there were no obvious union activities at the plant. In March, professional UAW organizers associated with Bendix Machine Company's UAW International Union in Elmira Heights started to distribute literature one morning each week. The literature outlined the merits of a UAW union and announced that our wages were well below those at Bell Aircraft of Buffalo where a UAW union was in operation. Apparently, the organization plan at SAC had been initiated by the Bell UAW union. Bell was sending subcontract work to SAC because it was more economical to do so, but the union was not happy with the work going to a non-union shop.

We hired James L. Burke, a local labor relations lawyer, to advise us. We worked with our supervisors and did a self-evaluation of our management style. Without promising additional benefits or making threats, we attempted to quietly correct legitimate inequities or problems. We also advised our employees that we did not think a UAW union was in the best interest of the employees or the Company.

A group of employees decided to start an Independent Union to fight off the UAW. The NLRB held a collective bargaining election in August. The choices were: UAW, Independent Union, or no union. The Independent Union won with 38% of the votes; the UAW received 34%; and no union, 28% of the votes. The NLRB said a majority vote was needed for certification of a union, and they scheduled an election between the Independent Union and UAW. The Independent received 60% of the votes. We attempted to work with the Independent Union, but the organization was ineffective. It lacked leadership, and employees did not want to attend meetings after working hours, nor did they want to accept union responsibilities. In addition, there was friction between the union and the supporters of the UAW cause. The only practical solution we could see was to have another election with the question: UAW or no union? It was necessary to wait over a year for this decision because the NLRB would not hold another election within a twelve month period. (In January 1953, the employees voted with a 2/3 majority against the UAW.)

During 1951, our work force grew from 165 to 258 employees and we were cramped for space. (See Appendix 1.) Our most pressing problem was lack of floor space for receiving, shipping and crating. For example, we were shipping 32 tow targets a month, and each one required a 18 × 4 × 3 ft. enclosed wooden shipping box. In the northwest corner of the plant, a 43 × 64 ft. receiving and shipping addition was built plus a 22 × 80 ft. carpenter shop. This increased our total floor area from 32,530 to 37,387 square feet. (See Appendix 2.)

The glider school activity was growing, but glider sales were very slow. Experimental glider development work was kept to a minimum because we were concentrating on getting our sub-contract work on schedule and making the Company profitable. We ended the year with a profit before taxes of $147,525, a 7.8% return on sales of $1,885,781. The tax rate was very high during the Korean War, and our after-tax profit was $51,445 which reflected a 65% corporate tax. The Company's employee bonus fund was $14,951 which was paid to 260 employees. The average bonus was approximately a week's pay, $57.50.

In 1952, Dwight D. Eisenhower and Richard M. Nixon were elected President and Vice President, respectively, of the United States. A serious polio epidemic spread throughout our country that year, and Peg and I were worried about our children. Thank God, this was the last major outbreak of polio before the Salk vaccine became available. Interest rates were low, but with the wartime inflation, they started to increase. The average rate charged by banks on a home mortgage was 3%. Savings banks in New York state were given permission to increase interest rates paid on accounts from 2% to a maximum of 2½%. Westinghouse Corporation built a plant in Horseheads to manufacture television tubes. They wanted to be close to the source of glass tubes, Corning Glass Works.

The tempo of the Korean War increased, and the government had established a national wage and price control system in an attempt to curb war-time inflation. The light aircraft industry was starting to recover, but the sailplane business was still depressed. SAC was busy even though the tow target project was phasing out in January. Our principal business included the Bell 47 Helicopter components and the Fairchild C 119 ailerons and rudders.

By the fall of 1952, Fairchild was building 30 large C-119 transport airplanes per month, and SAC had to build a minimum of 120 large control surfaces per month to keep up with them. This meant 30 left and right ailerons and 60 left and right rudders. The large volume of Fairchild repetitive production allowed us to break the project down into small work segments for each employee. The results were better efficiency than estimated and a very profitable job. The bulk of this profit was used to buy small hand tools, equipment and supplies which we could write off in one year. We did this to reduce the profit and to properly equip our expanding work force.

After I left Long Island, I started a quiet crusade to make SAC an airframe subcontract supplier to Grumman Aircraft Corp. Grumman had a proven, select list of suppliers which was developed during WWII, and it was hard for a new company to get on this list. In the spring of 1952, Grumman decided to evaluate Schweizer Aircraft. They sent up a four-man team to survey our facilities and our manufacturing control systems. They liked what they saw, and SAC was chosen to be one of the bidders on their Magnetic Airborne Detector Boom (MAD BOOM) which extended from the aft fuselage of the Grumman S2F-1 Tracker (*Figure 36*). This boom was part of a very important new U.S. Navy aircraft system to search for and attack submarines.

SAC was not the lowest bidder on the MAD BOOM; but Grumman liked our technical proposal which was a detailed report with sketches showing how we planned to tool and manufacture the boom. A week later, we were called to Bethpage to discuss our technical proposal. This went well and SAC was awarded the contract. The agreement called for building the production tooling and manufacturing 514 MAD Booms over the next three years (*Figure 37*). This project gave SAC an opportunity to prove ourselves to Grumman and to develop Grumman as a long-range customer.

Back in 1950, the U.S. soaring movement had received some international recognition when our friend, Paul B. MacCready, Jr., a Yale physics major, entered the first World's Soaring Championship held at Orebro, Sweden. His father, Dr. Paul P. MacCready, Sr., a well-known eye-and-ear surgeon, was his crew chief at the competition. Paul earned the right to represent the United States because he had won the 1948 and 1949 U.S. Soaring Championships. He was a very talented young college man who had beaten the best and most seasoned soaring pilots in the U.S. With a rented Swedish sailplane, Paul surprised the top European pilots by finishing in second place in the World's Championship.

The second World's Soaring Contest was scheduled for the first two weeks of July, 1952 at Carabanchel, Spain. The Soaring Society of America decided to sponsor a U.S. team for this event. The SSA wanted American pilots to fly American ships and asked for help from SAC. Our Company was then operating profitably, and we agreed to supply two sailplanes. This project looked to us like a worthwhile investment that would promote Schweizer sailplanes in the world market.

Two improved versions of the SGS 1-23 were built and sent by boat to Spain. One was flown by Paul MacCready and the other by brother Paul. They did not win the competition but made a good impression. Paul MacCready finished 6th and Paul Schweizer finished 19th. (Paul MacCready earned his P.H.D. from CalTech and today is a well-known atmospheric and aero research scientist in his own research company. Paul won worldwide recognition by designing and building two muscle-powered aircraft, the "Gossamer Condor" and "Gossamer Albatross." The former won the Kremer Prize in 1977 when it flew the required course, and the latter one made a flight across the English Channel in 1979. The ships had pedals similar to that on a bicycle that were used to turn the propeller, so the pilot pedaled to supply the power for take off and flight.) Ernie had made the trip to Spain with the team and served as an advisor and participated in a number of technical meetings. After the meet in Spain, Paul, Ernie and his wife Eileen went to Switzerland to visit our relatives and tour the Alps. This was the first real vacation my brothers had taken from SAC since they started the company, and it was well deserved.

In the fall of 1952, SAC received an interesting experimental assignment from General Electric, the type of project Ernie enjoyed. Companies such as Douglas and Boeing were starting to design jet transport airplanes, and GE was interested in getting into the jet aircraft engine business. GE's research engineers wanted to operate their prototype engines in flight before they installed them as the sole power source in an airplane. In order to do this, they asked SAC to design and build a jet engine mount which would support the engine below the belly of a B-29 bomber (*Figure 38*). During the test flight, when the B-29 reached the desired altitude, the pilot shut down the four radial engines, and the experimental jet engine took over. This allowed the engineers to observe the engine's operation in flight and to take measurements to determine its operating power, fuel consumption, etc.

The fall of 1952 also brought changes to my family. One noon at lunch, Peg told the three boys she was going to have a baby. Johnny, the youngest, looked up at Peg and asked, "Does Daddy know?" On October 3, 1952, Peg and I had our fourth child, Gayle, a pretty little girl whom the boys loved and later, loved to tease.

Four young children kept us both very busy, but it was a wonderful experience. Work and family responsibilities totally absorbed my time. Ernie had the same problem. The Schweizer brothers normally worked 50 to 60 hours per week (*Figure 39*). Occasionally, I gave glider rides to business visitors at SAC, and sometimes I took a recreational flight after work just to be alone and relax. It was a great form of therapy for me. Paul, a bachelor, was an ideal uncle to our kids. He spent his free time gliding and promoting soaring. He was a director of the Elmira Area Soaring Corp. and the Soaring Society of America.

Our employment for the year 1952 averaged 248 workers. Our diversified manufacturing operation required more floor space, so three building additions were built to increase our floor area from 37,850 to 46,000 feet. (See Appendix 2.) The additions:

A 63 × 90 ft. metal parts fabrication building with a truck height receiving dock,
A 30 × 90 ft. finishing building with two paint spray booths,
A 22 × 60 ft. office extension.

The glider sales showed slight improvement, and at our annual meeting, we told the stockholders that the military surplus gliders were gradually being absorbed, and we looked for reasonable glider demand by 1954. Seeking diversification, SAC purchased the rights and tooling for the aluminum milk case which we built for Glider Metal Products Corp. in 1947 and 1948. For a market test, a series of aviation metalworking kits with instructions were developed and sold to vocational training schools.

For the Company, 1952 was an excellent year. Our manufacturing capabilities (equipment and facilities) were greatly improved. A profit of $370,401 (16.5% on sales) was earned before taxes with a profit of $115,890 (5.2% on sales) after taxes. With the surplus profit tax in effect during the Korean War, 69% of our profit was paid to the government. A bonus of $38,005 was paid to 255 employees, which averaged $149 per employee, in excess of two weeks pay.

We planned a Christmas Party for the employees and their families and expected about 500 people. Bardwell, our Personnel Manager, took a survey the day before the party, and it looked as if nearly 800 people might come to the party, so he ordered 300 more ice cream Santa Clauses. He picked them up himself before the party and left them in the trunk of his car to keep them cold. Apparently, we did not need the extra ice cream, and Bardwell forgot about it. He did not open the trunk of his car until the next spring, when he smelled an odor. What a mess!

In January, 1953 the NLRB finally allowed the run-off election for the UAW union vote. Even though two thirds of the employees voted against the union, the Schweizers recognized that we needed to pay more attention to employee relations. Within a month, the Company organized an employee/management council composed of one elected member from each department including the office. Monthly meetings were held with only the three Schweizers representing management. In theory, each council member represented his or her department rather than himself or herself personally. The council worked out well and provided the employees with a chance to sound off and keep management aware of current problems.

Many historic happenings took place in the world during 1953. The Korean War was in full swing, and tensions were mounting with Russia. After 29 years of iron-hand rule in Russia, Joseph Stalin died in March. His successor was Malenkov, an inexperienced and unpredictable leader. There was great fear throughout the world that either Russia or the USA might panic and use an H-bomb. A number of our friends were building bomb shelters in their cellars and stocking them with food and water supplies.

That fall, Peg and I and our four kids drove to Syracuse to attend the Army-Syracuse football game. There was a sudden rainstorm just when we were ready to have our tailgate party. Peg and I had our whiskey sours in the station wagon's front seat, while the kids had their lunch in the back. After twenty minutes of teasing, wrestling, crying, and merrymaking, Peg looked at me and said, "Bill, don't ever build me a bomb shelter."

In January, Dwight D. Eisenhower was sworn in as President of the United States and Richard Nixon, Vice President. Eisenhower took a post-election trip to Korea to get the stalled peace talks going again. He instructed Secretary of State John Foster Dulles (who grew up in Auburn, New York and took his bar exam with Peg's father) to warn China that if it delayed the peace talks between North and South Korea, the U.S. would bomb the Chinese supply lines to North Korea. The talks then moved quickly, and a truce was signed in July of 1953. This agreement was a blessing to the world and to humanity because the Korean War could have led to an expanded war with China.

SAC management was aware that an abrupt end to the Korean War would cause some major business adjustment problems, therefore, we had been working diligently to develop new customers and subcontract products to replace the Korean war work. We acquired five new customers: Stanley Aviation, Republic Aviation, Kaman Helicopter, Link Aviation and American La France Corp.

It was obvious that the Bell 47 Helicopter and the Fairchild Flying Boxcar projects were vulnerable to a quick phase-out or cancellation. The Bell work actually phased out in October of 1953, except for the spare parts program (principally side doors) which was a little plum for SAC. When the war ended, Bell Aircraft Company of Buffalo was convinced that there was going to be a large commercial market for helicopters. They decided that an independent helicopter facility was required, so they established a division at Hurst, Texas. Unfortunately for SAC, the new facility had the capacity to manufacture their current requirement of commercial helicopters.

The USAF decided to complete the Fairchild C-119 surfaces on order, which meant our production would continue to midyear 1954. This gave us an additional year of work and was a great help to our business transition. The Grumman MAD Boom also remained in full production. It was not affected by the Korean War because it had an important anti-submarine mission in the Atlantic and Pacific Oceans.

I had been working hard for two years to acquire subcontract work from Republic Aviation Corp. of Long Island, but with little success. However, in the fall of 1953, we won a major new contract on the F-84 Thunderjet. The contract called for SAC to tool and build a large quantity of the top forward fuselage of the aircraft (*Figure 39*). This aircraft, a fighter bomber which was needed for the Cold War support, fit right into the hole left by the C-119 phase-out.

The sailplane business remained small even though SAC was the only active commercial manufacturer in the U.S. in 1953. To be a loner in a depressed industry is not normally considered a good business position. In retrospect, the Schweizer brothers had, by 1953, acquired excellent manufacturing experience and, in my opinion, were making good business decisions in all areas except in the sailplane category. This was because we had a love affair with soaring. Gliders had been responsible for getting us in the aircraft business and for making the Schweizer name well known in the aircraft community. So we had a tendency to make sailplane decisions based on emotion rather than on cold facts.

The 2-22 two-place trainer sales were very slow because the USAF surplus bargain-priced trainers were still satisfying the training requirements. Sales of the 1-23 high performance contest ship were improving. A total of twenty-five ships had been delivered over the past four years. Due to the low manufacturing volume, however, our sailplane prices were too high to stimulate volume sales. At that time, we were fortunate to not be competing with European manufacturers. Their hand-built ships were too expensive, and the shipping costs to the U.S. prohibitive.

In spite of the lack of unit sales, sailplane activity was increasing in the U.S. The Schweizer brothers felt there was a pent-up demand for a good low-cost sailplane, and since the Company was in good financial condition, we decided that the time was right to invest in the future. In the fall of 1953, we decided to design and build a prototype, the model SGS 1-26. It was designed so it could be built at the factory or sold as a kit to home-builders, with all the complicated parts made ready for assembly. We also designed and promoted the ship to be a one-design "class" sailplane so competition could be organized with all pilots flying the same ship with no aerodynamic modifications. The 1-26 proved to be a successful glider project and 700 were built over the next 25 years (*Figure 40*). (In 1965, the first annual 1-26 class national contest was sponsored by the Soaring Society of America. It is now an important annual contest and is held in a different geographic location each year).

The 1953 National Soaring Contest in Elmira received widespread publicity when three sailplanes (two Schweizers) landed at Idlewild (now J.F.K. Airport). Wind and cloud conditions were perfect for a flight to New York City, but airport officials were not happy with the unannounced landings. When they asked the pilots why they landed at Idlewild, their answer was, "Ran out of hot air." Later that same day, the New York Port Authority, which operates the New York airports, added the following sentence to its regulations, "No motorless aircraft may land or take off at a New York City Terminal without permission." (Today, even with our elaborate air traffic control system, aircraft without sophisticated electronics, including sailplanes, are not allowed to fly within 20 miles of New York City).

On that same day, brother Paul, who was flying in the contest, picked Grumman-Bethpage Airport as his goal. After Paul was in the air for a few hours, I called the subcontracts manager of Grumman Aircraft, who was a pilot and aviation enthusiast, and told him that Paul was on his way to Grumman by sailplane. Paul made his goal in six hours. It was the second longest flight of the day. Paul was wined and dined that evening by some of our Grumman friends.

The Long Island press also gave Paul's flight good press coverage. A byproduct of our sailplane business was the "free" publicity it generated about the Company and our products. Journalists were, and still are, always looking for an interesting story. To round out our public relations program and to inform the aviation industry of our product diversification, we ran a series of six ads in *Aviation Week* magazine during 1953. In 1953, brothers Ernie and Paul were jointly awarded the Warren E. Eaton Memorial Trophy by the Soaring Society of America. This award is given each year to persons who have made an outstanding contribution to the art, sport or science of soaring flight. Ernie and Paul were cited for the outstanding support given in 1952 to the U.S. International Soaring Team in Spain.

Because 1953 was a profitable year, we were able to complete our three-year plant expansion program which doubled the size of our original plant. (See Appendix 2.) In addition, we purchased new equipment that improved our manufacturing capabilities. Employment remained constant at 285, but in order to accomplish that, we returned to a 40-hour work week from the 45-hour week that was normal during the Korean War. The Company earned $339,027 or 14½% on sales before taxes. After Federal taxes and the Excess Profits Tax (for the Korean War), the retainable profit was only $107,208 or 4.5% on sales. (This amounted to a 69% tax rate on profits). A bonus was paid, which averaged $205 per employee, or a little over two weeks' pay.

29

29. *The Chase Aircraft family of prototype transport aircraft, with SAC components: Top—GC-18A, glider version to carry 20 troops; 2nd—C-122, powered version; 3rd—GC-20, glider version to carry 50 troops; bottom—C-123, powered version.* National Soaring Museum

30

31

***30.** The 29A Tow Target for practice combat by military fighters; SAC built 461.* ***31.** Fuselage assembly of the Bell 47 helicopter; SAC built more than 1,000.*

32

33

32. *The Bell 47, a star in rescue action in the Korean War—and later a star in the TV show, M*A*S*H.* **33.** *Another Korean War workhorse, Fairchild's C-119 transport, with SAC-built components.* Fairchild Aircraft Corp.

34

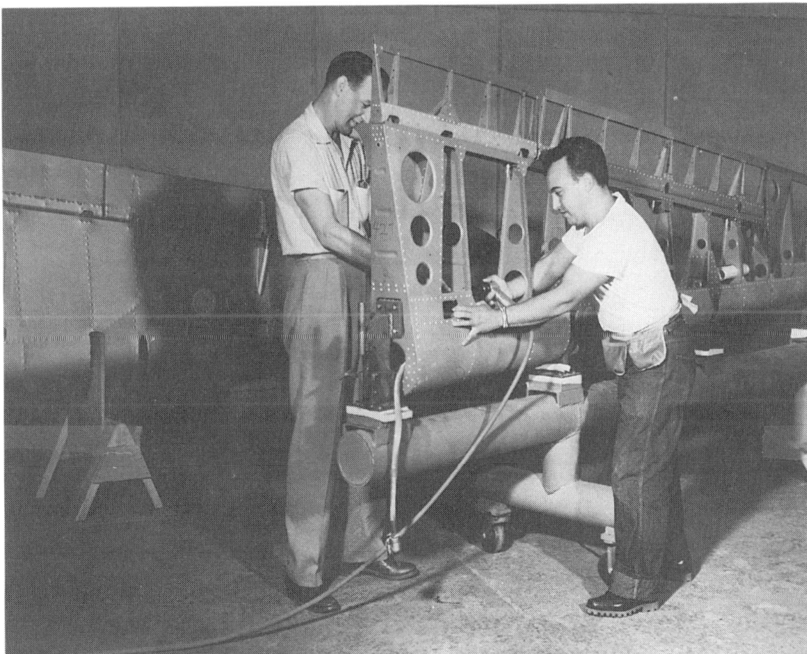

35

__34, 35.__ Schweizer workers building component parts (ailerons, rudders and trim tabs) for Fairchild's C-119 transport. This craft was an important forerunner to later huge transport ships.

36

37

***36.** U.S. Navy SZF-1 Tracker with Magnetic Airborne Detector (MAD) anti-submarine boom extended.* Grumman History Center ***37.** MAD booms under construction at SAC, whose contract ran from 1951–1966.*

38

38A

__38.__ In 1952, SAC designed and built an engine mount for testing General Electric's experimental jet engine beneath a B-29 bomber. __38A.__ The Schweizer brothers at a drafting table in 1952; from left: Paul A., Ernest, Bill.

39

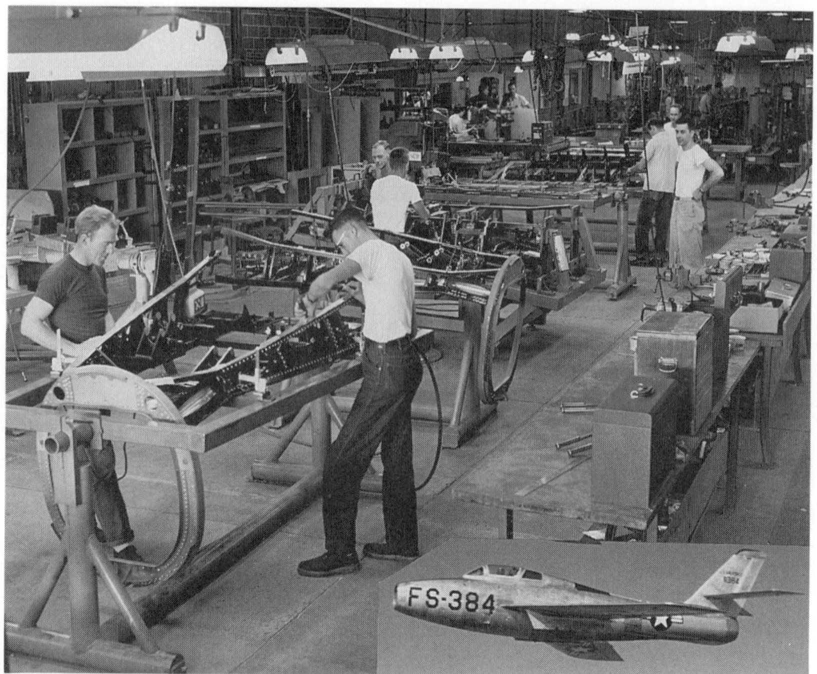

40

39. Building gun deck assemblies for Republic's F-84F fighter-bombers at SAC. ***40.*** *Classic of classics, the 126 "one-design" sailplane; Wally Scott at the controls above Odessa, Texas.* S.A. Aldott

7

BACK TO A PEACETIME ECONOMY 1954–1957

The year 1954 was one of change. I was elected to the West Elmira School Board and was trying to fight off consolidation of our school with the Elmira city system. There was still no vaccine for the crippling disease, polio. However, for the first time, group insurance plans covered polio victims, and we made this new benefit available to SAC employees. Fortunately, no one had to use it. Jonas Salk's polio vaccine was finally declared safe and effective. As soon as the vaccine was available in Elmira, we took our whole family to a local school and got our inoculations. Even before reaching the school building, we could hear the screams of the children getting their shots. It sounded like a torture chamber.

This was also a year of technical advances. The Korean War was over, and the country was readjusting to a peacetime economy. The aircraft industry was also changing rapidly. Military aircraft and airliners were converting from engines with propellers to jet propulsion. Much discussion focused on airplanes built from fiberglass or high strength plastics, ducted fans for power, and vertical take-off and landing (VTOL) airplanes that could be used in small airports the size of a football field. It was difficult for us at SAC to decide what effect these changes would have on our future, but this was not a new problem for a high-tech company such as ours.

The future is always elusive. For example, a Presidential Commission had been appointed by Herbert Hoover in 1929 to plot our country's scientific course for the following twenty-five years. The 500 researchers involved wrote a 1600 page report. Interestingly, there was not a word about jet propulsion, atomic energy, space travel, antibiotics or many other significant developments of importance in the 1950's.

The Schweizer organization decided that our best protection for the future was to improve our manufacturing fabrication capabilities. This meant adding some new machinery so SAC could assist prime contractors with some of their difficult manufacturing problems. It allowed us to handle many jobs that our competitors were not equipped to perform. This fabrication equipment is still in very active use today, 35 years later, except for the spot welder which has been replaced.

Two key pieces of equipment added in 1954 were an 800 ton hydraulic press with a 20″ × 54″ rubber pad and box for forming aluminum parts and a Ceco Stamp drop Hammer that was bought second hand from an aircraft company in Philadelphia for $16,000. The drop hammer had a 66″ × 44″ work table which gave us the capability to form large, complicated parts. The press weighed 47 tons and was 18 feet tall, which made it quite a project to move to Elmira. We built the recommended foundation for the machine outside of the plant, erected the machine and then constructed a building around it. In addition, we built a foundry next to it so we could cast large male and female dies for the hammers.

Except for a few large aircraft companies, SAC had the largest drop hammer east of the Mississippi available for aircraft subcontract work. With this new capability, SAC was able to acquire jobs that our competitors could not handle. As soon as the drop hammer was available, SAC received an order for the two camera door assemblies used on the Republic Thunderjet photographic airplane. Each assembly was built around a large compound-shaped stamping. This hammer has been in use practically every day for the past 35 years. Its tremendous mass and dropping action have caused the hammer with its foundation to sink about two feet into the ground. By pure luck, it has sunk straight down without a tilt. Twice we have dug around the machine and lowered the level of the floor for the operator.

With the war over, new aircraft subcontract work was scarce. Most of the available work was experimental and low-volume production only. SAC was fortunate, therefore, to have won the 1.2 million dollar Republic Thunderjet job. The tooling was complete in March, and the project accounted for 30% of our business for the year.

Other projects that continued throughout the year included the Fairchild C-119 ailerons and tail surfaces, Bell spare parts and the Grumman MAD Boom. Grumman was very pleased with our performance on the Boom project and sent us a letter of commendation. With our sailplane business and other small miscellaneous jobs, we had enough business to keep our organization intact.

Bell Aircraft Company of Buffalo gave us an interesting experimental job. They wanted to get into the vertical take-off and landing (VTOL) aircraft business. Bell decided to build a flying test bed at their own expense in anticipation of winning a military contract. Unlike a helicopter, which has one or two rotors that act as rotary wings, the VTOL has a conventional airplane wing which is fixed and two jet engines that will tilt 90 degrees.

Stan Smith, Chief Engineer of Bell and a Schweizer sailplane owner, came to SAC and asked us to build a modified 1-23 sailplane fuselage with a T-tail for their prototype VTOL (*Figure 41*). Bell added a Cessna 150 wing and a Bell Helicopter landing gear to our fuselage. They then installed a jet engine under each side of the wing. For take-off, the jets were pointed at the ground and then gradually, the jets were turned parallel to the ground for level flight. The ship had four compressed air nozzles which used bleed air from a third small engine in the fuselage. There was one nozzle in the nose, two in the tail, and one in each wing tip. By controlling the air flow to each nozzle, the pilot could control the flight attitude of the VTOL. The aircraft flew and proved Bell's general approach. However, on the take-off and landing it raised so much dust that it almost asphyxiated the pilot. Bell responded with another more sophisticated design but was unable to sell it to the military.

The prototype kit sailplane, the 1-26, made its first flight in January, 1954. We were pleased with its performance and general handling characteristics. During the next month, it was enthusiastically received by a number of experienced soaring pilots. In March, SAC announced that the Company would start taking orders with a price of $2,195 for the completed ship and $1,495 as a kit for the home-builder. The kit was designed so that it could be built by one man in his spare time in approximately six months.

The production decision meant the ship had to be FAA certified as a complete ship and then as a kit with an approved FAA construction manual. SAC had to build a complete set of production tools so the 1-26 could be built economically and kit parts would be interchangeable. The pre-production work was complete by the end of the year and brother Paul had come up with 40 firm orders.

The third World Soaring Championship was held in Camphill, England in 1954. Each country was allowed two single-place and one two-place sailplanes. In January, the Soaring Society of America asked SAC if they would consider building a two-place sailplane for the championship because there was no competitive American-built ships in existence. The Company decided that building such a ship would not only promote good public relations, but there might be other uses for the ship as well. The USAF was looking for an aircraft to do high-altitude wave research at Bishop, California.

The new two-place SGS 2-25 was built on an experimental basis with no production tooling (*Figure 42*). Stan Smith, the Bell Aircraft chief engineer, and his partner, Bob Kidder, flew it at Camphill. It performed well, but Stan had to drop out of competition due to a landing accident. He landed in a very small field and ran into a wooden fence. The canopy wedged under the top rung of the fence, so Stan and his partner could not get out. The two men sat there until an Englishman finally came along. He asked if they were all right, and when he was satisfied that they were not injured—he left. Brother Paul and Paul MacCready flew Schweizer 1-23's in the single-place competition. They did not do as well as expected because they were unfamiliar with the English wet weather soaring conditions. Ernie, who attended the meet as a technical advisor, called Camphill "Damphill."

In the spring of 1954, I was invited by Lynn Bollinger, Professor of Marketing, to be a guest lecturer at the Harvard

Business School. Lynn was also involved with Helio Aircraft in Norwood, Massachusetts for whom I had done consultant work when I lived on Long Island. While at Harvard, I led a two-day seminar on aircraft subcontracting. On the second day, I met with small groups and had question and answer sessions. It was an interesting experience. I have followed the careers of some of these students who are now top executives of large corporations.

SAC's employment averaged 252 individuals for the year. Sales amounted to $1.7 million for the year, and there was a small profit of $11,389 after taxes. This was the result of SAC's standard policy to charge off product development expenses in the year they are incurred. In 1954, we had the 1-26 development, FAA certification and tooling, as well as the construction of the experimental 2-25 sailplane.

From the Schweizer family standpoint, the race between Eileen and Peg ended in a four-four tie. Julie Louise Schweizer was born on the 25th of February.

Schweizer sailplanes were becoming well known in the soaring community because of their acceptance in the field. Numerous unsolicited articles about them appeared in several aviation periodicals. Since the bulk of our business was aircraft subcontracting work, we decided it would be wise to start promoting the Schweizer organization to the aircraft manufacturing industry. Starting in the fall of 1953, a series of monthly ads appeared in the industry's leading publication, *Aviation Week*. The by-line of the ad stated "Another SCHWEIZER Production Assist." (*Figure 43*) Each month the ad featured the production assist given one of our customers, such as Fairchild, Grumman, Republic, Link, Kaman, Stanley, etc.

Paul and I were members of the Elmira Rotary Club, and we had some world famous guest speakers. Remington Rand had a division in Elmira, and its chairman of the board, General Douglas MacArthur, was one of our speakers in the fall of 1954. In 1955, New York State Governor, Averell Harriman, who was a right-hand man to Presidents Roosevelt and Truman, spoke to the club. He also paid a visit to Big Flats farmer, Sloat Welles, in an attempt to solve a Route 17 problem. The new four-lane "limited access" highway that by-passed Big Flats and Elmira was nearing completion. Many farms along the way, including the Welles Farm in Big Flats just south of the airport, were denied farm crossings over the highway. Farmers were disturbed about the changes taking place in our area, but they were also well aware that their farm land was appreciating in value.

Bob McDowell had arranged the purchase of the original plant site in 1942 from farmer Kohan. In the early 1950's, Bob told Kohan that SAC might be interested in buying more land to the east for future expansion, and he gave Bob right of first refusal. In February, 1955, Steven Kohan called Bob and said his farm was for sale. We tried to buy part of his land, but for obvious reasons, he did not want to break up the farm. After some negotiations, Bob bought the 80-acre farm for $25,000. Nick Haich, our Treasurer, sold the 12 acre plot on the southwest corner of Chambers Road which had the house and barn on it for $14,000. This left SAC with 68 acres of additional land with a cost of $10,500 or $155 per acre. The twenty-seven acre portion of this land located on the east side of Chambers Road was sold to Elmira Industries in 1959 for industrial development. (See Appendix 6.)

One day that spring, Paul and I were driving to Elmira for a meeting. We stopped to pick up our *old* night janitor who was walking to his home in Fisherville a mile south of the plant. We considered him an old-timer because he was in his sixties and we were in our thirties. He had heard that SAC recently purchased the Kohan farm, and as he was leaving the car, he stopped to say, "This valley has a great future." Paul and I smiled at each other and hoped he was right. We thought then that the Kohan farm was a bargain purchase, but we did not realize just how good it was. Ten years later the land became the base for a very large shopping mall, known as the Arnot Mall.

Our business volume with Republic Aviation had expanded and had made that company our largest customer with 38% of our annual sales for the year. Grumman was holding its own, while Bell and Fairchild were decreasing. Fortunately, some new small jobs were developing which helped our volume and diversification.

All American Engineering Corp. of Wilmington, Delaware, came to us and asked for help on a new project. They had received a contract from the Marine Corps to build a portable land-based track with a catapult similar in principle to the track and catapult then used on Navy aircraft carriers. This system was designed to assist the acceleration of a jet aircraft fighter so it could take off in less than 600 feet on an underdeveloped airport. The track had to be fabricated in 30 sections, each 20 feet long, so it could be carried in a cargo airplane. All American Corp. needed help building the track because they had determined, after their bid, that it had to be made of aluminum rather than steel so it could be conveniently transported by air. A steel track would have been approximately three times heavier than one made of aluminum.

Our friend and former employee, Donald Doolittle, of Penn Yan, NY, was then vice-president and chief engineer of All American. Don had confidence in Schweizer and convinced his company to offer us the opportunity to do the detail design and build the prototype track at a negotiated price. We were pleased to accept the challenge.

The track looked like an open box from the top, with wing panels on each side to hold it in the ground (*Figure 44*). Because each individual track section had to be interchangeable with the other 29 track sections, the project required precision tooling and careful production workmanship. SAC built the track in nine months and All American installed it in the ground at Georgetown, Maryland. The airport was on the Eastern Shore of Maryland, and in the summer, the field was often covered with turkey buzzards.

In 1956, the Marines made over 100 jet airplane launches at Georgetown to prove out the system. I visited the site to see our track in operation and was impressed. The Marine pilots were well satisfied with the equipment. Although they were concerned about running into the turkey buzzards on take off, no accidents occurred. The Marines had originally talked about a production order for five to ten systems, but to our disappointment, no production order developed for the All American system. I believe this was the result of a U.S. budget problem.

In the fall of 1954, SAC received an order from Kaman Helicopter of Bloomfield, Connecticut, to tool and build 50 sets of entrance doors for their new search and rescue HOK-l helicopter. To save weight, the doors had magnesium skins which required some new fabrication techniques and controls at SAC.

The plexiglass windows were formed so they bulged outward, so we called them pregnant windows. The outward bulge allowed the observer on each side of the ship to have greater visibility, particularly under the aircraft.

For Link Aviation of Binghamton, New York, we built the canopy for their pilot and crew trainer, today called a simulator. The plexiglass canopy was formed to a shape that looked like a bathtub. We gave a rejected glass to one of our employees who boasted of having the only transparent bathtub in Horseheads.

Ernie and the chief design engineer of Piper Aircraft, Fred Strickland, had developed a good relationship. When they learned that they both enjoyed playing the electric organ, their friendship was cemented. In 1955, Piper was overloaded with development work. Fred asked SAC to design, stress analyze, and build a prototype of a new type of horizontal tail surface developed by the National Advisory Committee for Aeronautics (NACA) for their new high performance, four-place "Comanche." The conventional tail had a fixed stabilizer and movable elevators. Piper's new configuration was called a flying tail since the complete airfoil surface moves as a unit. It can rotate up to 20 degrees to control horizontal atitude of the airplane (*Figure 45*). The new tail proved to be an effective control and was aerodynamically efficient. This was a learning experience that proved to be quite beneficial to SAC. We used a similar design concept later on the 2-32 sailplane and on a number of other Schweizer gliders and airplanes.

During a late afternoon thunderstorm in June, I was driving past Paul's house when I noticed that the roof was on fire. Apparently it had been struck by lightning. I hurriedly parked my car and ran inside the house to find my father who was alone and in a daze from the thunderbolt explosion. I walked him to my car and then ran back inside the house to see what I could save. By that time, some other men had stopped and offered to help. They ran for the television, hi fi, and electric clocks, while I begged them to help me save the oil paintings—six large family portraits and some landscapes. We were able to rescue all but one large landscape that hung behind an open door. The only other things saved were the dining room furniture, the silverware and two canaries.

The oil paintings, particularly the portraits, were family

treasures. They had been painted by two outstanding artists, a German and a Pole, who had come to the U.S. before World War I. They had a studio near Carnegie Hall where my father's restaurant was located. After the U.S. entered the war in 1917, they were in disfavor in this country and were unable to find work. When they offered to paint for their meals, Papa took them up on it.

After the fire, Paul rented a furnished apartment in Horseheads and went right to work building a new, modern home on the original site. However, the fire was a traumatic shock to Papa who was then 74 years old. He rested for a month and then took a three-month vacation trip to Europe while the new house was being built.

Papa had lived with Paul since 1949 when Paul purchased the 150-year-old year old Owen farm from Matt Welles. Papa did all the cooking, and he loved it. He often put on gourmet dinner parties for the family and Paul's glider friends. During two winters, he taught a gourmet cooking class at the Elmira YWCA. To this day, I still meet women who talk in glowing terms about Papa and his cooking class of 35 years ago.

The grounds around Paul's house were extensive, and Papa loved flower gardening. He developed beautiful gardens and each year expanded them. Paul wondered how he would take care of them when Papa was not able to do it anymore.

When the new house was completed, Paul moved a job from the shop to his large basement to keep Papa busy in the winter time. The project involved cutting out and machine sewing the fabric covers for the airplane or glider control surfaces built by SAC. This was about a half week's work for the normal shop worker, but Papa did it in half that time.

The first 1-26 sailplane regatta was held on Labor Day weekend, 1955, at Elmira's Harris Hill. Seven ships were entered, and five of them were homebuilt from kits. The regatta demonstrated the fun and satisfaction that pilots and their crews receive from competing in a contest in which all the sailplanes are the same model. The 1-26 production started at SAC in January, 1954, and as of the date of the regatta, 39 kits and five complete ships had been delivered.

The 2-25 two-place sailplane built for the Internationals in England was rented in the spring by the USAF for their high-altitude Sierra-Nevada Wave Projects. Mountain waves or upcurrents sometimes extend to altitudes of over 80,000 feet. The USAF project goal was to find out what effect the wave had on the jet stream and ultimately on our weather. Airplanes and gliders were used for research flying, but the gliders proved to be more suitable to measure wave conditions. The glider flights were limited to 40,000 feet because gliders with pressurized and heated cockpits were not yet available. (Even with oxygen, a man cannot live in air pressures much above 45,000 feet.) Cockpit heat was another important factor at 40,000 feet because the average temperature is approximately -50°F degrees, and the temperature continues to decrease until the stratosphere is reached at about 52,000 feet. The USAF talked to Ernie about a larger version of the 2-25 that could carry the power and equipment to support a pressurized cockpit with heat. Ernie worked on a preliminary design, but because the USAF was not able to get the funding, the project was stopped. During the project, our 2-25 set an unofficial world's altitude record with a flight of 43,000 feet.

During the fall of 1955, the UAW launched a two-month campaign to organize a local at SAC. They passed out literature at our gate two or three times a week. We understood that the regional UAW professionals and the Bendix UAW union officers at Elmira Heights had promised the Bell Aircraft UAW union officials in 1951 that they would organize SAC because we had taken over a great deal of Bell work. They were embarrassed that they had lost two elections in 1951 and a third in 1953. Therefore, they were determined to make their word good. Basically, our approach was to talk frankly to our employees individually and as council members and tell them why, in our opinion, a UAW local at SAC was not in the best interest of the employees or the Company. The election was held in November, and 60% of the employees voted against the union.

During the year, the Company invested heavily in new product diversification and plant improvements. This reduced our profit after taxes to 1% on sales of 1.7 million. An employee bonus of $66.64 (about a week's pay) was paid to 229 employees. Thomas G. Craig, President of Chemung Valley Savings and Loan, was elected a Director to replace Alexander G. Long, who resigned because of ill health. (See Appendix 9.) The Company was honored by the induction of Ernest and Paul A. Schweizer to the Soaring Hall of Fame at the 22nd National Soaring Meet.

In 1956, Adlai E. Stevenson defeated New York Governor Averell Harriman for the Democratic presidential nomination. In spite of his heart attack in 1955, President Eisenhower decided to run for a second term and won by a landslide. Israel had become an independent nation in 1948, and by 1956 they had built a formidable army. They invaded Egypt's Sinai Peninsula in October. Nikita Khrushchev became Premier of the Soviet Union, and the Cold War really heated up.

In February, Bob Stanley, President of Stanley Aviation Corp., Buffalo, called Paul and asked if we had clearance for USAF secret information. Since we did, he invited us to visit his plant and look over his secret project. Bob said the USAF was talking about doubling the production of the project and his company did not have the capacity. He wanted to know if SAC would be interested in helping.

The project was located in a sealed-off area of the Stanley plant, and the entrance to the area was controlled by a guard and a USAF representative. The project turned out to be a small gondola approximately four by four feet in size built from aluminum parts which was part of a balloon system. There were two cameras in the gondola, one pointed toward the earth and the second pointed toward the instrument panel. The panel had a number of radios and instruments including an altimeter and a 30-day clock. It also had a bundle of electronic wiring and equipment because the balloon was monitored and remotely controlled by radio from a ground station.

Although we were not directly told its mission, it was obvious to us that the gondola was designed for a balloon that could fly over enemy territory (probably the Soviet Union) to gather photographic information. At that time, the news media reported that Khrushchev was complaining bitterly about U.S. spy planes and balloons over Russian territory. He was probably more disturbed because the Russians were unable to shoot them down. The U.S. ignored the Russian complaints. However, we now understood the reason for the secrecy of the Stanley project.

We returned with a complete set of drawings and then

prepared a cost proposal to build the gondola. Our estimators were assigned work on individual parts and sections of the job. It was done that way so estimators were unaware that the project was a balloon gondola. Just when the bid was completed, Stanley himself called and told us that the USAF had decided not to increase production. He instructed us to send the drawings and specifications back with a trusted messenger.

We learned 20 years later, when this information was no longer classified, that during a five-year period, 1956–1960, the USAF had been using balloons to spy on Russia. This was a backup operation to the CIA program that was using the secret high altitude jet airplane, the Lockheed U2. The pictures taken from the balloons and U2 flights apparently reassured the President and his advisors that Russia was a long way from mounting an ICBM missile threat. In 1956, the President felt that the number of flights being planned was excessive. This was the reason the USAF made a quick decision not to double balloon production.

The USAF high-altitude, photographic balloons were released in eastern Europe and the prevailing winds carried them eastward to the Pacific Ocean in three or four days. They flew at an altitude of over 100,000 feet and were tracked electronically. Because the USAF was able to reduce the amount of gas in the balloons, by the time they reached the Pacific, they were down to about 20,000 feet. They were then picked up while airborne by a Fairchild C-119 airplane that used an All American Engineering pick-up system.

Fairchild Aircraft received an USAF contract in 1954 to build the C-123A when their C-119 Flying Boxcar was being phased out. The C-123A was a derivative of the Chase Aircraft XC-20 cargo glider that SAC helped build in the late 1940's. It was initially called the XC-123 when Chase installed two engines on the glider but the X was dropped when it became a production airplane. After the war, the USAF still required an assault transport that could operate from unpaved runways on a relatively short field. The C-123A was still the best ship available for this mission. Fairchild had an excellent production record, and, with the C-119 phasing out, they had ample facilities to build the C-123. In 1954, the USAF negotiated a contract with Fairchild for a small quantity of C-123A airplanes which Fairchild planned to build at their Hagerstown, Maryland facilities. Brother Paul kept in close contact with Fairchild, and when they received a large follow-on order in 1956, SAC had the opportunity to quote on building all the moveable control surfaces (rudder, elevators, and ailerons) plus the rear cargo door. SAC won the competition and this work was moved to Elmira in June, 1956 (*Figures 46, 47*).

To offset Schweizer's good fortune of winning the Fairchild contract, Republic notified SAC during the same week that their F-84 Jet Fighter, which was our largest subcontract project, was being cut back and phased out in February, 1957. Republic's new F-105 supersonic jet fighter was replacing the F-84. Although SAC had developed a large amount of subcontract tooling work for the new F-105, we did not acquire any major production assembly work. Although Republic remained our largest customer again in 1956 (38% of sales), at year end the Republic backlog was small. Our Grumman, Bell and Kaman business remained at about the same volume as during the previous year.

For diversification reasons, SAC studied the market potential of the small pleasure boat. We thought it might be a logical product area because the industry was converting from wood to aluminum boats. During the previous year, we built two prototypes, one 12 feet long and the other 14 feet in length. We decided to test the market with the 12 foot model because it seemed to have greater sales appeal, and our design could be built economically. A production release was made to build 100 twelve foot boats during the spring of 1956. The boat hull was made from one 12 by 4 foot sheet of aluminum which was routed to shape and formed, and then the seams were welded. This created a better water-proof seam than did our competitors' riveted joints and resulted in a good looking boat (*Figure 48*). Our high aircraft-quality standards were evident in the boats we manufactured.

The 100 boats were sold by the following spring, but we could see business problems ahead with building pleasure boats in a facility that had an aircraft overhead and the accompanying aircraft quality standards. To be competitive, the boat would have to be built in a separate, low-overhead plant, but SAC did not have the capital to invest in another new venture.

An additional factor that discouraged us: Fiberglass boats were just starting to appear, and it appeared they would be less expensive to build and would have more sex appeal.

The sailplane business amounted to 7% of SAC's sales in 1956, and there were some encouraging signs for increased sales. SAC received an order from Argentina for ten 2-22 sailplane kits. The first fifty 1-26 kits or complete ships were sold by mid-year and the Company released an order to purchase material and make detail parts for a second fifty. Our glider school had a very busy summer. Some U.S. Air Force Academy representatives attended the school and asked our advice about how to start a program at the Academy.

In the summer of 1956, SAC received an USAF contract for the maintenance and modification of sixty-seven L-17 Navion aircraft (*Figure 49*). This program provided the Company with a new experience of running an airplane flight test program because the aircraft were required to be flight tested when completed. The L-17's were scheduled to be used by U.S. colleges that had Air ROTC programs. The plan was to give each student a few indoctrination flights as encouragement and to check their adaptability to flying.

During the year, SAC employment increased from 229 to 286, and our backlog of business increased from .9 to 1.4 million. The phase-out of the Republic F-84 project and the start up of the Fairchild C-123 were costly and reduced our profit for the year to a little better than a break-even.

During the summer of 1956, the plant's heating system had been converted from coal to oil. This was the first winter that the janitors did not have to shovel coal around the clock. Shoveling coal had really been a half-time job, but because the man on duty loved to sit in front of the fire when he wasn't shoveling, it often became a full-time job. Being creatures of habit, even with the new automatic oil system, the janitors still wanted to sit in front of the furnace and watch the fire.

President Eisenhower had been deeply involved in international affairs during his first term, and in 1957 he began his second term determined to correct some of the country's domestic problems. He made a bold move by sending troops to Little Rock, Arkansas to open the way for the admission of nine black children to the public high school. Eisenhower also initiated a general government economy drive which resulted in a reduction of military aircraft production and indirectly, business for subcontractors.

Fortunately for SAC, the C-123A Fairchild cargo aircraft production continued at the same rate and generated 55% of SAC's $1.9 million sales in 1957. This was a large project for SAC and required about 70 production workers. Our $1.9 million sales may not seem like a large dollar volume of business in 1989 dollars, but at that time our sales price for an hour of labor was $5.50, and our average hourly shop rate was $1.95.

SAC's new large drop hammer and foundry provided the capability to make dies and form many larger compound-shaped parts. As a direct result of this capability, Bell Helicopter negotiated a contract with SAC to tool and build the complete cabin for their new U.S. Navy instrument trainer, HTL-7. Unfortunately, there was not a large requirement for the HTL-7 and the contract was for only 18 cabins.

The Schweizer staff worked hard trying to develop proprietary products and commercial aircraft work. During the year, small orders were received from Piper Aircraft, Link Aviation, Star Instrument, Fairchild Engine Corp. and Hardinge Brothers of Elmira.

The Hardinge work developed when Mr. D.G. "Damn Good" Anderson, President of Hardinge Brothers and a former director of SAC, suggested that his purchasing agent, C. R. Bauman, and his chief engineer talk to us about making lathe guards. Mr. Anderson knew of our ability to form plexiglass windshields and thought the same technique could be used to make lathe guards. Hardinge manufactured precision production lathes and needed guards for their machines to protect the operator from hot chips and the liquid coolant that was applied to the lathe work. This precaution was a result of a new trend for the concern of the health and welfare of employees.

We worked with Hardinge's engineering department and developed a guard for their turret lathe. Mr. Anderson liked the guard and he told Bauman to get a quotation on 500. We quoted $50 per guard. Mr. Anderson said he could only pay $40 because he had to sell a guard for $80 to allow for a 25% markup for his dealers. The design was reworked and we came up with a $40 guard. Shortly after it was in production, our inventory started to build up because Hardinge was selling fewer than projected. We heard indirectly that Hardinge's price for the guard was $100 and our purchasing agent checked and confirmed that price. I called Bauman and told him I was surprised to hear that they were selling the guard for $100. He said he did not know but would check their sale price. Bauman called back and reported that "Damn Good" Anderson had said, "What Hardinge is selling the guard for is none of Bill Schweizer's G___ D____ business."

In the long run, the Hardinge guard business worked out well for SAC. Over the next 30 years, SAC built 12 different guards for a grand total of 16,000 units and a total sales of over $5 million. We developed a good working relationship with Hardinge, and Mr. Anderson was a good friend and mentor. C. R. Bauman, the former purchasing agent, became President in the mid 1970's, and I often teased him that the reason he became president was that Schweizer made him look good.

The sailplane business amounted to 6% of the Company's sales for the year. A total of 24 ships were sold: 1-26 (16), 2-22 (6) and 1-23 (2) sailplanes. This total included two 2-22 trainers and three 1-26 sailplanes for the Air Force Academy at Colorado Springs (*Figure 50*). The Academy was starting an experimental program to determine if a glider program would be a worthwhile addition to their curriculum. The objective of the program was to whet the cadet's appetite for flying and to sort out those students who did not show an interest in flying for a career.

During the year, Paul had been working to establish a Schweizer National Dealer Organization. The first meeting was held in Elmira during the fall, and the 1958 models were on display. Paul was also elected President of the Soaring Society of America, so he was busy seven days a week.

During the November meeting of the Schweizer Board of Directors, we showed them a preliminary design of a single-place airplane called the 1-30, and asked for their approval to build a prototype. The proposed airplane would use a 1-26 sailplane empennage and wing with minor modifications. We thought the aircraft would be an ideal glider tow-plane and could be used for air patrol, banner towing, pleasure flying, etc.

The board gave approval and we put it in work and planned to have a prototype flying by the summer of 1958.

Grumman Aircraft Engineering Corp was also looking for diversification and new products. Leroy Grumman, founder of the company, had not been active in the day-to-day operation of his company since WWII, but he was investigating potential products. His love was airplane design, and he had a talented, small group of engineers who worked with him on preliminary designs and product development. On an auto trip through the U.S. Gulf Coast area, Joe Lippert, the aerodynamicist of the group, noticed that the aerial applicators were primarily using biplanes, which were converted WWII flight training aircraft. Joe talked to Mr. Grumman about this situation and received permission to make a survey to determine the special requirements of a cost-efficient agricultural airplane. He then convinced Mr. Grumman that there was a market for a special-purpose ag airplane and that it should be a biplane.

Lippert picked the biplane configuration because it would provide an airplane with a shorter wing span and yet still carry the required load. The short span would result in a small turning radius and excellent maneuverability. The structure of the biplane would also provide the pilot with good crash protection. Another advantage was its safe stall characteristic. In a proper design, the top wing stalls first. Then only the lower wing is still flying and the lift is cut in half. As the airplane starts to nose down and pick up speed, the top wing starts flying again. Because aerial applicators fly over trees, roads, buildings and under wires, it is easy to stall an aircraft, especially with a heavy load aboard. Mr. Grumman was impressed with Joe's findings and let Joe and designer Art Koch configure an ag airplane. The project moved along quickly, and three months later, they were building two prototypes. They planned to take the ships on tour when completed to receive input and reactions from experienced ag-plane operators.

In the spring of 1957, Fred Eckert, who was my Grumman contact when I was with the State University and was familiar with SAC's subcontract performance, asked me to stop in and see him the next time I visited Grumman on subcontract business. He was then the assistant to Vice President George Titterton who was in charge of manufacturing operations at Grumman. Fred and his boss knew that a commercial ag airplane production could not be successful in their high-cost military aircraft environment. They wanted to have an alternate plan ready if Mr. Grumman decided to put the airplane in production at Bethpage. The Grumman management probably would have supported the project even if it had been illogical because it was labeled a "Mr. Grumman special project."

Fred took me to Hangar I and showed me two prototypes that were under construction. After I had an opportunity to carefully look over the airplane, Fred asked, "Do you think Schweizer could build that airplane?" I looked at him and said, "No problem." Paul and Ernie made trips to Grumman a week later to inspect the the G-164, and they also felt it would be an ideal project for our Company.

Fred Eckert suggested that we prepare a budgetary quotation on the project for planning purposes. The proposed program called for building the production tooling as well as manufacturing 100 airplanes. In June, I took three of our top manufacturing people to Grumman: Paul Pullen, Ernest Whidden and John Griswold. We spent all day Friday and Saturday studying the prints and the airplanes that were under construction.

The prototypes were completed in July, and they flew well. Grumman personnel took the two G-164s on tour, visiting ag operators in the Midwest and Gulf Coast areas. When the Grumman crew reported a positive reaction to the aircraft, Mr. Grumman made the decision to build the airplane.

The individuals at Grumman who wanted to build the commercial ag-airplane at Bethpage saw the light when our cost estimates were compared with the Grumman estimates. During September, we negotiated a contract for 100 airplanes. It was approved by the SAC board and Grumman management in late September. In addition to the contract, three Schweizers were asked to sign an agreement which restricted them as individuals and the Schweizer Aircraft Corp. from entering the ag-plane business for ten years after SAC stopped building the Ag Cat Airplane.

Because I had been birddogging the project, I went to Grumman during the first week in October to sign the contract.

I had lunch with Mr. Grumman and some of his executive team. I was seated next to Mr. Grumman who was a quiet, retiring gentleman. That day, he was upset because it had just been announced that Russia's *Sputnik I*, the first man-made satellite, had been placed in orbit. Mr. Grumman said that his company had made a number of unsolicited proposals to the Defense Department for a project similar to *Sputnik*, but they had all been ignored. Now, everyone was asking why the U.S. was not in the space race. Fortunately, *Sputnik* got the U.S. going, and NASA was immediately established. For that reason, I associate the timing and development of the G-164 project with our U.S. space program.

To round out our Grumman business, in March, SAC built its one thousandth MAD Boom for the U.S. Navy's Grumman S2F-1 anti-submarine warfare airplane. This project began in 1952 and the contract was extended in 1957 to assure boom production until 1960. The Russian submarine fleet was growing and the technology associated with the MAD BOOM apparently had proven to be an effective method for the U.S. to keep track of their locations. In the spring of 1957, the UAW organizers showed up at our front gate for the fifth time. They were determined to keep their promise to organize SAC. After a two-month campaign, the election was held in June and 60% of the employees voted no union. The union contested the election and accused Schweizer management of unfair labor practices. However, after a hearing, the NLRB ruled in favor of the company.

The year 1957 was an exciting and a reasonably profitable year for the Company. We had embarked on a new phase of aviation, manufacturing powered airplanes. Paul and I quickly earned our powered-aircraft ratings so we would fly the airplanes we built. In addition, an airplane could be convenient for our business transportation since most of our customers were located on airports. The ratings came easily since we both were commercial glider pilots and had soloed airplanes in the past.

My father, "Papa," passed away in July, 1957. It was a very sad day for all of us. He was a wonderful father, and he made great sacrifices for his family. The National Glider Contest was in process, and, on the morning of his funeral, they delayed the contest flying. During the grave/site ceremony, three sailplanes circled overhead. It was a very touching sight.

41

42

41. *Testing a Bell Aircraft Vertical Take Off and Landing (VTOL) craft, built around a SAC 1-23 sailplane fuselage.* Bell Aerospace Textron. **42.** *The high performance SGS 2-25, built for the 1954 world championship, later used in a USAF wave research project.*

Another *SCHWEIZER* PRODUCTION ASSIST* for a CRITICAL NEED!

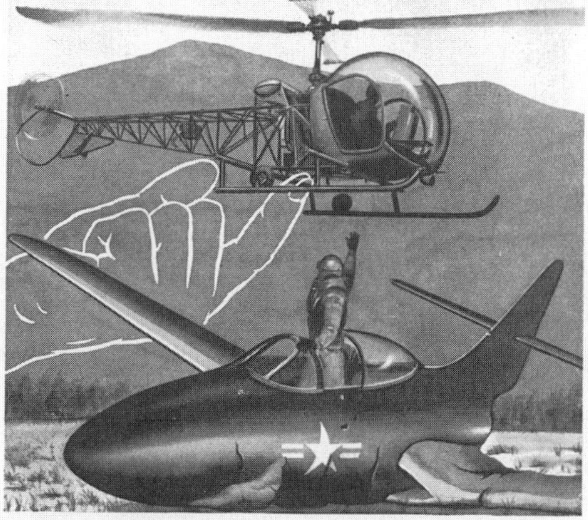

BELL HELICOPTERS play a vital part in rescue and liaison work. Schweizer Aircraft Corporation has given Bell a **production assist** by building the forward fuselage and cabin for the Model 47 Helicopter.

Since 1937 Schweizer engineering and production facilities have been used for a variety of sub-contract work in addition to manufacturing internationally famous sailplanes and gliders.

Call on us if we can assist you in your sub-contract production.

***Other SCHWEIZER Production Assists for Fairchild, Grumman, Republic, Link, Kaman, Stanley, etc.**

SCHWEIZER

SCHWEIZER AIRCRAFT CORP.
ELMIRA, NEW YORK

SCHWEIZER ADVERTISEMENT APPEARING IN AVIATION WEEK

43

43. *The M*A*S*H helicopter in action, one of a series of advertisements in* Aviation Week *reflected SAC's 1950s emphasis on specialty subcontracting for other aviation companies.*

44

45

***44.** SAC-built section of a track used in catapulting U.S. Marine jets from undeveloped air strips.* John Hirtreiter ***45.** SAC designed-and-built advanced tail surface for Piper Aircraft's Comanche.*

46

47

46. *Building control surfaces and cargo ramps in 1956 for the C-123 transport.* ***47.*** *A military vehicle rolls off the SAC-built C-123's ramp.* Fairchild Aircraft Corp.

48

49

48. *SAC's venture into the metal boat business succeeded on the water but not in the marketplace.*
49. *On familiar ground in 1956, inspecting and repairing USAF Navion trainers.*

50

50. *Wearing USAF insignia, a SGU 2-22 and SGS 1-26 were among SAC sailplanes delivered to the Air Force Academy as part of an experimental glider training program.*

8

THE BIRTH OF THE AG CAT 1958–1960

Alaska joined the United States as the 49th state in 1958. The U.S. *Nautilus* atomic submarine sailed under the North Pole that summer and British Overseas Airways began the first jet airline service between the U.S. and Europe. Our domestic airlines were expanding and starting to use jet transport airliners. The largest could carry 140 passengers. The airlines were gradually taking over the railroad passenger business. The Elmira-Corning area desired the service of a major airline but the Chemung County Airport did not have an instrument landing system (ILS), which was becoming a must for commercial airline operations. The FAA had matching funds available to help communities finance an ILS installation, and in 1958, the County Board decided to install the system.

Runway 24 (240 degrees) directly north of the plant was picked as the best approach for an ILS. To prepare for the installation, it was necessary to extend the runway to the northeast and to increase ground clearance 500 feet on each side of the runway. An additional air clearance corridor was also required outside each 500 foot ground clearance area.

In order to meet the ILS requirements, the County again needed some of SAC's land. SAC agreed to cooperate because we felt that airport improvements would be beneficial to the community, and ultimately, to the Company. The following agreement was worked out with the County. For $20,000 and our facility's permanent access to the airport, SAC agreed: (See Appendix 8.) Sell 9.15 acres of land parallel to the runway to provide the airport with a 500 foot ground clearance; give the County an air easement which restricted any building above an agreed upon slope line perpendicular to the ILS runway; eliminate the old road to the plant and deed a 50 foot right-of-way so a new plant entrance road south of the 500 foot ground clearance could be built.

The above changes were completed during the next year and the ILS runway 24 was in operation in 1960. The pine trees near the glider school area adjacent to the airport were removed. The trees beyond this point were trimmed by airport personnel to conform to the slope line.

We have respected the slope line in our plant construction to date, but airport personnel have allowed the trees to grow above the slope line. The permanent access from our plant site to the airport has proven to be a valuable asset to the Company.

The first Schweizer airplane, the experimental single-place 1-30, made its maiden flight in July (*Figure 51*). We found it to have excellent flight characteristics and to be great fun to fly. The high-lift sailplane wing gave it excellent take-off characteristics. It also had sailplane spoilers on each wing so the pilot could increase the sink rate of the airplane as required for a short field landing. These features allowed the 1-30 to land and take off from an airport the size of a football field. The 1-30 was built as a test vehicle for future airplane development, and it gave the Company some actual powered-aircraft experience. It also allowed SAC to be classified as a power-aircraft manufacturer.

During the next few months, a number of experienced pilots flew the 1-30. Their general comments included, "It is a great flying airplane. Why don't you make it into a two-passenger ship?" Our market analysis indicated there would also be a greater demand for a two-place version of the 1-30. However, this approach meant a more expensive airplane and more competition because there were a number of good two-place airplanes on the market. After a great deal of thought, we decided for the time being to set aside our original idea of manufacturing a special-purpose, low cost, single-place airplane. A decision was made to design and build a prototype two-passenger airplane with side-by-side seating, the 2-31.

In the meantime, however, we continued to fly the 1-30 and to make minor modifications. The power was increased from 65 to 90hp and the wingspan was reduced from 40 to 36 feet, which increased the cruise speed to over 100 mph. I used the airplane for a number of business trips to companies such as Grumman, All American and Piper.

Eisenhower's economy drive started in 1957 and continued through 1958. The volume of military aircraft subcontract work let out by prime contractors was drastically reduced because they needed work for their own factories. The military budget crunch forced the USAF to phase out the Fairchild C-123 cargo airplane, which they had planned to keep in production until 1960. This created a problem for SAC because our C-123 project produced 50% of SAC's sales in the first six months of 1958. We were forced to make some drastic adjustments and were scrambling for new commercial work. This was the first time since 1950 that our employment dropped below 200. (See Appendix 1.)

Les Clute, owner and operator of the area's largest Ford dealership and a director of SAC, was impressed with the van body the Company built for our new pickup truck. He felt that SAC should consider marketing this truck body-top as a Company product. The design was simplified to reduce cost and a production prototype was built. The proposed sales price was based upon a projected shop release of 100 units. Our commercial salesman took the truck on a tour of the major auto dealers in up-state New York. The reaction was positive, so we made a shop release to manufacture 100 truck bodies. All the truck bodies built were sold, but the volume was not sufficient to allow us to continue building them at a cost-efficient rate. To increase the volume, the product had to be sold on a regional or national basis. This would require SAC to hold its sales price in order to be competitive and yet increase the dealer cost allowance. The result would have been an unprofitable product. Our truck body dilemma was similar to what we experienced with our boat production. Again, we had too much quality in the product. Today, 30 years later, I still see our truck bodies on modern trucks because they simply don't wear out.

In January, the Grumman contract to tool and build one hundred G-164 agricultural airplanes was moving full-speed ahead, and our personnel were enthusiastic about the project. There was a general feeling at SAC that airplane manufacturing would be a very stable part of the aviation business, a lot like building farm tractors. It was a very busy time for me because I was responsible for manufacturing and getting new products into production at SAC. The employee acceptance of the airplane made the hard work a pleasure.

At that time, the G-164 airplane did not have a name because the Grumman personnel could not agree on one. Mr. Grumman wanted to call it the Grass Hopper but the name did not excite the advertising and sales people. Then someone came up with the name that satisfied everyone, the Ag Cat. This tied in with Grumman's practice of giving a cat family name to their fighter airplanes such as: Wild Cat, Hell Cat, Tiger Cat, etc.

According to the general Ag Cat operating plan, Grumman, the owners, managed the program and controlled the design. They also handled the marketing and aircraft sales. Schweizer manufactured the airplane per schedule which included flight testing and presentation to Grumman of a FAA certified airplane. At that point, Grumman paid for the aircraft.

The Ag Cat was designed by military aircraft designers and in some areas, the cost to build was apparently not the prime consideration as it had to be with a commercial product. Grumman had Arthur Koch, chief Ag Cat designer, stationed at Elmira so Schweizer-suggested changes could be evaluated and, if approved, incorporated on the drawings before tooling started.

Building the manufacturing tooling for the complete airplane was a big job for SAC. Our estimate was 15,000 hours or 10 men working nine months. Our goal, which we accomplished, was to complete the basic tooling and to fabricate five sets of parts by July. Assembly work started in August and the first flight was made on October 17, 1958 with Clyde Cook, SAC airplane test pilot, at the controls (*Figure 52*). There were about ten Grumman representatives at Schweizer's first Ag Cat flight ceremony including Terrell Kirk, the designated Ag Cat sales manager and acceptance pilot. The Grumman personnel were impressed by SAC's performance. Four FAA certified Ag Cats were delivered to Grumman by year end.

After the first flight, I invited the Grumman guests to my home for a drink before dinner. I arrived home about five minutes before the guests were scheduled to be there and found out that we did not have any gin. I raced to the liquor store, got caught in an electric speed trap and received a speeding ticket. After the party I learned that no one even drank gin.

SAC's gliding and soaring business made progress in 1958. A total of 31 ships were sold, compared to 24 the previous year. The glider school, which operated from June through September, had 109 students and made 1485 flights which was a big gain over previous years.

In 1958, the Company had an operating loss of $30,000. This was the first time since 1950 that the Company had ended the year in the red. Two major reasons for the loss included the abrupt end of the C-123 project in July and the high starting load cost of the Ag Cat.

Under Eisenhower's leadership, the United States realized the military importance of the Alaskan and Hawaiian territories. Alaska joined the Union in 1958, and Hawaii became the 50th state in March of 1959. The jet transport airplane and improved electronics communication were making the world seem smaller. As a result of this new electronics technology, SAC received an order from Sperry Gryroscope of Long Island for four 36 foot IFF antennas for the U.S. continental defense system. This new experience opened the door to SAC to some big antenna projects in the 1960's.

On a snowy winter afternoon, I had an appointment to meet with Sperry's Vice President in charge of the Great Neck plant. I took the airline to La Guardia Airport and rented a car. When I got close to the plant, I stopped at a gas station to wash up. I entered the men's room entrance on the side of the building. After I washed up, I found I could not unlock the door. I pounded on the door and wall and yelled, but there was no response. Finally, after about a half hour, I climbed to the top of the stall so I could look out a transom window and try to attract some attention. A gas station attendant finally heard me. It took two men with crow bars to open the door. When I arrived at Sperry a half hour later, I had a good story to tell them.

The Ag Cat production, less the agriculture spray and dust system, was starting to move according to the contract schedule. It called for one aircraft per week by March and two by October. By the end of March, a total of 12 FAA certified Ag Cats had been delivered to Grumman. The contract called for the hopper, which carried the agricultural material, to be installed in the Ag Cat, but it did not include the spray and dust system. This was considered accessory equipment which Grumman felt could be installed later. As a result, Grumman engineering had put off development of dispersal equipment. When they finally got involved, they found it to be a more complicated job than they expected. Grumman had customer orders for Ag Cats but could not deliver airplanes until ag-dispersal equipment was available.

Grumman and Schweizer knew how to design and build airplanes but were "babes in the woods" when it came to developing a practical ag-dispersal system. There were two basic requirements which created our problems. First, the airplane and the pilot had to be protected from the toxic ag-chemicals. Second, the dispersal system had to provide an even distribution of liquid or dust over the application area. In addition, the volume of chemical output per acre had to be controllable to the desired amount.

To solve these problems, Grumman and Schweizer worked hand-in-hand developing and testing equipment. Grumman also brought in some experienced aerial applicators to advise and assist with the development. Just when we thought the spray system was acceptable, we learned that the environmental regulations in some states demanded that the spray booms have a suck-back system. This meant that the air spray pressure had to be reversed to suck the liquid out of the booms when the pilot shut off the system to avoid dropping chemicals in areas where it might be objectionable.

When the first dust spreader was ready for a test run, we learned that there was no inert foundry talcum powder, which is normally used in testing, to be found in the Elmira area. Terrell Kirk, Grumman's service test pilot, said, "Get a ton of lime. It will be okay." We put 500 pounds of lime in the aircraft hopper and Terrell took off. When Terrell opened the dust gate, the lime came out of the spreader but some was sucked back into the tail section of the airplane and seeped into the cockpit. Terrell almost suffocated. When he landed the airplane, he looked like a giant snowman. We quickly realized the open cockpit was a low-pressure area which sucked in dust. The problem was solved by adding a dust-seal bulkhead behind the cockpit and inducing air into the cockpit to create a high-pressure area. This was just one of the many learning experiences we went through to of develop an efficient spray and dust system.

By the end of April, Grumman and Schweizer felt the dispersal system had been debugged and was ready to market. Grumman started to deliver Ag Cats to customers. To our dismay, when the operators put their new Ag Cats in the field, they were unhappy with the spray and dust system.

When ag-aviation started after WWII, the majority of ag operators bought surplus military biplane trainers for less than a $1,000, which was about 5% of their original cost. They normally bought two airplanes. One was modified as a sprayer and the other as a duster. Then they purchased equipment (from ag suppliers) such as hoppers, fans, valves, pumps and spray nozzles, and then installed their own systems.

Each took pride in the fact that his dispersal system was his own design, so he was more easily satisfied with its performance and willing to overlook its shortcomings. Had these dispersal systems been tested to meet state ag-requirements, as was our Ag Cats, their systems would probably not have passed the test. Grumman sent out technical representatives to investigate the complaints. Some were legitimate, but many were not. Each operator seemed to have a different idea of what was wrong with our dispersal system and how it should be redesigned. They seemed to be prejudiced against any system which was different from their own concept or the one they were using. In fairness to Grumman, the Ag Cat was one of the first special-purpose ag airplanes in the world to be marketed with an installed production universal dust and spray system.

Operators with WWII surplus airplanes had a relatively small investment, and they had a hard time justifying a $15,000 Ag Cat, even though our aircraft had the capability of providing two different dispersal systems and had passed stringent testing. Grumman management was unhappy with the Ag Cat's lack of acceptance. They decided to slow down production at SAC to one ship per month until the sales resistance could be overcome. By the end of 1959, a total of 35 Ag Cats had been built but only 10 were in customers' hands.

The Ag Cat slowdown at SAC meant a great loss of business, but to compensate for the scheduled reduction, Grumman gave SAC the opportunity to build the complete tail and ailerons for their new million dollar executive turbo-prop airplane, the G-159, also known as the Gulfstream (*Figures 53, 54, 55*) . This airplane turned out to be the worldwide, top-of-the-line executive airplane in the 1960's. The Gulfstream was a seventy-man project for SAC and allowed us to make the transition without a major layoff.

The Remington Rand factory on the Southside of Elmira was the world's largest office equipment plant in 1955 with a peak employment of 6600. They manufactured mechanical calculators and typewriters. Because Rand was not out front in the electronic equipment field, their employment level gradually decreased, and there were rumors that the plant might close. To counteract this situation, our community leaders were looking for ways to attract industry. In the spring of 1959, the Chemung County Chamber of Commerce decided that an industrial park was needed to provide land and incentives to new businesses. The Chamber was considering the land on the east side of Chambers Road in Big Flats. This included 27 acres owned by SAC. (See Appendix 6.)

In anticipation of a potential sale, our Board set a price of $15,000 for that parcel, or $555 per acre. SAC's cost in 1955 had been $4,200 or $155 per acre. Nothing happened on this issue during the next few months. However, at the October Board Meeting, Director Harry Moseson, who represented Elmira Industries on our board, suggested that SAC consider exchanging our 27 acres for the 1395 shares of Schweizer Stock owned by Elmira Industries. This organization had become inactive in the 1950's, and the Chamber of Commerce had taken over the industrial development function.

The SAC Directors approved the exchange of land for stock. Harry Moseson rounded up the inactive Elmira Industries directors, and they too approved the exchange. To their chagrin, however, no one knew where the stock was located.

The lawyers worked out the problem. As a result of the transactions, there were fewer outstanding shares, which increased the value of each share of Schweizer stock by 21%. During 1960 and 1961, the Thatcher Glass Administrative Offices and Research Center plus the Buckley-Nylok plant were built on part of the 27 acre plot. Later, the portion that was left was used by the Arnot Mall project.

That U.S. glider movement was growing was substantiated by a 50% increase in activity at our glider school. A total of 3,038 flights were made from June through September, and 259 students took flight training lessons. Clarence Chamberlin arrived at our school that summer for a soaring check ride (*Figure 56*). Chamberlin set a world's distance record on June 4, 1927 by flying the 3,911 miles between Long Island, New York and Mansfeldt, Germany in 43 hours. His flight took place only two weeks after Lindbergh's historic flight.

My oldest son, W. Stuart, reached his 14th birthday that summer and worked at the glider school as a ground crew member to pay for his glider flight instructions. He made his first solo flight at 14, and when he was 16, he earned his private license. Stu became a flight instructor when he turned 18. The same pattern was followed by my sons, Paul Hardy and John as well as Ernie's son, Leslie, and my sister Emily's son, Paul Martinez. They all soloed gliders before they drove automobiles.

In spite of the rapid growth of gliding and soaring activity in the United States, SAC had a very small increase in sailplane sales. A total of 32 ships were sold that year. Our new competition were the all-wood, high-performance sailplanes being imported from Germany. The German sailplane manufacturers were located in rural areas of Germany, and their labor rate was less than half of SAC's. We were building our all-metal, high-performance SGS 1-23 in about 800 man-hours. The Germans were taking about 1600 hours to build a competitive ship with a sales price below ours even with the shipping costs included.

In 1959, the fourth 1-26 One-Design Regatta was held at Elmira's Harris Hill. Its great success was a credit to our glider sales manager, W. E. "Tony" Doherty, and brother Paul. There were 19 ships entered in the competition (*Figure 57*). A painting of a regatta scene by Frank Hurtt was presented to the winner. The winner keeps the painting for one year and then gives it to the next year's winner. Each is listed on a brass plate attached to the picture frame.

I earned my Silver C International Soaring Award on a cold, windy day in March by making a five hour duration flight on the Harris Hill ridge. A few years earlier, I had completed the other requirements. These included a cross-country flight of at least 32 miles and a gain in altitude of at least 3281 feet after release. For the duration flight, I borrowed Clyde Cook's winter flying suit and was crammed into the 1-23 cockpit. The zipper stuck and the pilot relief tube was useless. Word got around fast in the shop, and the next day I was subject to some good-natured ribbing.

In spite of the Ag Cat struggle, we ended the year in the black with a 1½% profit after taxes on sales of $1.8 million. A bonus of $9,300 was paid to 264 employees, the equivalent of two-thirds of a week's pay. We were saddened by the death of SAC Director, George S. Chamberlain, who was very helpful to SAC in acquiring the original Bell Helicopter work in 1948.

In 1960 two airliners collided over New York City killing 127 people. The Russians sent two dogs into space. They made 17 orbits in 24 hours and returned to earth in good health. In November, John F. Kennedy defeated Richard M. Nixon to be elected President of the United States. The Xerox process, which makes dry copies of printed and written material on ordinary paper, was perfected in the late 1950's. It soon after revolutionized office work. SAC acquired its first Xerox Copier in the early 1960's.

In the spring of 1960, a United States Lockheed U-2 high altitude reconnaissance aircraft was shot down while flying over The Soviet Union. Premier Khrushchev's and President Eisenhower's dispute over the U-2 incident broke up the Paris Summit in May. It also indirectly contributed to some international problems during the World Soaring Championship held in Cologne, West Germany one month later. One of the American pilots, Dick Schreder, got lost and landed in East Germany. Paul, who was the non-flying captain of the American team, was involved with some complicated diplomatic discussions with the American Embassy, and Schreder was released with his sailplane two days later.

Even though the commercial aircraft industry was at a

standstill, in January Grumman announced a 12% price increase for their Gulfstream I executive transport airplane. This worried us. It turned out, however, to have little impact on sales or their backlog of orders because their major customers were Fortune 500 companies which needed fast, safe and comfortable corporate air transportation.

SAC successfully negotiated a follow-on contract for three ship sets of Gulfstream control surfaces per month through 1962. To expedite the original project, Grumman had provided a $100,000 advance to finance the first production deliveries. However, for this follow-on order, Grumman expected SAC to work out its own financing.

The local Chemung Canal Trust Co. had been the Company's bank for nearly twenty years. We had a $50,000 line-of-credit, but because of the Gulfstream order, we asked Chemung Canal to increase our line to $150,000. The loan committee turned down our request. Chemung Canal had made a few large loans that turned sour, so they were cautious about financing commercial airplane projects which they considered highly speculative. They encouraged us to press Grumman for the financing. That was not a viable alternative, so Paul went to Elmira's branch of the state-wide Marine Midland Bank. They agreed to the loan, but they wanted all of our other banking business as well, including payroll and checking accounts.

The Chemung Canal came back and offered to increase our credit limit to $100,000, but because that amount was still inadequate, we decided to switch to Marine Midland. It was a difficult decision to leave Chemung Canal, since over the years we had established a good relationship with the bank personnel. We based our decision to switch solely on our belief that the Chemung Canal was too small to finance our expanding business.

Our friend, TWA Captain Robert N. Buck, wrote an article on soaring entitled, "Come Sail in the Sky", which was published in January, 1960 *Reader's Digest.* His article was a boost to soaring in the U.S. The nice things he said about Schweizer sailplanes and our soaring school helped make 1960 a record year. The school provided training for 412 students and had more applicants than it could handle. Over 4,100 flights were made that year.

At year end, we received an order for 60 sailplanes from the U.S. Air Force. The ships were to be used in a foreign country for a youth flight training program. Although the name of the country to receive the sailplanes was not public information, we knew it was Indonesia because the USAF gave us the shipping labels to put on the crates. Apparently, the U.S. was trying to support President Sukarno, who was fighting an internal communist movement in his country. The order called for 30 two-place 2-22 trainers and 30 single-place 1-26 training sailplanes to be delivered during 1961 and 1962.

During the spring of 1960, the UAW International Union launched its fifth campaign to organize SAC. They were at our gate passing out literature two or three times a week. We understood that only a small group of employees wanted a union, but the UAW professionals and the Elmira Bendix Plant UAW officers were bound and determined to organize our plant to keep the promise they made in 1951 to the Bell UAW. Apparently, the union organizers were embarrassed because they had lost four previous elections at SAC: two in 1951, one in 1953 and one in 1955. The election was held in June, and 75% of the employees voted no union. Even though only 25% of the employees voted for the union, it concerned us, so we tried to find out what steps should be taken to improve employee relations. Our Personnel Department carried out an employee attitude survey and found out that the majority of our employees felt that our biggest deficiency in employee benefits was the lack of a pension plan. In the fall of that year, a Connecticut General Insurance Company Pension Plan was established, and It is still in effect today. Because of the large expense of funding the plan for all the past service years of our employees, we were forced to start out with a very modest benefit. Nevertheless, the Pension Plan was well received.

In July, 1960 the second Schweizer experimental aircraft made its first flight. The Model 2-31 was a side-by-side two-passenger airplane (*Figure 58*). Although its flight performance compared favorably with competitive production airplanes, the development and tooling cost plus the bill-of-materials and production labor estimates to build the aircraft were too high, and the resulting sales price was not competitive. We decided that it would be necessary to amortize the development and tooling cost over a greater number of ships, but this approach concerned us. Our organization was busy getting the Gulfstream project running smoothly, and the two-place airplane market was not bullish. So we decided to put the 2-31 project on hold.

Grumman and Schweizer were looking at the Ag Cat as a piece of flying farm machinery. Production was held at a rate of two ships per month, and our goal was to make the Ag Cat a cost-effective agricultural tool. Field suggestions and complaints were carefully evaluated. The product was debugged and improvements were continually incorporated. Brother Ernie was a big help to Grumman with his suggestions for cost savings design improvements. In addition, Ernie was an FAA approved DER (Designated Engineering Representative). This allowed him to approve design changes to the Ag Cat so they could be incorporated immediately in Elmira and then filed with the FAA.

In 1960, Ag Cat sales amounted to 29 airplanes. This was an improvement over the ten sold during the first sales year. By year end, a total of 64 Ag Cats had been built, which resulted in a Grumman inventory of 25 airplanes. This was a problem because, the Ag Cat had an open cockpit, and Grumman felt they should be hangared during the winter. SAC did not have the required hangar space and neither did our airport. Therefore, during the winter, the Ag Cat inventory was stored at Hornell and Ithaca Airports. To help keep Grumman's cost down, I volunteered to assist Terrell Kirk with the ferrying responsibilities. We had great fun. We even had occasional dog fights. Terrell would always try to get on my tail, and he was very hard to shake.

Sales for 1960 amounted to a record $2.4 million and the profit after taxes was 2% of sales. A bonus of $20,000 was distributed to 260 employees, equivalent to over a week's pay. Up to this time, a local CPA had been performing our annual audit on SAC. The Board of Directors felt that an audit by a nationally recognized audit firm would make a favorable impression on the banks and our customers. Lybrand, Ross Brothers, and Montgomery (which became Coopers and Lybrand) was engaged to perform this function.

51 

52 

***51.** SAC's experimental SA 1-30 airplane takes off in 1958. **52.** Also in a maiden 1958 flight, the first production Ag Cat roars off the ground. Between 1958 and 1989, 2617 Ag Cats were built by SAC—workhorses of agriculture and of Schweizer's corporate development.*

53

54

55

__53.__ The Grumman G-159 Gulfstream I, top executive airplane of the 1960s flew on 200 sets of fins, rudders, elevators, stabilizers and ailerons built by SAC between 1959 and 1968 (plant details, __54, 55__).

56

57

58

56. Clarence Chamberlain, foreground, the second aviator to cross the Atlantic solo, with Tony Doherty of SAC. 57. Regatta for the 1-26 class in 1959. 58. Bill Schweizer and son, Paul Hardy, in the experimental 2-31. Howard Levy

59

60

***59.** The MARS missile range station (1960-1962) for tracking spacecraft; SAC-built antennas are mounted amidships.* ***60.** A 40-foot MARS antenna under construction at SAC.*

9

THE SAILPLANE MARKET FINALLY ARRIVES 1961–1965

In January, 1961 the United States broke diplomatic relations with Cuba when the revolutionary dictator Fidel Castro took over the remaining U.S. owned businesses in Cuba. Although the Eisenhower administration had promised military and air support to the Cuban exiles, our new president, John F. Kennedy, refused to send military personnel to support the exiles in their Bay of Pigs invasion. Castro's forces crushed the invasion and created an even further break in U.S. relations.

Paul Bikle, NASA's aircraft flight test director at Edwards Air Force Base, set a world's glider altitude record in February, 1961. He used a Schweizer 1-23E sailplane with a low-pressure oxygen system. By utilizing high altitude waves created by the Sierra-Nevada Mountain Range, he reached an altitude of 46,267 feet. Bikle gained 42,300 feet from his airplane tow release point and could have gone higher, but he had reached the upper limit of the altitude possible without a pressure suit or pressurized cabin. This record stands today.

In April, 1961 a Russian astronaut, Yuri Gagarin, made the world's first successful manned space flight. He was rocketed into space and made a single orbit around the earth. The first American space flight was made a few weeks later by Navy Commander Alan B. Shepard, Jr. with a sub-orbital flight which lasted 15 minutes. He was rocketed to a height of 116 miles, flew

300 miles in space and then re-entered the earth's atmosphere. NASA's goal for this initial flight was to prove out the hardware and guidance system before a U. S. astronaut orbited the earth. The Russians were out front in the space race, and the American people were unhappy about this situation. NASA was under great pressure to catch up. They appeared to be overly cautious and afraid to stub their toes. However, NASA had already scheduled a series of space orbital flights for 1962. Only twenty days after Shepard's flight, President Kennedy gave his State of the Union speech to Congress in which he challenged America to send men to the moon and return them safely by the end of the decade.

In the spring of 1961, Sperry Gyroscope Corp., plus a battery of other companies, received a multi-million dollar order to convert two large troop transport ships into ocean-going missile and space vehicle tracking stations (*Figure 59*). This was called the MARS project, an acronym for Mobile Atlantic Range Station. The prime requisite was mobility; the ship had to be able to move to the most advantageous communications position in thousands of miles of ocean.

Sperry's job was to develop the sophisticated long-range tracking radar systems with the capability of instantaneous data transmission to Cape Canaveral or other control centers. The Sperry system required three large antennas on each ship, two with diameters of 30 feet and one 40 feet in diameter (*Figure 60*). They were the largest seagoing antennas to date. Sperry had been favorably impressed by SAC's performance in building their 36 foot IFF antennas during the previous two years. In the summer of 1961, Sperry negotiated an eighteen month contract with SAC to build the six antennas required by the MARS project plus an extra static test unit. Because tolerances were extremely tight, SAC was required to make a healthy manufacturing advance in precision tooling, fabrication, assembly and quality control. The antenna's reflecting surface or dish contour had to be built within 30 thousandths of an inch to the theoretical contour (*Figure 60*). This accuracy was necessary because the data from the antenna had to be continually adjusted by computer to compensate for the roll of the ship at sea. This project created jobs for about 40 shop workers at SAC.

Our hours were long and demanding, but as always, the Schweizer brothers felt that family responsibilities came first. After all, we were a "family" company (*Figure 61*). In the winter of 1961, my oldest son Stuart, a junior in high school, was thinking about college. He was interested in Dartmouth College, so we made a family ski/college trip to New Hampshire. When we stopped at a rest stop to have a picnic lunch, Stuart asked, "How do you like your hot chocolate? I ran out of chocolate so I used some Ex-Lax. Is that okay?" That gave us a hilarious start for our trip and made it easy to leave my business concerns in Elmira.

Ag Cat production was kept at a rate of three ships per month, and 34 were manufactured in 1961. Late in the spring, sales started to pick up and 56 Ag Cats were sold during the year. This reduced Grumman's inventory to three aircraft, and they had a backlog of 30 orders to be delivered in 1962. Both companies finally felt that our efforts to improve and debug the Ag Cat were starting to pay dividends.

In the summer of 1961, we negotiated an order for a second hundred Grumman Ag Cats (S/N 101 - 200). As expected, the increased demand for agricultural aircraft created new competition. In the fall of 1961, Piper Aircraft Corp. announced that their new special-purpose agricultural airplane would be coming off the production line at year end. It was a smaller and lower cost airplane than the Ag Cat.

To help stimulate sales, Terrell Kirk, Ag Cat sales manager, was working with Grumman's advertising agency on a new ad. They wanted a picture of an Ag Cat spraying corn. Terrell picked out a lush corn field about 400 feet wide which was located between old Route 17 and the Erie Railroad tracks in Big Flats. Because it was so narrow, poles were not required to support the guy wire that ran across the center of the field; so Terrell was not aware of the wire. The cameraman was set and Terrell started his spray run with his wheels just above the top of the corn. He hit the wire—bounced down in the corn and then up in the air. Terrell flew home as if nothing had happened—in an Ag Cat that had swept-back wings and corn leaf streamers.

Our national glider dealer organization was starting to

show results. A record 45 sailplanes were sold in 1961 and with the 60 U.S. Air Force glider order for Indonesia, our glider sales amounted to 29% of our total sales.

In spite of large facility and equipment expenditures, 1961 was a successful year. A 2% profit after taxes was earned on sales of $2.1 million. A bonus of $16,922, the equivalent of a week's pay, was paid to 240 employees. Because of our growing sailplane and Ag Cat business, more manufacturing and storage space was needed. A 90 × 90 foot hangar with a 60 foot door was built on the west end of the plant, and 1500 square feet of stockroom space was added with a second story over the present stockroom. This increased the plant floor area to 75,376 square feet. (See Appendix 2)

In February, 1962 John H. Glenn, Jr. became the first American astronaut to orbit the earth and was followed by Scott Carpenter in May. The U.S. space program was in high gear and had caught up with the Russians. NASA wanted two floating, shipboard mobile range stations in operation by the fall of 1963 to track their planned space missions. They put the pressure on the MARS team, which included SAC to achieve its schedule. With a herculean effort, SAC built the six shipboard antennas on schedule.

President Kennedy's challenge to send a man to the moon by the end of the decade created a surge of new activity at NASA. Much was written about how this goal could be accomplished. My daughter, Gayle, our youngest child, was in the fourth grade and brought home an article in her *Weekly Reader* about sending a man to the moon. At dinner, she asked me if I thought Kennedy's challenge could be accomplished. I told her, "It is impossible." Gayle had a wonderful memory and dutifully reminded me of my prediction several years later when Neil Armstrong stepped on the moon. She still kids me about it.

During 1962, 92 Ag Cats were manufactured, and a total of 77 were sold. Up to August, Grumman Ag Cat sales were ahead of our production. Grumman was willing to accumulate an inventory of 25 airplanes by year's end so that Ag Cats were available for what they believed would be a surge in sales during the spring. By the end of December, we had built our 190th Ag Cat since the program started in 1958. A follow-on order for an additional 100 aircraft (S/N 201 - 300) was received in September.

Although the soaring business amounted to only 8% of our total sales in 1962, the demand for sailplanes was increasing. It was a record year for ships sold to the civilian market. A total of 51 gliders were delivered: 1-26's (30), 2-22's (18) and 1-23's (3).

We added a new sailplane to our line, the SGS 2-32, an all-metal, high performance two-place aircraft that could carry a third passenger in the rear seat. This design had been developed in 1961, and the prototype was built during the first six months of 1962. The first flight of the 2-32 (Zero Zero Romeo) was made in July and the aircraft was most enthusiastically received by sailplane dealers and the gliding public (*Figure 62*). The production decision was made in August. It required extensive tooling and production development during the next 12 months, which was all costly to the Company. It also meant that the 1-30 and 2-31 airplane projects were temporarily put on hold. We felt the investment was justified, since we believed that two hundred 2-32's could be sold over the next 10 years. Thirteen firm orders had been received by year end at $8,000 each. Because of the complexity of the design, the cost of producing the ship was greater than our original estimate. Therefore, we had to increase the selling price and a total of only 87 ships were built. The 2-32 has excellent flying characteristics and, in my opinion, is the most outstanding Schweizer sailplane, a real "Cadillac." Today, a 2-32 in good condition is worth over $50,000. They are now in demand because sailplane operators can put two passengers in the rear seat and make a good operating profit selling rides. With current production costs, a new 2-32 would have a price tag in the neighborhood of $70,000 to $90,000.

The complete tail and ailerons for the Grumman Gulfstream executive airplane continued in production at a rate of two ship sets per month. This project amounted to 15% of our business in 1962. To round out our production, SAC continued to make parts for Bell Helicopter and Fairchild Aircraft, plus lathe guards for Hardinge Brothers and MAD Booms for Grumman.

At the August meeting of the Soaring Society of America, Paul was named non-flying captain of the U.S. soaring team for the World Championships to be held in February, 1963 in Argentina. This turned out to be a difficult assignment because the pilots were picked by their standings in recent U.S. glider meets, and some turned out to be real primadonnas. In addition, there was a strong anti-American feeling at that time in Argentina, and there were many "Yankee Go Home" signs.

In April, my oldest son, Stuart, was accepted for admission to Dartmouth College. He enrolled in September in a five-year dual major program, Liberal Arts and Engineering. I was elected president of Capabilities, Inc. and served in that office until 1965. Capabilities is a local non-profit organization which operates a workshop in Elmira to provide work for more than a hundred physically disabled persons. That year the three Schweizer brothers received the Community Builders Award from the Association of Commerce.

In 1962, our general manufacturing business was quite profitable, but our profit was reduced by the high development cost of the 2-32. SAC had a record sales of $2.7 million but earned only 1 1/2% on sales after taxes. Over the years, we have been able to keep out of financial trouble because the Company established a good internal cost-control system. This allows the Schweizers to continually see how experimental and developmental costs are affecting the bottom line and provides time to make adjustments when necessary.

Some of the most momentous events of this century took place in 1963. Increased communist threat to take over South Vietnam created great concern in Washington. Civil rights demonstrators were active throughout the country. In August 200,000 whites and blacks joined together to march to the Lincoln Memorial in Washington, D.C. Their "Freedom March" dramatically demonstrated the blacks' demand for equal rights. This event was highlighted by Martin Luther King, Jr's, historic speech: "I Have a Dream." On November 22nd, a sniper's bullet killed President Kennedy. The country was in shock and there was great sadness throughout our land. Lyndon B. Johnson became President in a moving ceremony that took place aboard "Air Force One" while enroute from Dallas to Washington, D.C. Although the Vietnam War expanded, it did not create military business for SAC as WWII and the Korean War had. The only exception was a small increase in the Bell Helicopter business.

Subcontract work amounted to 47% of our business volume. A seventh Sperry antenna, which was built for static test analyses, was delivered in February. This completed our Sperry MARS project. The Grumman Gulfstream tail surfaces and MAD Boom business continued as did our Hardinge guard and Bell and Fairchild projects. Unfortunately, there were no new major projects developing.

Sailplane business amounted to only 12% of our 1963 sales volume. However, it was another record year with 77 ships delivered. A breakdown of unit sales and prices were as follows: (The shop hour rate in 1963 was $2.20 per hour.)

Model	*Description*	*Deliveries*	*Sales Price*
1-26	Training Sailplane	42	$3575
2-22	Basic Trainer	29	3795
1-23	High Performance	6	6000

During the year, the glider school made 4233 flights, and there were 275 students from 26 states and six foreign countries. The FAA sent a number of their test pilots to our school to provide them with another type of flying experience. Bill Cullen, a CBS-TV personality, visited the glider school and told the Schweizer story on his program. This gave our school some valuable free publicity.

The 2-32 sailplane production development, which included tooling, static test, FAA certification and production start-up costs, proved to be more expensive and a bigger job than we estimated. The design required 400 drawings and 14,000 man-hours of engineering and drafting. The tooling required an additional 16,000 man-hours. In an attempt to keep the Company from having an operating loss for the year, we had to slow down the project. By the following February, the 2-32 was FAA certified and five aircraft were in work. The first delivery was scheduled for March, 1964.

With 244 aircraft in service, our Ag Cat spare parts business was growing and amounted to 7% of the Company's volume. A total of 72 Ag Cats (41% of our sales volume) were delivered in 1963, which was slightly below the 77 for the previous year. There were also some foreign orders waiting for payment at year end. All Ag Cat and sailplane deliveries at SAC were, and still are, made on a C.O.D. basis.

A Japanese company ordered an Ag Cat in January, 1963

and made a down payment. The ship was disassembled and crated, but in December, it was still in our shipping area. Someone asked Clyde Cook, our final assembly inspector and test pilot, what was holding up the shipment. His reply was, "Apparently the Japanese have no 'yen' for the Ag Cat."

In the fall, ten Ag Cats were delivered to a very large operator in the cotton plantation area of Guatemala. Normally Ag Cat deliveries that were required to cross the Atlantic or Pacific Ocean were crated or containerized. However, the ships purchased for Central or South America were normally flown by ferry or the customers' pilots (*Figure 63*). Because of the long distance between airports outside the United States, extra fuel was carried in the plane's hopper. A hand-operated wobble pump arrangement was used to transfer the fuel from the hopper to the main gas tank in the upper wing. In underdeveloped countries south of the border, the U.S. dollar was the common exchange vehicle. Therefore, each pilot was given a brown paper bag which normally contained about 1,000 U.S. one dollar bills to pay for his gas and traveling expenses.

The Ag Cat salesmen were feeling the competition from the new, smaller and lower cost 180hp Piper Pawnee. Its hopper capacity was 150 gallons compared to 215 in the more expensive Ag Cat. Grumman management felt that with some minor changes the Ag Cat structure could carry more load and become a more cost-effective aircraft.

Starting with the new contract (S/N 301-400) the 220hp Continental engine was replaced with the WWII surplus Jacobs 300hp engine. The increased power allowed us to increase the hopper size to 245 gallons. The hopper was fabricated from aluminum and completely welded to provide a better seal. The most important sales feature was the hopper's capacity to hold a ton of water-soluble ag material. We also developed a cockpit canopy as a production option and as a kit that could be retrofitted on airplanes in service. The enclosed cockpit was so well received that it soon became a standard installation (*Figure 64*). Those features and some other service improvements were tooled for production and FAA certified during the fall of 1963. The new model was ready for the spring market.

That fall, Wally Neth, who handled Far East Ag Cat sales, had a sales lead for six planes in the Philippines. He took his wife with him and on the way vacationed in Hawaii. Wally wore his normal uniform, a dark suit and tie with a white shirt, but his wife talked him into buying a flowery Hawaiian shirt. When Wally wore the shirt to lunch the next day, he discovered that all the waiters were wearing exactly the same shirt.

The UAW attempted to organize our plant for the seventh time in the spring of 1963. During the 1950's and 1960's, the UAW was not used to losing certification elections, and they were bound and determined to catch us. We used our standard approach which stated that, in our opinion, we did not think a UAW union at SAC was in the best interest of the employees and the Company. The election was held in April and 59% of the employees voted NO union. The UAW promptly protested the election. The charges were investigated by, in our opinion, a prejudiced NLRB representative and the election was set aside. A new election was scheduled for June. Our eighth election resulted in a 61% NO union vote. We were pleased that our employee/management council was apparently meeting the needs of our employees.

The Federation Internationale Aeronautique presented Ernie with the Paul Tissander Diploma for outstanding work in sailplane design. This was the same year that astronaut Alan B. Shepard, Jr. received the same award for his contribution to the space program.

The 2-32 sailplane development plus the disturbance of two union elections were costly to the Company. With $2.3 million in sales, we had a break-even year. Our employment remained stable at 255 employees. When my son Stuart came home from college for the summer, he was hired to work in the machine shop under John Flood. This proved to be a valuable part of his education.

The Warren Commission, appointed by Congress to investigate the Kennedy assassination, determined that Lee Harvey Oswald was guilty and that he had acted alone. Scientific analyses confirmed that the bullets that killed Kennedy were fired from Oswald's rifle.

The Vietnam conflict continued, and the U.S. role intensified when President Johnson ordered U.S. planes to attack North Vietnamese bases.

That spring Chemung County's sagging economy received

some good news when the A&P Company announced that they planned to build a gigantic 1.5 million sq. ft. plant two miles east of SAC in Horseheads. They said it would be the largest food processing facility in the world and employ over 2000 workers by mid 1965.

The year 1964 was the 25th anniversary of SAC and also the 34th anniversary of the first glider built and flown by the Schweizer brothers at Peekskill, New York. SAC's business volume was growing, and our staff increased from 247 to 288. This growth was the result of a strong market for sailplanes and Ag Cats plus some new subcontracts from Corning Glass Works and Bell Helicopter. However, the Company was having a financial struggle because of the extremely high production start-up cost of the new 2-32 sailplane. Unfortunately, the other sailplanes and the Ag Cat product line were closely priced, so the Company's profit was less than one percent profit on $2.6 million of sales. This created a financial strain because the profit was not sufficient to meet the capital requirements of our growing business.

The sailplane sales amounted to 15% of the Company's total business volume in 1964 and set a new record with 90 units delivered. A breakdown of the deliveries was as follows:

Deliveries	*Model*	*Classification*
33	2-22	Two-place trainer
47	1-26	Single-place training sailplane (one design class)
2	1-23	Single-place high performance contest ship
8	2-32	Three-place top of the line high performance ship

SAC had monopolized the training glider market in the U.S. and Canada since WWII. Commercial glider operators and clubs preferred our 2-22 and 1-26 for flight training because of their rugged all-metal construction, safe flight characteristics and competitive prices.

Beginning in the early 1960's, however, SAC gradually started to lose its position in the U.S. high performance sailplane market to European manufacturers. Our high performance 1-23 was no longer a top competitive contest sailplane.

The Europeans had new designs available at attractive prices which included the cost of transporting the aircraft to our shores. The European manufacturers' labor rate was approximately 50% of our cost. Their all-wood sailplane structures could be modified with less development and tooling expense than SAC could with our all-metal ships. Their relatively low labor cost also made it possible for the Europeans to utilize more hand craftsmanship on finish and appearance details, which increased the sales appeal of their aircraft.

We thought the 2-32 would be a challenge to the European ships because, at that time, it was the highest performance two-place sailplane in the world. It had a glide angle of 36 to 1, which means that in still air, a 2-32 one mile high could glide 36 miles. It had a luxurious interior and comfortable seating arrangement similar to that found in the finest private and executive powered aircraft. We saw the 2-32 as a sailplane that would attract sophisticated commercial and airline pilots to the sport of soaring and, as a result, expand our market.

The 2-32 was a big bird with a 57 foot wing span, dual controls and room for two people in the rear cockpit. It had taken approximately twice as many manhours to design, prototype, tool and build as had our other sailplanes. This meant a sizeable investment, which turned out to be a larger one than we could then afford. Historically, the development cost of new Schweizer-owned products was absorbed in the Company's overhead. Unfortunately in the case of the 2-32, our increased hourly cost of doing business and reduced profit made it harder for us to compete for new business.

To compound our problem, in order to make the 2-32 price more attractive and to increase projected sales, we based our price on a program to build 200 gliders. This decision was substantiated by what we believed to be a meaningful market survey. For pricing, we then used the generally accepted 80% manufacturing learning curve theory which results in a loss on the first 25% of the ships to be built (50), a break-even on the next 25% (50), and a profit on the last 50% (100) large enough to recover the loss on the first 25% built.

In retrospect, it is clear that the Schweizers over-estimated the growth of the U.S. soaring movement. It was probably due to our enthusiasm for the sport. Unfortunately in the case of the

2-32, only 87 were built, so SAC had no recovery of the start-up costs. Had the program been based on a smaller number of ships to be manufactured, the price would have increased approximately 25%. But then it is anyone's guess how many ships would have been sold at that higher price. On the other hand, the 2-32 actually proved to be a good investment. It led to very valuable spin-offs and by-products for the Company during the following 25 years.

Until 1964 the sailplane business was at best a break-even operation. However, there were some significant advantages of being the No. 1 sailplane manufacturer in the United States. The aircraft manufacturing industry was relatively small and each company was known throughout the world by its products. SAC was building a good reputation in the industry because our sailplanes and now the Ag Cat were known for being a rugged, safe and good performing aircraft. Being recognized as an established aircraft manufacturer opened the doors to the top people in large companies and helped us acquire aircraft subcontract business. In addition, SAC received a great deal of free advertising in aviation periodicals from articles about our products.

The Ag Cat with the Jacobs 300hp engine and larger 245 gallon hopper was well accepted. A customer who was picking up a new Ag Cat that spring said to me, "Your ship is now a practical piece of farm machinery." I considered his comment a real compliment. A total of 80 Ag Cats were delivered in 1964. Our spare parts business was also increasing. At year end, 324 Ag Cats were out working in the fields.

In 1964 the Vietnam War was expanding, and the helicopter was playing an important role in the United States' military support program in Vietnam. Bell Helicopter had more business than they could handle building military helicopters, so they decided to subcontract the cabin and tail boom of their four-passenger commercial 47 J2 helicopter. As a result of our good record with Bell, they offered SAC the job. A contract was negotiated in the spring of 1964 and the project was transferred to Elmira. The project was completely tooled and in production at Bell so it was just picked up and moved. The transition was made without any major hitches, and within a month we met their production rate of one ship per week (*Figures 65, 66*).

We were continually on the lookout for commercial products for business diversification. Our most successful non-aircraft commercial project to date had been the family of lathe guards which SAC manufactured for Hardinge Brothers, a local concern. Since the early 1950's, we had tried to find a production project at Corning Glass Works similar to our Hardinge project. Occasionally, the Laboratory Glass Division asked us to do some sheet metal design and to fabricate prototypes. In the summer of 1964, they asked us to design and build a prototype cabinet for a laboratory still. The distillation unit could produce ten liters of pure water per hour, and its planned market would be college and small commercial laboratories. Our job was to produce the aluminum cabinet with the electrical controls; Corning would make the glass apparatus. Corning liked the prototype and ordered ten sample production stills. In November, 1964 Corning gave SAC an order to build 500 stills during 1965. SAC "home brew" makers took more than a passing interest in this project.

In order to support the new business, it was necessary to purchase some new state-of-the-art equipment, and the plant was expanded by 14,200 sq. ft. to a total of 89,598 sq. ft. The expansion was financed by using depreciation funds and by increasing the mortgage by $75,000 at an interest rate of 5½%.

My son, Paul Hardy, graduated from high school in June, 1964. He wanted a college like Dartmouth but one where there were no other Schweizers. He could not find one he liked, so that winter he applied to Dartmouth even though it was said it might be more difficult for a second member of the family to be accepted. (With 6000 applicants and only 900 openings, Dartmouth attempted to achieve a geographic and social cross-section in each class.) There was a little tension around our household on the spring day that all of the Ivy League colleges send out their acceptances or rejections. Paul made it and registered for the same five-year program in Liberal Arts and Engineering that Stu was taking.

On the afternoon of November 9, 1965 the largest power failure in history blacked out nearly all of New York City and parts of nine northeastern states including Chemung County. The lives and work of perhaps 25 million people were affected for 6 to 24 hours. Also in 1965 Germany entered the first fiberglass sailplane in the World Soaring Championship thereby starting a trend in European sailplane construction. (Even now, U.S. sailplane and light airplane manufacturers that build FAA Certified airplanes still do not use fiberglass for their primary structures. The stringent FAA design and production reliability requirements are extremely difficult to meet and result in a heavy and very costly product. In my opinion, this is an example of FAA over-regulation of airplane manufacture. One of our quality control managers referred to the FAA as the guys who show up after the battle and shoot the wounded.)

Production was moving well at SAC, and employment reached 300 in March, a new high. The starting load loss on each 2-32 sailplane was decreasing because fewer man-hours were required, and the Company was now profitable again. Much of the profit was reinvested in equipment, shop tools and supplies which had been neglected during the past two years. Our backlog of business for the year was solid, and we had record sales of 3.2 million for 1965. However, we were concerned about the next year because the Bell 47 J2 fuselage project was phasing out and the Grumman Gulfstream I empennage schedule had been cut from 2 ships to 1 per month. Current orders would run out in June, 1966 and Grumman had follow-on orders on hold. This project was especially important because the Grumman Gulfstream I had produced 25% of our business since 1959.

In the fall of 1965 we developed some new business with a new customer, the General Electric Missile Division of Burlington, Vermont. They had developed a 20 MM aircraft "gatling" gun or cannon which would shoot 6000 rounds per minute (100 per second). This type of cannon was normally built into our fighter airplanes. GE was directed by the USAF to mount some of their cannons in a detachable pod which would be hung under the wing of an airplane. This was known as the "canned" cannon project. This new idea allowed the military to switch pods, thus allowing a single airplane to be converted from a close-support fighter to a light bomber or a reconnaissance plane.

GE asked Grumman for help in designing and building the detachable gun pod. Because they were very busy, our good friend at Grumman, Fred Eckert, suggested that GE talk to SAC.

We convinced GE that our Company could give them the assistance they required. We received a contract to assist in the design and manufacture of a section of the pod. The "canned" cannon was used successfully in the Vietnam War, and the project was in production at SAC until 1972.

In 1965 there were three leading U.S. aircraft companies building small private and business airplanes: Beech, Cessna and Piper. SAC had been working for Piper Aircraft Corp. of Lock Haven, Pennsylvania on and off since 1947. The organization was controlled by the Piper family and actively run by Bill Piper, Sr., and his three sons, who were about the same ages as the Schweizer brothers. Up until 1965, our Piper work had included assisting with aircraft design details as well as production tooling and prototyping. In spite of our good relationship, we had not been able to develop any Piper subcontract production work. They had ample space and a good supply of competitive skilled labor available. In the fall of 1965, however, we were asked to assist with the tooling of the fuselage for their new light passenger Navajo executive airplane (*Figures 67, 68*). The plan was to tool the forward and aft fuselage structures, and to sweeten the pot, SAC received an order to build 100 assemblies of each fuselage section. This helped build up our backlog of business and avoid layoffs.

The Ag Cat continued to produce our largest volume of business, 31%. However, deliveries decreased from 80 to 58 airplanes for the year, but with more aircraft in service, spare parts business increased. Ag Cat dealers felt the sales decrease was due to improvements made by our ag plane competitors which made their aircraft more cost effective. The Ag Cat was a quality airplane with an excellent safety record which is hard to measure in dollars and cents. An ag operator who owned an Ag Cat, as well as other competitive models, normally flew the Ag Cat himself.

In June, 1965, SAC received a follow-on order for 125 Ag Cats (Serial No. 401-525). As part of the new contract, SAC agreed to work with Grumman Engineering to incorporate a larger hopper and a more powerful engine into the airplane. These two changes would allow the Ag Cat to carry a payload of 1¼ tons and would make it a more productive piece of farm machinery. The new hopper was made from acid resistant fiberglass and had a volume of 300 gallons. The 300hp engine was replaced with the 450hp Pratt and Whitney R985.

The new modified Ag Cat was called the Model A and required FAA certification because with the additional power, the aircraft could fly faster and carry a heavier payload, a general "beef up" of the basic structure including a stronger landing gear were required. The Model "A" was FAA certified in the fall and deliveries started in February, 1966. It was approved to operate in the field at a new, increased gross weight of 6075 lbs.

The sailplane business broke all previous records in 1965 and 101 new sailplanes were delivered. This amounted to $452,224 or 14% of our total sales. Over 5000 flights were made at SAC's glider school. The One-Class Design 1-26 was the best seller with 51 delivered. At the SAC 1-26 Regatta on Harris Hill, 30 ships entered the competition. The sales price of the 2-32 was increased by $1000 to $8,995, and a total of 18 were delivered.

Over a three week period in June, the Schweizer brothers attended the World's Soaring Championship at South Cerney, England. Paul was asked to serve on a committee that would fly and evaluate some new European sailplanes built to the new International Standard Class Specifications for One-Design Class competition. Paul's first-hand knowledge of the new European sailplanes was of great interest to SAC. This was important information because, at that time, the European share of the U.S. sailplane market had reached 40% and was growing. Eighty six sailplanes from 26 countries including the Soviet Union entered the competition.

On a pilot rest day during the meet, the president of the leading British sailplane manufacturer, Slingsby, encouraged me to fly his new single-place high performance ship, the "Dart." I was very happy to have this opportunity. It was a misty day with sun streaks coming through holes in the clouds. The cloud base was about 1500 feet above the beautiful green landscape. The president personally gave me a cockpit checkout and briefed me on the flight characteristics of the Dart. I found out later that he had never flown the ship and was not even a pilot. On takeoff, the airplane tow pilot flew straight out until we got to the cloud base. I looked around for the airport and could not find it. Normally the U.S. tow pilots circle the field so you can keep the field in sight. I released and fortunately there was lift under the clouds so I could maintain my altitude. After flying around for a half hour, I finally found South Cerney Airport. I was greatly, relieved because I did not want to make an off-field landing in a borrowed ship in a foreign country.

After the meet, Ernie and I visited the Slingsby company. They were interested in a license arrangement so they could build our 2-22 training sailplane in England. Ernie returned to Elmira, and I attended the Paris Air Show and then visited my mother and father's homeland, Switzerland, for the first time. I arrived in Zurich, and as I walked through the airport, I noticed that most of the people looked like me. I guess my Swiss heritage is fairly apparent after all.

We later learned first hand that the aviation public recognized the Schweizer name when Peg and I flew to Cumberland, Maryland to pick up a St. Bernard pup (*Figure 69*). Five miles out of Cumberland I called the airport to receive landing instructions and to close my flight plan from Elmira. The airport did not have a control tower but had "Unicom," a two-way radio, in the manager's office. The radio voice asked for the name of the pilot. I said "W. Schweizer." The voice came back and asked, "Are you the missionary, Swiss cheese maker, or the sailplane manufacturer." I said, "Swiss cheese maker" knowing full well he knew who I was because he had my flight plan in front of him. As I landed, I saw two Schweizer gliders on the field.

61

62

***61.** Bill and Peg Schweizer's family, from left: Gayle, Stuart, John and Paul Hardy.* ***62.** SGS 2-32, with Paul A. in the rear seat giving a flight check.*

63

64

63. *Ag Cat en route to Uruguay, South America—10,000 miles from SAC.* **64.** *Bill Schweizer flying the first Ag Cat with an enclosed cockpit.* Garland Heistand

65

66

__65.__ Bell Helicopter's 47J2 commercial ship. In 1964, Bell subcontracted the cabin and fuselage tail section to SAC (__66__).

67

68

*67. The first 100 Piper Navajo executive airplanes had major fuselage sections (**68**) tooled and built by SAC.*

68A 

69 

68A.** Model "A" Ag Cat with 450hp engine and 300 gallon hopper ready for a test flight.* ***69. *Peg and Bill Schweizer arriving at Cumberland, Maryland, in a Piper Arrow.* Anne Antell

10

THE ADJUSTMENT PERIOD 1966–1969

In the 1960's, Elmira had the reputation of being a strong union area, which discouraged some industries from locating there. Union pressure forced factory wages up faster than general inflation. In the Elmira area the industrial wage rate was higher than in Binghamton and all of the other cities in the southern tier of New York State. By 1966 a number of Elmira's major manufacturing concerns were having difficulty competing for business. Some of them are no longer in business in the Elmira area, including American La France Fire Engine Co., American Bridge Works, National Homes, GE Foundry, Eclipse Machine Co. (Bendix) and Remington Rand Business Machines Co. During this period, there was labor unrest, and the community had numerous strikes. American La France had strikes in 1960, 1965 and 1966; Westinghouse TV Tube plant had strikes in 1963 and 1966; and Kennedy Valve had a four-month strike in 1966.

In the spring of 1966, for the ninth time, the UAW professional organizers were at our gate trying to organize our plant. Their general approach was to pass out literature regarding the merits of a union shop and to attempt to develop a friendship with our employees. They were also assisted by the union officers of our local Bendix union. Meetings and beer parties were held for our employees at the local Bendix union hall. The UAW had a well organized game plan. They waited three months before asking for an NLRB election, because they felt time was on their side. SAC, however, was anxious to have the election because the long campaign was causing employee unrest and confusion, which was having a negative effect on plant operating efficiency.

The ninth election was held in late June, and finally the union won by a narrow margin. In retrospect, we felt that we had become too complacent after winning eight previous elections. We were probably too cautious in our response to union propaganda, since we did not want to give the UAW any basis for unfair labor charges.

After the election, the Schweizer brothers took a good deep breath and thought the new situation through. We realized that according to law, our new union was the sole bargaining agent for wages, fringe benefits and working conditions for SAC's production and maintenance employees. Therefore, we had to accept the union as part of our organization and learn to work with them.

The contract negotiations got underway in July. The Company was assisted by labor attorney James L. Burke of Elmira, and the union was assisted by two UAW professionals. Our Employee-Management Charter had been continually updated since 1951 and in many ways was similar to a union contract. The Company negotiated from the rules, regulations and benefits called out in the Charter. This document provided a foundation from which to work and helped speed up the negotiations.

Four months later we had a contract that was a good practical working agreement, and I believe fair to both parties. The contract was approved by the employees in November, 1966. I believe that our management and the union have developed mutual trust and a good working relationship. There have been some major disagreements, but there has never been a work stoppage or a strike at SAC.

Unionism reached its peak in the 1960's and since then has lost ground nationally. During the past thirty years trade union participation has shrunk from a third to a sixth of the work force. Some social scientists say there are fewer reasons for unions today because of two new conditions. First, management is more responsive to the workers' needs. Second, new state and federal legislation provides more protection for the worker from unresponsive management. They refer to new laws such as the Civil Rights Act of 1964, the Occupational Safety and Health Act of 1970 (OSHA), the Employee Retirement Income Act of 1974 (ERISA) and the laws covering human relations concerns such as race, color, sex and age discrimination.

Between 1959 and the end of 1966, a total of 180 Grumman Gulfstream I turboprop aircraft had been sold. During that time, the price of the Gulfstream had gradually increased from one to two million dollars. The Gulfstream I was then the world's leading executive transport airplane, and the complete tail and ailerons were built by Schweizer.

There was also considerable discussion that Fortune 500 executives were now ready for a jet-powered airplane rather than a turboprop, so Grumman's management was concerned about releasing additional Gulfstream Is for production. A 20-ship manufacturing release was the minimum quantity for efficient production, and Grumman did not want to have unsold inventory that could amount to $40 million. Therefore, Gulfstream I production was on hold at S/N 180, and our orders were completed in June. This project required 40 Schweizer employees, so we had to make some manpower adjustments. Fortunately, the new Piper Navajo project that was then accelerating helped to avoid layoffs.

Ship S/N 180 was scheduled to be completed at Grumman in December. When the news got out during the summer that Grumman was considering a halt to the Gulfstream I production, a surprising volume of orders developed. In November, Grumman made a production release for 22 additional Gulfstream I airplanes. We were pleased to have the problem of getting the Gulfstream project started up again.

In December, SAC won a competitive Bell bid and was awarded a contract to manufacture 1700 elevator control surfaces for the UH-1B "Huey" Helicopter. The "Huey" played an important role in the Vietnam War. The elevators were subject to a great deal of damage from ground handling and in-flight bullet hits. In Vietnam they did not repair the damaged elevators, but just replaced them with new ones. This created a large volume of spare parts business for Bell and Schweizer (*Figures 70, 71*). For the next five years, we had about 25 workers continually building "Huey" elevators. After the war, we continued to build elevators for various versions of Bell's 214, 204 and 412 helicopters. (All these years later, this project is still going on at SAC on a smaller scale.)

The glider school had a busy season in 1966, and a record 5,847 flights were made. Among the students at the school were Thomas J. Watson, Jr., chief executive officer of IBM, and our mutual friend since the mid 1930's, Eliot Noyes. Eliot was then a world-famous architect and industrial designer who did consultant work for IBM.

Sales for 1966 were $2.8 million, down 10% from the previous year. The average employment dropped from 292 to 262. (See Appendix 1.) The profit margin was low due to the inefficiency caused by the long union campaign and the subcontract product line changes. The overall sales volume of the Ag Cat and sailplane business remained about the same as 1965, even though the number of new aircraft delivered was slightly lower. The dollar volume held because of an increase in spare parts business and higher aircraft sales prices.

Leslie, Ernie's son, was accepted at the New York University College of Engineering. He majored in aeronautical engineering as had my brothers, Paul and Ernie. John, my third son, applied to Dartmouth College and was accepted. He entered the five-year Liberal Arts and Engineering program and followed in the footsteps of his two older brothers. That September John was a freshman, Paul a junior and Stuart was a fifth year student at Dartmouth. Peg and I had some financial constraints, but we were pleased to have the problem.

In January, 1966 I was elected a director of the Elmira Savings Bank. It was then a mutual savings bank owned by the depositors with 18 employees and assets of $33 million. When I retired as a director in 1988, the bank had been converted to a stock ownership bank with 120 employees, three branch offices and assets of $177 million.

Two representatives from a Washington, D.C., electronics company arrived at SAC on the morning of June 23, 1967 on Mohawk Airlines to talk to us about building a large experimental antenna. When we finished our discussion, I gave them a plant tour and offered them a glider ride, which they were somewhat reluctant to accept. Soaring conditions were excellent and the two rides took a little longer than I expected. Their 2:35 p.m. Mohawk flight was taxiing out when they arrived at the airport. They had to wait for the evening flight so they rented a car and drove up to see the Finger Lakes. They turned on the car radio and found out that the 2:35 p.m. flight out of Elmira had crashed at Blossburg, PA, 40 miles southwest of Elmira. Everyone aboard was killed—30 passengers and the crew of four. A mechanical malfunction in the tail section was blamed for the crash of the British-built BAC-111. My friends stopped their car and made three phone calls: to their homes, to their offices and to me. They could not thank me enough for the glider ride.

The Elmira Area Soaring Corp. changed its name to Harris Hill Soaring Corp. in 1967 to reflect its location. The gigantic Arnot Mall, located east of the Schweizer Plant on Chambers Road, opened for business in 1967, the first enclosed shopping mall between Rochester and New York City. The Arnot Mall evolved in 1965 when the JC Penney Corp. was seeking a location for a new store between Elmira and Corning. In the spring of 1967, the Arnot Realty Corp. purchased 5 acres of land from SAC, on the West side of Chambers Road, to build a warehouse for Penneys. (See Appendix 8.) The five acres were sold for $32,000 which we thought was a real bonanza since we paid $155 per acre in 1955. The funds from the sale were used by SAC to pay for a new shipping and receiving building addition.

The January, 1967 issue of the *National Geographic* magazine featured an article about soaring entitled, "Sailors of the Sky." It was written by Gordon Young, who became fascinated by soaring as a spectator and convinced his editor to run a soaring story. Young visited soaring sites throughout the country and then came to our soaring school for a month as a student. He became a licensed glider pilot and earned his Silver "C" soaring rating. His article was accurate and well written, with outstanding descriptive drawings and photographs. He wrote in glowing terms about the Schweizer Soaring School and our products. This publicity windfall had a great impact on our 1967 soaring business.

Our soaring school, which had been in operation for 20 years, had its busiest year. The school made 9,573 flights in 1967 compared to 5,760 the previous year. We had more student applications than we could handle. The soaring school serviced 332 students from 37 states and 6 foreign countries. Our glider sales also set a record; a total of 104 sailplanes were sold. SAC sailplane business amounted to a record $686,730 or 19.1% of our total business.

The new 2-33, a two-passenger training sailplane, was added to our product line in 1967 (*Figure 72*). This aircraft also contributed to the record sailplane sales. A total of 55 were delivered, primarily to sailplane operators who used the ship as a business vehicle for rides and training. The 2-33 was basically a 2-22 with a new wing, and some improved styling and refinements. Because many of the 2-22 components and wing parts were used, this greatly reduced the cost of getting the new model into production.

Ten 2-32, three passenger top-of-the-line, sailplanes were sold at the 1967 price of $10,995. One was built especially for Jim Bede, who planned to convert it into an airplane which he intended to use for a non-stop flight around the world. Bede picked the 2-32 airframe because according to his calculations, the efficient 57 foot sailplane wing and the aerodynamically clean fuselage and tail would allow his proposed airplane to maintain altitude with a small amount of power. This meant the engine would require a small amount of fuel per hour, and with large gas tanks the aircraft could fly great distances.

When we built Bede's wings, they were modified internally and all joints were sealed with a compound so each wing would become a gas tank, or what is known in the trade as a "wet wing." Theoretically, his modified 2-32 airplane could carry sufficient fuel so he could stay in the air seven days (168 hours), fly at 150 mph, and travel 25,000 miles. It had the latest electronic navigation equipment and an autopilot which Bede could use when he planned to rest or sleep. Potentially, the Bede ship could fly non-stop around the world assuming the pilot had the physical stamina to stay in the air six and a half days, the weather was favorable and that no mechanical problems developed.

Bede never accomplished the global flight, but he did set a world's distance record for propeller-driven aircraft with a flight of 8,974 miles in 1969. On this flight, his goal was 11,500 miles, but it was cut short due to an electrical problem. The actual gas used for the record flight was 3½ gallons per hour, which gave the aircraft a potential range of 25,000 miles. We and others tried to convince Bede to get an astronaut, who is trained for this type of mission, to make the global flight. Apparently, Bede wanted to make it himself, and it never happened.

Of the ten 2-32's sold in 1967, three were delivered to Lockheed Missiles & Space Company, Sunnyvale, California for what was then a classified military research project. Like Bede, Lockheed engineers theorized that the aerodynamic efficient 2-32 sailplane could be converted into an airplane that could maintain flight on a small amount of power and fly quietly. The military needed a reconnaissance airplane in Vietnam that could fly as low as 1,000 feet above the ground without being heard. (Military helicopters were noisy and the Viet Cong would hide when they heard them coming). The proposed airplane would be equipped with the new forward-looking infra-red night vision sensing devices, allowing an observer to detect and track night troop movements without tipping off the enemy below.

Lockheed modified each 2-32 sailplane into an experimental quiet observation airplane called the "Q Star." (*Figure 73*) The engine was located behind the cockpit for balance and the power was delivered to the propeller in the nose of the ship through a long shaft over the pilot's head. They also used some new techniques to mute propeller and engine exhaust noises which made the aircraft very quiet in flight. The military was favorably impressed by the "Q Star." This was how SAC got into the quiet-airplane business.

Ag Cat sales were disappointing in 1967 with only 40 airplanes sold to customers. However, in the late fall, the market changed, and Grumman received orders to deliver 22 aircraft during the first two months of 1968. This took care of the airplane inventory and allowed SAC to continue to build six Ag Cats per month.

Our subcontract business was steady and well diversified. Only one new job in the $100,000 per year sales range was received, the left and right pallet or housings for the classified "Black Boxes" used on the Grumman A6A attack airplane. This was the first year in the history of the Company that no single project amounted to more than 20% of our business. Our 1967 sales breakdown was as follows:

Sailplane Business	$686,730	(19.1%)
Ag Cat	599,938	(16.7%)
Subcontract:		
A. Grumman	711,515	(19.8%)
B. Bell	513,870	(14.3%)
C. Piper	665,671	(18.5%)
D. Miscellaneous, including General Electric, Fairchild Hiller, Mercury and Hardinge	415,639	(11.6%)
	$3,593,363	100%

The year 1967 was good for the Company and its employees. Our employment was steady and averaged approximately 300 workers. (See Appendix 1.) The Company's earnings after taxes were 3½% on a record sales of $3.6 million. A $33,000 bonus was paid to our employees. The Company ended the year with a $4.0 million backlog of orders.

In June, Ernie's oldest child, Susan, graduated from Keuka College and joined the staff of the Corning-Painted Post school system. His third child, Sally, entered Green Mountain College. My son, Stuart, graduated from the Thayer School of Engineering at Dartmouth College and received a summer job at the Thatcher Glass Research Center. In July, he married Lucia (Lucy) E. Torres, a high school classmate and graduate of Russell Sage College. Stuart received a National Science Foundation graduate scholarship and entered the Forrestal School of Engineering at Princeton University in September with a major in aeronautical engineering.

On Saturday, December 2, 1967, my brother Paul A. (age 54) was married to Virginia (Ginny) M. Mayer in a small family wedding. Ginny was a glider pilot and had known the Schweizers for years. The ceremony was held at the Community Chapel, New York, NY with SAC's personnel manager, the congenial Rev. Eugene S. Bardwell, officiating.

On the day of the wedding, most of us walked to the chapel from the hotel, but the bride and groom and the Bardwells arrived in a black limousine. As the car drove off, Bardwell realized he had left his robe in the limousine. Stuart was walking toward the church when he spotted us chasing the limousine down the street. He yelled at the driver to stop and saved the day for Bardwell. This wedding was a very big deal for Bardwell. He liked to perform marriages and kept a special list in his office of all the SAC employees he had married. Ernie and I did not make his list.

In 1968, the Hong Kong Flu claimed the lives of 34,000 Americans. Ten years earlier 70,000 died from the Asian Flu, while the 1918 flu epidemic resulted in 500,000 deaths in our country. New medical technology, vaccinations and control of secondary infections by antibiotics has been responsible for the declining death rates of major influenza epidemics.

In 1968, the first direct airline service opened between the United States and the Soviet Union. In April, Martin Luther King, Jr. who preached non-violence and racial brotherhood, was slain in Memphis. Robert F. Kennedy was shot and killed in June a moment after he had made his victory statement in the California Democratic Presidential Primary. Richard M. Nixon won the 1968 presidential election by a thin margin over Hubert H. Humphrey, and Spiro T. Agnew became Vice President. Nixon's major goal was to settle the Vietnam War as quickly as possible. In spite of his efforts, however, the war dragged on. The U.S. Army's need for a quiet reconnaissance plane was urgent, and the experimental "Q Star" project proved it could be done. As an outgrowth of this project, Ernie worked with Jack Baumann, Design Engineer of the Lockheed Missiles & Space Co., on a production version of this airplane. By using the modified 2-32 sailplane for the basic structure, the product development time was reduced and the Army was allowed to have an operational aircraft in a much shorter time.

According to the performance requirements spelled out by the Army, the aircraft had to have the capability of maintaining altitude with a small amount of power so at 1,000 feet above the ground it would be inaudible. For night operations, the aircraft would carry the very new development, forward looking infrared (FLIR). The military identification for this special purpose aircraft was labeled by the Army as the YO-3A (*Figure 74*).

In February, 1968, SAC received the first YO-3A order, which grew to 16 airplanes. The contract was classified as a secret military project. At SAC the YO-3A aircraft was so secret that not even the employees knew what they were working on.

It was called the PRO-83 project, and there was no mention of the end user or the aircraft's mission. Only a few individuals at SAC who were cleared for secret information by the Department of Defense knew what was going on.

That fall I was at Lockheed's Sunnyvale plant working on some production tooling and coordination problems and I was invited to go along on a chase helicopter flight following a YO-3A during a test flight. Stanford University was nearby, and we observed a large group of people milling around the college campus. After the test flight was completed, we made a low pass in the helicopter over the Stanford campus. We could then see there were about five thousand people involved in an anti-war demonstration.

The Vietnam War was an unpopular war in the United States. As it dragged on, more and more people felt the nation was supporting a corrupt undemocratic and unpopular government in South Vietnam. What I saw on the Stanford campus was a typical reaction to the war by college students throughout the country.

In his graduation address, the valedictorian of Paul's graduating class at Dartmouth told his classmates to avoid the war even if it meant leaving the country to dodge the draft. Although the Dartmouth graduation is typically a very dignified ceremony, the audience reaction was quite vocal. United States Senator Jacob Javits was the commencement speaker. He threw away his prepared address and answered the valedictory speaker. Basically he said, if you don't like the way the country is run, get active in politics and do something about the situation.

A new sales first was achieved in 1968 when five Ag Cats were delivered to Yugoslavia. Ag Cat sales were increasing and a total of 84 ships were delivered, amounting to 33% or $1.5 million of our annual sales. At the Annual Ag Cat Dealers' Meeting, I asked Dick Reade, of Hayti, Mo., our leading dealer, to explain the sales increase. He said, "The Ag Cat's biggest selling point is its built-in safe flight characteristics and structural integrity. This has resulted in an outstanding safety record which also means lower insurance costs to the operator." Apparently our joint effort with Grumman was finally paying off.

The 1000th Schweizer sailplane, a 2-32, was built in January, 1968. Our sailplane business continued to grow, amounting to 19% or $842,395 of our total business. There were 130 ships delivered which breaks down as follows:

Model	*Description*	*Deliveries*	*Sales Price*
2-22*	Two-Place Trainer	2	
1-23*	High Performance Single-Place	1	
1-26	Training Sailplane Single-Place	51	$ 4,775
2-32	High Performance Two-Place	10	11,995
2-33	Two-Place Trainer	66	5,995

*Ships being phased out of production

SAC had 57% of the U.S. sailplane market, estimated to be 230 ships. The balance amounted to 63 ships imported from Europe and 37 built by other U.S. manufacturers and home builders. We had controlled all of the training and pleasure sailplane market with the 2-33 and the 1-26. However, we had gradually lost out in the single-place, high performance contest market because our 1-23 was an updated 19-year-old design. During a two-year period in 1967 and 1968, (to spread out the development cost) SAC had been working on a replacement for the 1-23. The new ship was the 1-34, a high performance, standard class contest ship. It was scheduled to be FAA certified, tooled and in production by January, 1969 (*Figure 75*).

Paul along with Tony Doherty, Sailplane Sales Manager, had worked hard at developing a national sales organization that was now producing results. One of the biggest sales deterrents was the high cost of transporting completed ships. Truck and railroad shipments were investigated and tried but were not completely satisfactory. The best answer turned out to be an auto trailer which could carry two or three ships.

After nine years of producing the Gulfstream I executive transport, Grumman decided to phase it out by the end of 1968, which meant production would stop six months earlier for SAC. It was replaced by a jet version, the Gulfstream II. We were offered the opportunity to build the complete tail for the new jet airplane. However, to acquire this contract SAC would be required to invest in the development and the success of the Gulfstream II. It meant that SAC would have to amortize the tooling cost over 100 ships which would result in a gradual payback over a four-year period. In addition, SAC was required to risk one-half of the tooling cost if the project failed. After a careful analysis of the potential loss which we estimated to be over two million dollars, we decided the gamble was greater than we could afford to take. A failure could put SAC out of business. Twin Coach Corp. of Buffalo, a much larger company than SAC, took on the project, and the Gulfstream II was a success.

Even with sailplane and Ag Cat sales expanding, subcontract work was still 50% of our total business. During the year, the Company provided steady employment for approximately 340 employees. However, we did have a setback in December when Piper told us they planned to take the Navajo airplane work back to their Lock Haven plant due to union pressure. There was a clause in their labor contract which stated that if employment decreased at Piper, they would call back subcontract work. Piper did not want to move the job because they felt their layoffs were temporary and it would be costly to relocate the project. However, it happened.

Peg and I normally took two or three long weekend trips each year to New England. They were related to our subcontract work at the GE plant in Burlington or to our large Vermont sailplane dealer at Sugarbush. We would also visit our sons at Dartmouth. On one particular trip, on our way home from Dartmouth, we stopped at Sugarbush on a Sunday morning. Daughter Gayle was with us and Peg said, "It is 11:00 a.m., and we should leave at noon because Gayle has homework." The girls left for the airport restaurant, and I returned to the airplane to get my camera. I found that the airplane was locked and the key was in the ignition. I was furious with myself. I walked around the locked Piper Arrow and did not know how to get in. I finally decided to remove the door. I borrowed some tools from a friend who was assembling a sailplane. With some delicate work, I removed the door and recovered the key. Just as I got the door back in place, Gayle and Peg arrived and said,

"Let's go." I was so mad at myself that I did not say a word about what I had done. We got in the Arrow and flew home without even talking to the operator at Sugarbush.

This was a successful year financially in spite of major development expenses for the new 1-34 sailplane. In addition, important new equipment and plant improvements were made. A second 90 × 60 foot cold storage building was built in order to free up valuable manufacturing space that was being used for storage. Sales for the year amounted to $4.4 million, and a 2½% profit was earned after taxes. A $53,000 employee bonus equivalent to two weeks' pay was distributed to 340 employees.

We were saddened by the death of two SAC directors. Thomas S. Craig, a good businessman, aviation enthusiast and a substantial investor in SAC, died in April. Robert P. McDowell died in September. He was one of the founders of SAC and probably more responsible than any other individual for convincing the Schweizers to locate in Elmira. He was community-spirited, an eternal optimist and a fine gentleman. To replace Mr. McDowell, attorney Kenneth Tifft was elected to the board and to the position of secretary. (See Appendix 9.) When I think of Bob McDowell, I always remember this experience. During the last two years of his life, he was in poor health. His wife would drive him to meetings, and I would take him home. On a snowy, icy winter evening, he got out of my car before I could get around the car to help him. His feet went up in the air and he fell flat on his back. I knew he had a bad back so I was concerned. He said he was okay so I helped him up carefully. The next time I saw Bob he said, "That fall apparently was good therapy; my back feels great."

Charles Manson, Woodstock, Miracle Mets, Chappaquiddick, and men on the moon; it was hard for me to believe it all happened in the summer of 1969. On Sunday, July 20th, two American astronauts, Neil Armstrong and Buzz Aldrin, landed on the moon and then four days later returned safely to earth. Man's first step on the moon, a quarter million miles away, was witnessed on television by millions of people throughout the world. The lunar module had a special cathode ray tube that picked up the TV camera signals on the moon and sent the signals to earth. Then the pictures were transmitted by television. The special cathode ray tube was developed and manufactured at our local Westinghouse Electronics plant. Our country's incredible success with the manned spaceflight program made the public more aviation-minded and indirectly stimulated airline industry growth during the 1960's. As a result, 1969 was the last year of railroad passenger service to Elmira.

Late in January, 1969 the news media reported that Chris-Craft Industries had targeted Piper Aircraft Corp. for a takeover. Chris-Craft, a diversified conglomerate, had a subsidiary which was one of the world's leading manufacturers of pleasure boats, and they wanted to get into the aircraft business. The president of Chris-Craft called William T. Piper, Jr. and told him of their intentions. This unfriendly takeover attempt was a complete surprise to the Piper president. Piper was ripe for a raid because it was in good financial shape and had a surplus of cash, and its stock was undervalued on the New York Stock Exchange.

We were concerned because not only was Piper a business customer of ours, but we had been long-time friends with the Piper family. Bill Piper, Jr. took the leadership in the family's fight to retain ownership of Piper Aircraft. While he was working on alternatives, another conglomerate, Bangar Punta, got into the act and started buying Piper stock. Under great pressure, the Piper family agreed to sell its 30% interest in the company to Bangar Punta if, with the Piper stock, it could acquire enough other stock to have a majority interest in the company. Bangar Punta was successful and eventually bought Chris-Craft's holdings, so they owned 100% of Piper Aircraft.

Since the Bangar Punta takeover, the ownership of Piper Aircraft has changed hands four times, and the company has gradually run down and now has serious financial problems. In my opinion, the organization misses the Piper family's management and their drive to develop and reinvest profits in their aircraft business. Lock Haven, Pennsylvania had been the Piper home for nearly a half century, but during the late 1970s their headquarters and manufacturing plants in the area were gradually abandoned.

Some good has come out of this very sad story. As the result of the Piper corporate raid and others like it, the Securities Exchange Commission now requires corporate raiders to notify the takeover candidate of their intentions when they have control of more than 5% of the stock in a company.

While the ownership control fight was in process, SAC received a new major subcontract from Piper for planning, tooling and production of two major fuselage sections of the new eight-passenger PA-31P pressurized Navajo. The order called for 100 sets of assemblies to be delivered over a two-year period. This was the last major project SAC received from Piper. In the mid 1970's, when we had an overload, Piper became one of Schweizer's subcontractors. They built the tail surface of the Ag Cat.

Some of the 16 Lockheed YO-3A quiet observation aircraft were now operational in Vietnam. There were good reports on the aircraft and the new night-vision infrared (FLIR) system. After the YO-3A project had been declassified, the October 13, 1969 issue of *Aviation Week and Space Technology* magazine reported the following information:

> Night-Vision sensor package earmarked for the Lockheed YO-3 quiet aircraft has completed 150 successful flights in the new aircraft with only a single failure. Developed by Xerox, the sensor system contains a 100-w tungsten searchlight with an infra-red filter, a periscopic sight using a direct-view image intensifier, and a Martin-Orlando yttrium aluminum garnet laser target illuminator/designator. The system is housed in the nose of the Army and Marine Corps YO-3 aircraft. Its line-of-sight is gyro stabilized.

Lockheed said that the U.S. Army was about to order 50 to 100 additional YO-3A aircraft over the next three years. We told them that some duplicate production fixtures would be required to meet their proposed schedule while enabling SAC to maintain our 2-32 sailplane production. Lockheed then gave us the order to build the duplicate tooling we requested, which included a complete set of wing assembly fixtures.

There were numerous newspaper stories and magazine articles about Jim Bede's airplane, a 2-32 sailplane derivative capable of flying non-stop around the world. A number of other airplane designers became interested in the 2-32 because of its long-span efficient wing and its tail, as well as its rugged aluminum construction. They saw the possibility of a low-cost military airplane such as the Lockheed YO-3A quiet airplane.

LTV Electrosystems, Inc. (LTVE) for example, was interested in the 2-32 as a poor man's U-2 (high altitude electronics aircraft).

Ernie worked with LTVE project engineer, Cliff Slagle, and staff and made a preliminary design of a 660hp turbo-prop configuration of the 2-32. The design of the wings was modified so each wing (L&R) became a sealed gas tank. As a result, the ship was capable of carrying 565 gallons of jet fuel. LTVE gave us an order in the spring of 1969 to build a prototype of their special-purpose airplane which was later called L450F (*Figure 76*). LTVE invested their own funds in this airplane development because they planned to use the L450F as an aerial platform in an attempt to sell a gigantic military electronic surveillance system to the government. The L450F airplane was designed to be piloted during testing and ferry flights. However, on its intended mission, it would be an unmanned, radio-controlled drone that would fly over 40,000 feet and have an endurance of more than 24 hours (*Figure 77*). The prototype was completed in the fall of 1969, disassembled and shipped to LTVE for the electronics installation. Flight tests were scheduled to start in March, 1970.

In December, 1969 the Company built its 1200th sailplane. The soaring movement was growing in the U.S., and the Soaring Society of America (SSA) reported 8,815 members. However, our sailplane deliveries dropped from 130 the previous year to 79 in 1969. The principal reason for this reduction was that the new 1-34 standard class contest ship was eight months behind our projected schedule for FAA approval and production. We were trying to get back into the contest market but were experiencing some problems. SAC designed the 1-34 to meet the new international standard class requirements, which proved to be a handicap when competing with the European ships then in production.

In January, 1969, before the production model was complete, we had fifty 1-34 orders, but by year end only seven aircraft had been delivered. This was a disappointment because we hoped to have some of our customers flying the 1-34 in the 1969 National Soaring Championship held at Marfa, Texas in July, but none were contest-ready. Of the 82 ships entered in the contest, only 22 were built in the United States and the top five places were European sailplanes.

At the National Agricultural Aviation Association Convention in Las Vegas in December, 1968, the 1969 Ag Cat model with a 600hp engine was introduced. It created a great deal of interest and sales orders. Grumman delivered a record 118 Ag Cats in 1969, and the project amounted to 54% of SAC's total business. Ten ships per month were rolling out of our hangar, which had made it possible to set up a production line. This helped to reduce our man-hours per ship and increased our productivity.

We found that the ag operators continually wanted more powerful airplanes. The original Ag Cat had a 220hp engine. Then in 1963, it was increased to 300hp and in 1964 to 450hp. For the 1969 model, the structure was beefed up so it could utilize the 600hp Pratt-Whitney R 1340 engine. The new model allowed the operators to carry a full hopper load of 1¼ tons and to operate safely from small grass fields near their application areas rather than from airports. It also improved the pilot's safety because he had reserve power to pull out of tight places.

Brother Paul was an active member and a director of the Harris Hill Soaring Corp. (HHSC), a non-profit gliding and soaring club at the Harris Hill glider site and park in Chemung County. HHSC had the use of the Harris Hill administration building and hangars, which had been built by the county in the 1930's to attract gliding activity to our area. Paul had been a director of the SSA since 1946 and was aware that the organization was looking for a permanent home for their records and historical documents. The Harris Hill organization had similar interests.

In 1968, Paul encouraged HHSC to start a soaring museum, library and archives at Harris Hill. The hangar was used to store some historic ships, and one room in the administration building was also set aside for this function. In 1969, in support of the progress made by the HHSC, the directors of SSA voted to make Harris Hill the official site of the SSA museum, library and archives. (A great deal of progress has been made at the museum in the last 20 years, and today it is an outstanding museum and tourist attraction. Paul deserves a tremendous amount of the credit for the development of the museum.)

The year 1969 would have been a very profitable year, but we had made a major investment in the 1-34 sailplane program.

Sales for the year amounted to $4.3 million, and only a 2% profit was earned. Our employment remained steady and averaged 328 workers. Two new directors were elected to the Schweizer board: Edward A. Mooers, president of Elmira's Hilliard Corp. and Alpheus F. Underhill, a local architect. (See Appendix 6.) After 27 years as SAC's personnel manager, Eugene S. Bardwell retired in March. He was replaced by his assistant, Americo "Ricky" Tagliaferri. Leslie D. Clute, president of the Arnot Ogden Memorial Hospital and a director of SAC, recruited me to serve on the hospital board. I accepted the challenge and found it to be an interesting and rewarding community service.

In January, 1969 my son Stuart completed his master's degree in aeronautical engineering at Princeton University. A month later, he joined the Boeing Airplane Company in Seattle, Washington. He was assigned to the (SST) supersonic transport airplane project. When he and Lucy left for Seattle, they took their only piece of furniture with them, a six-foot-high grandfather's clock. Stuart built a box for it and mounted it on top of their compact car. I am sure all the way across the country people wondered what was in the "coffin."

Son Paul was completing his fifth year at the Dartmouth's Engineering school that spring. Lauren Jo Whittier had graduated from St. Lawrence University in June of 1968, and she and Paul had been married at Christmas. Paul found a very small apartment off-campus, which he called the "love nest." They thought that two could live as cheaply as one if Lauren had a job while Paul was finishing school, but in February, before Lauren could find a job, she broke her leg skiing. About a week later, our third son John broke his leg in a ski race at Dartmouth. This was just normal operations for the Schweizer family. Paul graduated in June and also went to work at Boeing. He was assigned to the Remotely Piloted Vehicle (RPV) section.

70

71

70. *Bell UH-B "Huey" Helicopters, famous for action in Vietnam, arrive at an advance training base. Huey elevators were made by SAC (**71**).*

72

73

72. The SGS 2-33 in 1967, an immediate success in the booming sailplane market; 579 were built by 1984. 73. Early "stealth," a Lockheed Q Star, an odd-looking, quiet observation craft built on a modified SAC frame.

74

75

74. *Next generation stealth: Lockheed YO3A quiet observation airplane, built on SAC's 2-32 airframe for reconnaissance in Vietnam.* **75.** *An SGS 1-34 over Tempe, Arizona.*

76

77

76., 77. *Manned and unmanned versions of the LTV L450. The former established 16 world records for turboprop aircraft. The latter made a 22-hour flight and reached 52,000 feet. Both were derived from SAC's 2-32.* LTV Electrosystems, Inc.

11

THE VIETNAM WAR PEAKS 1970–1973

The first Boeing 747 jumbo jet went into operation for Pan American World Airways in 1970. It was capable of carrying 362 passengers. The 747 is still in production, but it now has more powerful engines and has had some airframe modifications which allow it to carry up to 500 passengers, depending on its configuration.

In 1970, Elmira's Sperry Rand plant laid off 1,300 workers when it discontinued manufacturing its line of desk top electro-mechanical calculators which sold at a retail price of $350 to $750. The Elmira firm could not compete with calculator manufacturers who started to utilize the new electronic and computer technology developed during the 1960's. Today, ten dollar hand-held calculators can perform more mathematical functions than did the large Sperry Rand machines.

The unpopular and costly Vietnam War was still dragging on, and, to make matters worse, the United States was having a recession. In an attempt to reduce the Federal deficit, Congress and the Nixon administration reduced aerospace and military airplane production. The YO-3A follow-on contract of 50 to 100 airplanes was put on hold. This was a blow to SAC and more so to Lockheed. They felt so sure that the contract would be renewed that in 1969 they released an order for additional 2-32 tooling at their expense. The first order of 16 quiet airplanes was completed the previous year, and our only Lockheed business in 1970 was spare parts support for the YO-3A's then operating in Vietnam.

The LTV Electrosystem's L450F high altitude airplane flight test program got underway in February, 1970. The first airplane which was owned by LTVE crashed during the early stage of the flight test program.

The ship was flying at a high altitude when it stalled and went into a spin. The pilot tried unsuccessfully to recover and decided to eject when he was at very high altitude. He came down safely in his parachute but the aircraft crashed. The flight was monitored by a flight recorder in the L450F and from the ground by radar and radio. Fortunately for the project, the post-flight investigation determined that the crash was not the fault of the aircraft, but of pilot error. According to the LTVE briefing, the investigators said that the test pilot should have ridden the ship down to a lower altitude where the air was thicker and then made his recovery. Earlier tests indicated that the ship had good spin recovery characteristics.

LTVE immediately ordered a second airplane to replace the original. The proving out of the LTVE's electronic surveillance system was put on hold until LTVE received its aerial platform. With a super fire drill by both companies, the second ship was ready to fly by July. For the balance of the year, the L450F was thoroughly tested with a pilot at the controls and then as an unmanned radio-controlled drone. In December of 1970, the U.S. Air Force became increasingly interested and ordered two L450F prototypes so they could evaluate the aircraft themselves.

The cut in military aircraft production also had a negative impact on SAC's opportunity to develop new subcontract business. Some of our orders were reduced, and schedules were stretched out. Because of the Vietnam War, however, the Bell Helicopter spares volume increased in spite of the general cutback. We produced large numbers of elevators for the UH-1 "Hueys" and the side doors for Model 47 observation helicopters (the ship used on the M*A*S*H TV show). "Huey" elevators with bullet holes were frequently replaced in the field, and Model 47 doors were continually being replaced. It was common practice for pilots of Bell 47's to remove the doors before flying over water or to jettison them while in flight if necessary. They did the same thing during hot weather.

Free market civilian airplane sales were down from 11,268 in 1969 to 6,759 in 1970, a 41% decrease. (See Appendix 5.) The market changed so fast that Beech, Piper, Cessna and most other manufacturers were caught with large inventories of unsold airplanes. Piper stopped their production line in July, 1970 for four months. The Navajo fuselage project, our second largest subcontract project, was also stopped for that period.

Fortunately for SAC, the Ag Cat sales held up fairly well. It amounted to $1.8 million dollars in sales, or 50% of our business. A total of 91 ships was delivered, down from the previous year's high of 119 airplanes. The market for ag-airplanes was 455 in 1970, and the Ag Cat share was 20% of that total. This represented growth from 7% in 1965, so Grumman and SAC were pleased with the results. Our average Ag Cat production was two ships per week which meant at least two flight tests each week.

As part of the FAA approved flight test, each Ag Cat would takeoff with a load of water, fly to the test area, south of Cayuta Lake, make a dive and release the load, which would make a big splash. Our airport manager reported that he had a call from an elderly woman in a rural area south of Cayuta. She said, "About twice a week a man in the same yellow and gray two-winger flies over and drops water on my property." After that we instructed Clyde Cook, our test pilot, to move around the area a little.

In 1970, Joe Lincoln and a passenger set a world record in a Schweizer 2-32 sailplane. They flew from Santa Fe, New Mexico to Saledo, Colorado and returned, a soaring flight of 404 miles. Only three 2-32 civilian sailplanes were sold that year, but we did have some sailplane derivative military airplane business. There were two factors which affected the 2-32 civilian sales. First, it was necessary to keep prices for the soaring public in line with what the military was paying. Therefore, the price was raised to $15,000 per ship. Second, the two-place category was no longer a class in national and international soaring competition.

A total of 85 sailplanes were delivered for the year, which breaks down as follows:

Deliveries	*Model*	*Classification*
14	1-26	Single-Place (One Design Class)
3	2-32	Three-Place High Performance
31	2-33	Basic Two-Place Trainer
37	1-34	Single-Place High Performance

By year end, the 44th new 1-34 sailplane had been built, and we were getting close to a break-even point on production. Therefore, the pressure was on Paul and the sales department to generate 1-34 sales. (See Appendix 4.)

A log cabin style glider school administration building was completed that spring. The building, adjacent to the airport, greatly improved SAC's ability to service glider school customers and the public. A total of 6,773 flights was made in 1970. We had some very distinguished visitors who included Werner von Braun, world renowned NASA space scientist, and Alexander de Seversky, a World War I ace with 13 kills and author of the widely read book published just before WWII, *Victory Through Air Power*. I had the pleasure of giving de Seversky, the founder of Republic Aviation Corp., his first sailplane flight (*Figure 78*).

SAC sales for 1970 were down from previous years, to 3.6 million dollars. (See Appendix 4.) Due to the reduction in business volume and the 1-34 sailplane starting load cost, profits amounted to only 1% on sales. Attorney Harry Moseson, an original Director of the Company and representative of the stock owned by Elmira Industries, retired in October after 30 years of service. Harry was a helpful advisor and a friend of the Schweizer brothers. Attorney Douglas P. Craig, son of former Director Thomas S. Craig, joined the SAC board in December. Doug was general counsel for U.S. Industries of New York City.

In September, Gayle, our youngest child, entered Wheelock College in Boston. Peg and I took her to Wheelock and then continued on to Cape Cod for a second honeymoon. We visited Wellfleet and Corn Hill where, in 1929, Navy Captain Ralph S. Barnaby set a new soaring record with a 15 minute flight along the sand dunes. He broke Orville Wright's 9 minute and 45 second soaring record set at Kitty Hawk in 1911. In addition, he earned the first "C" soaring award in the United States. This was the same Captain Barnaby who accepted the first Schweizer 2-8 or LNS-1 sailplane for the U.S. Navy in 1941.

Les Schweizer, Ernie's son, graduated from the New York University Guggenheim School of Aeronautics in June and joined SAC's engineering department. On his own time, he designed and started to build a sailplane with a 75 foot wingspan that was projected to have a glide ratio of better than 40 to 1. The U.S. Congress cancelled the Boeing SST, and Stuart was transferred to Boeing's rocket engine plant in Huntsville, Alabama. This time Boeing moved the grandfather clock "coffin."

Since 1944, our sailplane business had accounted for 5 to 20% of our annual sales, and the balance had been attributed to subcontract work. The sales volume of our own product line was not sufficient to support the well-rounded aircraft facility required to develop and build competitive sailplanes. Therefore, subcontract work was essential. During 1970 and 1971, congressional action had dried up new military aircraft funds except for research and development contracts. The commercial airplane and airliner business was also depressed. To make matters worse, Congress also cancelled the SST development program.

The companies still in business which had been major airframe subcontractors during WWII had been forced to change their product lines or go out of business. Therefore, SAC's major competitors in 1971 were companies which were not dependent upon airframe subcontract business alone but considered it as add-on business. Examples were Twin Coach (a bus manufacturer in Buffalo, New York) and Mercury Aircraft (manufacturer of business machine cabinets in Hammondsport, New York). Twin Coach was building the tail surfaces for the Gulfstream II, and Mercury was building the heat shields for the Grumman's A6E Navy Intruder.

SAC was fortunate to have the Ag Cat project with its increasing volume. However, we were becoming too dependent on it. It was still a Grumman subcontract project. SAC did not own it, so we could not control its destiny. Grumman had acquired a commercial aircraft facility in Savannah, Georgia where the Gulfstream II executive transport airplane was being built. Some of the Grumman executives talked about moving the Ag Cat to Georgia, and this subject came up during Ag Cat contract negotiations. To counter this argument, we pointed out that SAC had fourteen years of built-in know-how on the project which would be lost in a move and that the move would be costly to Grumman. In addition, the transfer would probably create delivery problems which might jeopardize the Ag Cat's position in the market. Apparently Grumman agreed with our rationale because they kept ordering Ag Cats.

The message was loud and clear to SAC management that we must diversify and find some new proprietary products. In our search, we came across Dave Thurston and the Teal Amphibian. Thurston Aircraft Corp. of Sanford, Maine had the Teal airplane design FAA certified, tooled and in production. A total of 18 ships had been delivered to customers, but the company was on the verge of being forced out of business because it could not raise sufficient capital to absorb the high start-up cost of developing a production airplane.

Designed as a sportsmen's airplane, the Teal was a two-place amphibian which could operate from land or water. SAC management talked to the Teal owners, studied the project carefully and arrived at the following conclusions which were reported to our Board of Directors:

> The Teal program could be purchased for a very reasonable price;
> The all-aluminum airplane design would fit our production capabilities;

We estimated that there would be a market for a minumum of 25 airplanes per year during the next 10 years; The Teal project would provide diversification and help stabilize our employment and sales.

Satisfactory purchasing arrangements were worked out in the fall of 1971, and the purchase was authorized by the Schweizer board. The project included the Teal design, FAA certification, tooling, inventory of parts and one airplane which was used as a demonstrator. Dave Thurston, an aeronautical engineer and founder of the Company, agreed to join SAC as the engineering manager of the Teal project. Dave worked for Grumman during WWII and was responsible for their post-war amphibian designs. The project was moved to Elmira in the late fall, and we expected production to start in January, 1972. My son, Stuart, was interested in the Teal project and left his Boeing job at Huntsville to join SAC in January, 1972.

In December, 1971, the aviation public was notified of the Teal transfer through an industry-wide press release which appeared in practically all of the aviation periodicals throughout the world. The airplane was then named the Schweizer Teal Amphibian.

The No. 3 and 4 LTVE high-altitude L450F drones, ordered by the USAF late in 1970 for their own evaluation program, were delivered in the fall of 1971. Military planners were interested in the high altitude unmanned drones because they were looking for ways to avoid some of the past problems with manned aircraft reconnaissance flights over hostile territories. When they were intercepted, captured, or destroyed with a crew aboard, it often created an international incident. The Gary Powers U-2 incident was a good example. The political impact of operating an unmanned reconnaissance aircraft was considered to be much less of a problem.

In line with this rationale, the USAF had organized two experimental high-altitude, unmanned drone programs: Compass Dwell and Compass Cope. The Compass Dwell program required a drone to carry an electronic payload of 700 pounds and to operate at an altitude of over 40,000 feet for a duration of 24 hours. The LTVE L450F drone was designed to meet this mission. The Compass Cope program required a drone that could carry a 1,500 pound electronic payload and to operate from 50,000 to 70,000 feet for a duration of 24 hours. The Boeing Company and Teledyne Ryan Aircraft Corp. had individual contracts to build prototype drones for the Compass Cope program. A fly-off was planned and the winner would receive the potential production contract. The altitude requirement for the Cope program dictated jet engines. My son, Paul, who was working in the Boeing RPV division because of his involvement with sailplanes, was given the opportunity to assist with the development of the configuration and the preliminary design of the Boeing drone. The Boeing drone looked like a big sailplane with a 90 foot wingspan.

Until June of 1971, LTVE was the only company building drones for the Compass Dwell program. The USAF notified the aircraft industry that they were prepared to release a Request for Quotation (RFQ) to another company for a second experimental prototype drone which met the Compass Dwell specifications. A number of companies made proposals, including the Martin Marietta Corp. of Baltimore, Maryland.

In January, Martin Marietta representatives visited SAC and wanted to know if we had a sailplane design that could be converted into a pilotless drone. They also wanted to know if SAC would be willing and able to work with Martin on a ship that would be in direct competition with the LTVE drone. We could see no conflict as long as the 2-32 design, used on the LTVE drone, was not used by Martin. The 1-34 sailplane design appealed to the Martin project engineer. He liked the fuselage lines and the small cross section which would decrease aerodynamic drag. With no pilot, the cockpit area would still provide ample room for the electronic payload.

Ernie turned over the coordination of the Martin project to his son, Leslie. He worked with Martin on the preliminary design of their drone for the technical proposal to the USAF. Martin Marietta with their Model 845 proposal won the USAF contract for the second Compass Dwell drone project and in June of 1971, SAC received a contract to design and build three drones for Martin (*Figure 79*).

The 1-34 fuselage was modified to accept an engine and electronic payload plus a landing gear. The wing span was increased from 50 to 60 feet and the wings were redesigned as sealed gas tanks. The drones were required to be delivered to Martin by February, 1972 (*Figure 80*) because the USAF had scheduled a fly-off between the LTVE and Martin Marietta drones in June. SAC felt a little smug about this situation because if there were a production contract for Compass Dwell drones, we would win either way.

In 1971, the U.S. sailplane market dropped from approximately 200 to 150 ships. SAC sales amounted to 64 units, the same percentage of the market we had the previous year. Sixty high performance sailplanes were imported, principally from Germany, and the balance was made by three other U.S. manufacturers. Sales of SAC's high performance standard class 1-34 sailplane were disappointing. Only 16 were delivered in 1971, which amounted to a total of 50 1-34's sold since 1969. We expected by this time to have absorbed our start-up costs and to have at least 100 ships in service, but, in order to spread the product development cost, it had taken SAC an extra year to get the 1-34 into production.

We learned the hard way that very few sailplane buyers competed in contests and that many sailplanes were purchased for prestige reasons. The smooth looking fiberglass imports had sales appeal. During the previous four-year period, fiberglass technology had given the Europeans an advantage; they could make minor aerodynamic changes without affecting the basic structure of the aircraft. The result was a sleek looking bird.

FAA regulations made it uneconomical for SAC to even consider fiberglass as a basic structure. So even though the 1-34 was priced competitively and was an excellent sailplane, by 1971 it was no longer the last word in performance and styling. In addition, the 1-34 was designed to meet the stringent International Standard Class requirements, while the European designers were taking a more liberal interpretation of the rules. It is interesting to note that with increased aerodynamic and fabrication technology, the top sailplanes in each era have gradually increased their glide angles: 1940, it was 25 to 1; in 1989, 50 to 1.

The Ag Cat business was holding at a steady production rate of nine airplanes per month. A total of 103 were delivered to customers and the Ag Cat had 22% of ag-plane sales. Each year a number of product improvements were made to increase the Ag Cat's service life and productivity in the field. For example, in 1971 a new urethane-resin paint finish was incorporated to inhibit oxidation of all the metal parts of the aircraft. The fuel supply was increased from 46 to 80 gallons by adding two optional fuel tanks in the upper wing panels.

In 1971, OSHA (Occupational Safety Health Act) became law, and the Company was faced with some major equipment and plant modification expenses. SAC sales for the year were $4.2 million, and a 4% profit was earned on sales. A breakdown of the year's sales was as follows: (See Appendix 4.)

Ag Cat	46%
Sailplane	15%
Military Related Sailplane	8%
Subcontract	31%

In June, my son, John, completed his five-year engineering program at Dartmouth. He had a very low draft number and was inducted into the U.S. Army a month later. While in boot camp, he found out that the Army's Cold Weather Research Laboratory needed some engineers. Being a rock mountain climber and skier, he jumped at the opportunity. John spent the next two years working in Alaska and Canada on winter warfare problems.

On a fall weekend in 1971, I made a pilgrimage to the Wright Memorial at Kitty Hawk, North Carolina. I left Peg visiting her sister in Richmond and flew to Kitty Hawk with my niece, Ruth Antell. The airport was one paved strip next to the Memorial, and it was a thrill to land my plane in the same field where the Wright Brothers had flown 68 years earlier. I remember reading that on the Wrights' first visit to Kitty Hawk in 1900, they took the train to Elizabeth City, North Carolina. Then they missed the boat to Kitty Hawk and had to wait a week for the next one. This seemed odd to me. However, on my flight there, I flew to the radio range station at Elizabeth City and found that Kitty Hawk was a 30 mile flight over water. I understood why they had to wait a week for the next boat.

In June, 1972, Tropical Storm Agnes created the worst natural disaster in the history of the Elmira-Corning area. The Chemung River rose 25 feet and went over the dikes built after the 1946 flood. On the 23rd of June, the downtown business section of Elmira was covered with 6 to 10 feet of water. Many buildings and a number of bridges were destroyed. When the water subsided, the Lake Street Bridge was the only Chemung River bridge approved for truck crossings. About 15,000 people were driven from their homes. My son, Stuart, who had just moved to West Elmira had four feet of water on the first floor of his house.

Fortunately, at SAC the Agnes flood damage was minimal. Water surrounded the plant, but we had no water in the building except for two inches in one warehouse built a few inches below the plant elevation. However, some parked cars in low areas of the parking lot received water damage, and Stuart's car was among them. The insurance company declared it a total loss, but he bought it back for 75 dollars. He used the car for the next three years until it was totaled again by the 1975 Sing Sing

Creek flood. He had a second insurance claim on the same car against the same insurance company.

In January of 1972, the world-famous Morrow bicycle coaster brake production was moved from the Eclipse-Bendix plant in Elmira Heights to San Luis Potosi, Mexico. The coaster brake was developed in 1895 by the Eclipse Machine Company, and was their principal product until WWI. After the war, automotive component products gradually became their principal business, but until the move in 1972, the coaster brake production still provided work for 100 to 200 employees. Bendix moved the project to Mexico to take advantage of the lower labor rates so their prices would be more competitive with those of European manufacturers. Unfortunately, the high labor rates and unproductive work practices at Bendix were geared to the Detroit automotive industry controlled by the UAW. Since we shared the same labor market, SAC's sailplane business also suffered from the same condition. We, too, were competing with manufacturers whose labor rates were much lower than ours—which gave us great concern about the future of our sailplane business.

The fly-off between the LTVE and Martin Compass Dwell drones took place at Edwards Air Force Base during the summer of 1972. It was like a big model airplane contest. *Aviation Week* magazine reported that the Martin piston-engine-powered entry demonstrated an endurance of 28 hours but fell short of the 40,000 foot altitude requirement. The unmanned LTVE turbine-engine-powered L450F exceeded the altitude objective by 12,000 feet but could not match the endurance of the Martin 845.

Prior to the competition, the Defense Department announced that the winner would be awarded an order for ten aircraft. It was understood that LTVE was the winner, but due to budget constraints and new altitude considerations, the production order was put on hold. When the FAA and the international airline organization heard that the military planned to fly unmanned drones at 40,000 feet, it got their attention. In their opinion, this altitude was not high enough to keep the drones out of the commercial aviation environment of 20,000 to 45,000 feet.

The 1,000th Ag Cat was built by SAC in October, 1972. This segment of our business was rapidly expanding, and it appeared as if it would continue. The Ag Cat amounted to 62% of our sales volume for that year. The Schweizers had mixed feelings about this situation because, in theory, we did not want any product that was not owned by SAC to account for more than 50% of our total business. We enjoyed the increased sales volume, but it forced SAC to expand so rapidly that other business opportunities were neglected. However, we did not want Grumman to set up their own Ag Cat facility, so we invested and expanded our facilities, equipment and personnel to meet Grumman's ag-plane requirements. During 1972, our Ag Cat production rate was increased from two to three ships per week, and deliveries totaled 141 airplanes. The ag-plane sales for 1972 were 565 units, and the Ag Cat share had increased to 25% of the market.

In December, 1972 SAC completed the 1500th sailplane since SAC's founding. That year, 91 ships were sold, a 50% increase over 1971. SAC had four different models in production (1-26, 2-32, 2-33 and 1-34) and dominated the U.S. training and recreational sailplane market. However, because the 1-34 never really caught on, the Company was losing out in the high performance market.

Les Schweizer, who had done an excellent job on the Martin drone, with his father came up with a preliminary design for a 15 meter class contest sailplane which appealed to us. It looked like it would be a step ahead of the field. In the fall of 1972, it was decided to build a prototype for flight evaluation. This model was called the SGS 1-35 and was scheduled to fly in the spring of 1973.

By mid-January, the Teal Amphibian demonstrator and four truck loads of material arrived at SAC. It was a big job to sort things out, classify them, and inspect all the aircraft material, parts and tooling. The Teal project was not a top priority job since we had to accelerate the Ag Cat and sailplane production to meet the recent increase in orders. Our objective was to set up the Teal project carefully for long-range efficient production.

Prior to the purchase of the program, we contacted the owners of the 18 Teals built by Thurston and found they had some legitimate complaints and ideas for product improvements that should be incorporated into the design. In addition, from our review at Thurston Aircraft, we were aware that some of the tooling was inadequate and must be improved to build the aircraft efficiently and to our quality standards. By June, the design changes, retooling, and the production control and inspection systems were in order, and Teal production was started on a limited basis.

In the meantime, we had the Teal demonstrator flying. Clarence See, a professional seaplane pilot, was hired on a part-time basis to train some of us so we could obtain our FAA seaplane flight rating. Erwin Jones, test pilot; Tony Doherty, sales manager; and Stu and I earned our seaplane ratings in the spring of 1972.

The first Schweizer-manufactured Teal Amphibian (Serial No. 20) was ready to fly by the end of July (*Figure 81*). During the next month, the ship was thoroughly flight tested and flown for evaluation by all of the Schweizer pilots and a number of professional seaplane pilots. After studying the flight reports, Schweizer management concluded that the Teal Amphibian was not ready to be marketed. The basic problem was that a minimum airspeed of 60 mph was required for takeoff. That was not a problem on land, but on water, it was a long ride to obtain the necessary speed. We believed that in rough water 60 mph could be a dangerous speed for a small flying boat. In fairness to Dave Thurston, the designer, the original Teal was a better amphibian at 1800 pounds gross weight. Unfortunately, it gradually grew in weight at Thurston Aircraft, and with our modifications to improve safety and maintenance, the gross weight increased to 2200 pounds. This increased the take-off speed from 54 to 60 mph, and obviously we could not put the ship on a diet.

On August 29, 1972, the No. 1 Schweizer Teal Amphibian was lost in 500 feet of water in Seneca Lake. I was the pilot, and Donald Quigley, our chief tool engineer, was the passenger. I wanted to familiarize Don with the retractable landing gear system because he was responsible for the retooling and building the equipment. We took off from the Chemung County Airport about 4:30 p.m. and headed north to Seneca Lake. Over Watkins Glen, I checked the wind direction and water conditions, retracted my landing gear and landed two miles north at Painted Rock.

The water was rougher than I had anticipated, and I was concerned about our take-off. My choices were to taxi back to Watkins and beach the airplane or to make a quick take-off and go home. I chose the latter. On the take-off run, as soon as the amphibian got on the step, I experienced severe pitching and heaving which made it difficult to control the flying boat. When I reached 55 mph, I hit a swell which threw the ship four or five feet into the air. It was not going fast enough to fly so the nose dropped. Upon re-entering the water, the aircraft flipped over. I found out that when you hit water at 55 mph, it is "really hard."

Fortunately, the canopy doors opened when the plane flipped. As soon as we hit, I released my safety belt, got out of the Teal and looked for Don. He was not around, so I went back into the cockpit and found him hanging upside down from his safety belt with his head in the water. As soon as I released his belt, he fell into the water and immediately started to swim. Thank God! We hung on to the Teal until it started to sink. Just then a boat arrived and rescued us. The Teal Amphibian sank. We were both injured but not seriously. I felt like someone had beat me with a baseball bat. Don spent ten days in the hospital, and I spent four.

After the Teal accident, the project was put on hold. We had been aware that the take-off speed was too high and SAC decided to add a new type of high-lift wing tips and slotted wing flaps to the amphibian. These modifications were incorporated in a prototype airplane and the take-off speed was reduced by 10 mph. The changes were FAA certified by the spring of 1973 and the ship was ready to market. For marketing purposes, we created a new name for the modified aircraft, the Teal II (*Figure 82*).

Several weeks later, I talked to some Hobart College scientists who had made a study of Seneca Lake. They showed me the contour of the lake from the south end to the north which along the track of my takeoff run. In the Painted Rocks area where the Teal flipped, the depth of the lake drops from 200 to 500 feet. This creates a steep 300 foot underwater cliff, and with a strong north wind, a treacherous cross-rib wave pattern with large swells develops. (I was also interested to find out about five years after my accident that three of the original Teals had also flipped in a rough water takeoff run.)

Two years later, we sold the rights to the sunken Teal for one dollar to a Seneca Lake diver who said he could recover the aircraft. A legal sales agreement was worked out which held SAC blameless during the recovery operation and prohibited the new owner from ever flying the aircraft. Personally, I never thought it would be recovered. Yet while I was writing this account, in May, 1990, 18 years after the accident, the ship was found by another diver at a depth of 450 feet. In a professionally constructed home-made submarine, salvageers hooked a line to the aircraft and used special equipment to raise the aircraft. Then they towed it to shore. I witnessed the final stage of the recovery. My radio headset was found on the cockpit floor, and the diver presented it to me. This was a traumatic moment for me, and I swallowed hard as the memories of the accident flooded my mind. My major interest in examining the recovered Teal was to see if the tail landing gear had retracted during my take-off run. As the result of damage caused by the recovery procedure, however, I could not determine if it had been retracted. After the recovery, there was a big rhubarb because the diver who bought the Teal for a dollar claimed all rights to the recovered aircraft. He eventually got it, but in the meantime, the area press made the most of the story.

Stuart was interested in the manufacturing end of the business and was moved to this area to assist me. He pointed out that with 350 employees it was becoming more difficult to manage the business by feel and suggested we consider a computer. In June of 1972, the Board of Directors authorized management to lease an IBM System 3/Model 10 computer. This was a far-reaching decision. First, it meant a minimum annual commitment of $40,000. Second, practically all accounting and production control systems had to be modified to conform to the computer system. Our payroll system was easily converted, but because the cost accounting and production control data was more approximate, the computer output was not meaningful until we could establish an accurate base. The adjustment to the computer did not come easily, but indirectly it disciplined the organization to keep more accurate records and to follow established procedures.

The Company's 1972 sales were a record $4.8 million. (See Appendix 4.) This is the equivalent of $18 million in 1989 dollars. Our average hourly labor rate was $3.50 per hour, and we sold an hour of labor with profit for ten dollars. Due to a large investment in the product development of the Teal and 1-35 sailplane, our profit was only approximately 2% of sales income.

Two plant additions were built that year. One was a 600 sq. ft. air-conditioned room for the computer and the other, an 8000 sq. ft. assembly addition. This increased our total plant area to 110,000 sq. ft. which was about the size of three football fields.

In September, Nicholas Haich, the treasurer of SAC since 1941, retired. He was an excellent financial man. His well-trained assistant, Joseph Kroczynski, replaced him. In October, Leslie Schweizer married Bonnifer Smith, daughter of New York State Senator William T. "Cadillac Smith" and Dorothy Smith. The Big Flats farmer and senator got the name "Cadillac Smith" in national headlines in 1961 when he bought a new Cadillac for $6100 and put the following sign on his car and drove his family to Washington. "Thank you JFK and Orville. We bought this car with the money we received for not growing corn." (Orville Freeman was the Secretary of Agriculture.)

A cease-fire agreement was reached with North Vietnam in January, 1973. On May 1, President Nixon was accused of attempting to cover up a break-in at the Watergate offices of the Democratic Party in 1970. On October 11, Spiro Agnew resigned the Vice Presidency and pleaded *nolo contendere* or no contest to a government charge that he failed to report $29,500 of income received in 1967. Gerald Ford was named by Nixon as successor to Agnew, and on December 7, Congress approved the appointment and Ford became Vice President.

With the war ending for the U.S., military procurement funds were further reduced. The Compass Dwell production drone program was put on the shelf, and our subcontract parts business decreased to 11% of total sales, the lowest percentage since WWII. Fortunately for us, the farm economy was strong, and SAC had all the ag-plane business it could handle. The Ag

Cat represented 69% of our total sales, though for stability, we were trying to diversify our business.

The ending of the war also touched off inflation. In 1971 and 1972, the U.S. inflation rate was 3.3 and 3.4%, respectively, but during 1973 it increased to 8.8%. Labor and material costs grew rapidly and reduced the profit margin on the Ag Cat and other fixed-price business. The 1973 Ag Cat contract was negotiated in April, 1972, eight months before the first airplane was delivered in January. During the negotiations, we asked for inflation protection, but since there had been no change in the inflation rate in 1972, we backed off on this demand in favor of solutions to other pricing problems. The SAC operating profit was needed to fund the two development programs in process that would, we hoped, provide business diversification. They were the new 1-35 sailplane and the Teal II. Our estimate to fund these programs was well over a half million dollars in 1973. We felt these programs were important to the future of our Company, so they were kept on schedule. The development cost ate up all of our 1973 profit; so with a record sales of $5.6 million, the Company had a break-even year financially.

Grumman's new commercial airplane division in Savannah, Georgia, Grumman American Aviation Corp. (GAAC), had corporate responsibility as well as the direct sales responsibility for the Ag Cat program. GAAC manufactured the Gulfstream II executive jet transport and was then developing a line of small private and business aircraft.

During the 1970's there was a large demand for agricultural products throughout the world. Prosperous U.S. farmers were utilizing advanced ag-technology, including ag-planes, to expand their output. Grumman dealers were selling more airplanes than we could produce. Our 1973 contract called for 150 Ag Cats, and even though we pulled out all the stops and built 171 ships (three and a half Ag Cats per week), we still could not satisfy the demand. Our employment grew to 395 workers, and we were reaching the maximum capacity for our facilities and equipment. (See Appendix 1.)

In the spring of 1973, prior to the 1974 negotiations, we met with the president of Grumman American. We told him that SAC had to have a long-range production commitment from

GAAC so we could prepare properly to meet their requirements. They came back with a proposal to buy 200 Ag Cats in 1974, 245 in 1975 and 300 in 1976. We told GAAC that SAC would agree to the three year commitment if the following contract clause was accepted: "It is understood by SAC that GAAC intends to have Ag Cats built at SAC's Elmira plant through 1976. In addition, should GAAC decide to move the Ag Cat project, GAAC will give SAC two years advanced notice prior to 1976." After a week of long, hard negotiations, a contract agreement was reached including the price on the 1974 Ag Cat. The contract called for 200 aircraft to be built in 1974, a production rate of four aircraft per week. In addition, GAAC agreed to give SAC an advance of $200,000 ($1,000 per aircraft) to help SAC finance the inventory. This would allow SAC to purchase raw material and equipment in the most cost-effective quantities. GAAC also agreed to invest $45,000 in some duplicate and high-production tooling so a 300 aircraft rate per year could be achieved efficiently in 1976. As a result of this agreement, SAC launched a $200,000 plant expansion program in June which was as follows: (See Appendix 2.)

A 600 sq. ft. sandblast building with dust collection system to meet OSHA standards;
A 6,200 sq. ft. finishing building with infrared paint drying system for large assemblies such as wings;
A 6,200 sq. ft. welding building.

Our biggest production bottleneck in building four aircraft per week was a shortage of certified aircraft welders. We had 35 welders and needed 45. There were no aircraft welders in our area, so it was necessary to train our own. This took time and money. We learned that Piper Aircraft had a surplus of welding capacity; so on a subcontract basis, they agreed to build the welded Ag Cat tail surface structures for us. This solved our immediate welding problem.

A total of 91 sailplanes, comprised of four different models, were sold in 1973. This amounted to 17% of SAC's business. The 1-35 Standard Class Contest sailplane prototype made its first flight in April, 1973 (*Figure 83*). After 50 hours of flying and many comparison flights with the top European fiberglass ships, we decided in May to put the 1-35 into production. Our goal was to have the new model tooled and FAA certified by the spring of 1974. Our sales department felt there would be a market for 100 1-35 sailplanes per year for the next five years. This helped us justify the half million dollar investment.

Our soaring school had another successful year. Ten thousand flights were made at the school during its five- month operating period in 1973 (*Figure 84*). This amounted to 75 flights per day when the weather was suitable for flying. I was out at the school late one afternoon to take a flight and a very attractive woman, whom I did not know, ran up to me and gave me a kiss. Sometimes it is an advantage to look like my brother Paul.

In August of that year, our soaring school made its 100,000th flight. The regional director of the FAA flew to Elmira for the occasion and presented SAC management with a safety award for operating the school for 28 years without a serious mishap (*Figure 85*).

The Teal Amphibian sales for 1973 were disappointing; only six were sold. We looked for a market of at least 25 per year to sportsmen pilots and to seaplane trainer facilities. The original Teal sold at $16,995 and our price two years later with improvements was $24,950. We still felt that with proper marketing, the Teal had worldwide sales opportunities. Therefore, we decided to keep it in production another year. We were encouraged by a sale of a Teal to a Swedish school teacher who ran a seaplane flight training school. He took delivery in Elmira and put an auxiliary gas tank in the fuselage and flew to Sweden. His route was as follows: Elmira to Northern Newfoundland; to the west side of Greenland, around Greenland to the east side; to Reykjavik, Iceland; to northern England; to Denmark and home to Sweden.

My third son, John, the winter warfare specialist, married Jennifer Lucas, a Mount Holyoke College graduate and native Elmiran, in August, 1973. He received an early release from the Army so he could enter the Tuck Graduate School of Business at Dartmouth College that September. Like Lauren, Paul's wife, Jenny got a job at Dartmouth to support the family; but unlike Lauren, Jenny did not immediately break her leg while skiing. She broke it while horsing around with John on the golf course. She fell into a ditch.

78 

79 

78. *Aviation pioneer author and builder, Alexander de Seversky, about to make his first sailplane ride with Bill Schweizer.* Elmira Star Gazette **79.** *Martin Marietta 845 unmanned drone, derived from the SAC 1-34 and built in conjunction with SAC to provide a high-altitude surveillance craft.*

80

81

82

80. *The Martin Marietta 845 drone ready for a test flight.* Martin Marietta, Inc. ***81.*** *SAC Teal 1A Amphibian, purchased from Thurston in 1971. Despite an improved version (**82**), the market for the Teal never developed.*

83 

84 

85 

*83. SGS 1-35 prototype flown by designer Leslie S. Schweizer; 101 were built 1973-1982 and proved to be top competitors. **84.** Lined up and ready to go at the SAC Soaring School, 1974. **85.** SAC's school receives 100,000-flight safety award from the FAA.*

12

THE AG CAT TAKES OFF 1974–1977

The Watergate investigation continued into 1974. On March, 2 six of President Nixon's aides were charged with obstruction of justice. On August, 6 Nixon admitted that he ordered a halt to the inquiry of Watergate six days after the break-in. Nixon, expecting impeachment, resigned on August, 9. Vice President Gerald Ford was sworn in as President, and, shortly thereafter, Nelson Rockefeller was named Vice President. The Watergate nightmare was over, and our great political system adjusted and grew stronger with some new safeguards to prevent the misuse of power in the future.

A fuel shortage had developed in the U.S. during the last half of 1973, and, as we entered 1974, it was at a crisis stage. Year round daylight savings time was adopted to save fuel but was repealed later in the year. The Federal Government asked for a 50% reduction in the use of fuel for pleasure and personal activities which included flying. We felt this restriction would reduce sailplane activity since travel to and from soaring sites and contests would be scrutinized. However, it did not work out that way. Apparently, the energy crisis gave soaring a boost because some aviation enthusiasts were beginning to realize that a great deal of flying time could be achieved in a sailplane for only the small amount of gas required for the airplane glider tow.

During this period an interesting glider sales opportunity landed on our doorstep. A well dressed, good looking young man about 35 years old flew into Elmira with a corporate airplane and pilot. He said that with the fuel shortage, he expected gliding and soaring to expand rapidly. He also said that he wanted to set up a sailplane operation outside of Denver with 12 of our sailplanes. Paul and sales manager Tony Doherty were six feet off the ground. They gave him all the information he requested, and the young man told them that his orders with down payments would be sent to SAC within a week. Nothing happened for the next ten days, so Tony did some checking on the prospect. Tony found out that two days after the man was in Elmira he was picked up for embezzling over a million dollars from the brokerage house where he worked in Denver.

Worldwide inflation was running wild in 1974, and it caused a dramatic increase in the cost of food, fuel, and material. The U.S. inflation rate was at an unprecedented 12.3%. This condition affected SAC's profitability since a large percentage of our business was based on fixed-price contracts. Our sailplane business had a similar problem because prices were set for one-year periods. Historically, our sailplanes were marginally priced anyway since we were attempting to help expand the gliding and soaring movement in the U.S. Obviously, we thought this would be to our advantage in the long run.

In spite of a 10% increase in sailplane prices, 120 units were sold in 1974. It was our best glider sales year since 1968. A breakdown of our sales was as follows:

Deliveries	*Model*	*Classification*
47	1-26	Single-Place One-Design Class
2	2-32	Three-Place High Performance
56	2-33	Two-Place Basic Trainer
3	1-34	Single-Place Standard Class
12	1-35	Single-Place 15 Meter Class

Although we had orders for and had scheduled 32 of the new 1-35 sailplanes for 1974, only 12 were delivered. The FAA certification and the production tooling which we expected to be ready in May was not completed until September.

A total of 201 Ag Cats were manufactured by SAC in 1974, which made a grand total of 1394 built since 1958. (See Appendix 3.) The Ag Cat production rate for the year averaged 4.28 aircraft per week. The Grumman schedule called for 255 Ag Cats in 1975 and 300 in 1976, which meant further expansion for SAC. The new welding and paint buildings were completed in the spring of 1974, and they worked out well. To meet the expanding ag-plane market, Grumman American initiated a program that created three different Ag Cat models. Again Schweizer had mixed feelings about further expansion of the Ag Cat project. We feared it would have a negative effect on SAC's product diversification goals. However, our rationale was that ag-aviation was one of the most stable segments of the aircraft industry so we should stick with it.

The three new models planned had the following configurations:

A Model—The current production model with a new sealed cockpit for pilot comfort and safety from the chemicals. All aircraft had the 600 hp R1340 Pratt & Whitney engine;

B Model—Wing span was increased from 36 to 42¼ feet so it could carry the same load as the "A" model with less power. It also had a wider spray swath to increase productivity. All aircraft had the 450hp R985 Pratt & Whitney engine;

C Model—This aircraft had a new fuselage design which would allow it to carry a 500 gallon hopper. Wing span was 42¼ feet. The engine was the 600hp R1340 Pratt & Whitney.

Grumman American's goal was to have the Model "A" ready in 1975, Model "B" in 1976, and Model "C" in 1977. They brought in two large trailers in September and a staff of seven engineers to work with us on the design and FAA approval of the new models.

On Easter Sunday afternoon, when no one was at the plant except the guard, thank God, a small, narrow tornado came across the airport and hit the west end of our plant. It took the roof off our 8,100 sq. ft. final assembly hangar but fortunately left the steel beams intact. Completed aircraft were tied down outside, but because they were not in the direct path of the narrow twister, aircraft damage was not serious. However, an enclosed glider trailer with its end door open was in the path of the storm and was blown for a quarter mile flight and over some twenty-foot-high obstacles. It took about a week to clean up and consolidate the final assembly operation in another area. Some production was lost, but with outstanding help and cooperation from our employees, we recovered our schedule. We also had a period of nice spring weather, which allowed us to do some of the final assembly work in "God's Hangar" outside. The roof was quickly rebuilt, and the final assembly operation was back in the hangar by mid-June. SAC had building and business interruption insurance, but it only covered part of the loss.

Only four Teal Amphibians were sold in 1974, and a production of at least one ship per month was required to get our costs in line. We thought there should be a market for our amphibian in Canada. We looked to the sportsmen who fish in the lake regions as potential customers. Our salesman took the ship on a demonstration tour and found out that the Canadian pilots preferred the high wing float airplane to the Teal. Their rationale was that they could bring one of the aircraft's floats up parallel to the dock and, with the wing over it, load or unload conveniently. The Teal's shoulder-high wing with a float at the tip made it difficult to get next to the dock for loading.

We also had a very sad incident happen in connection with the Teal. A very nice young Norwegian pilot picked up a Teal in November and planned to ferry it to Norway. He took the same route that our Swedish pilot took the previous year. He got lost in instrument weather over Iceland, flew into a mountain and was killed.

At year-end, we decided that the Teal was not going to be a profitable project for SAC and that we should look for a buyer and sell the program. We were prepared to follow T. Boone Pickens, Jr.'s, philosophy, "I hate to fail, but when it is time to take a bath, I get in the tub."

The computer installed at SAC in 1972 had been developing into a very useful tool for the day-to-day operation of the Company. By 1974 it was being used to control payroll, labor distribution and production efficiency of all shop jobs and automatic pricing of parts and material. The big challenge before us was to bring the computer up to speed on the current parts and material inventory to assist with our complicated production control operation. SAC was still using manual methods to control 35,000 different items required to build five sailplane models, the Ag Cat and parts for our subcontract business. In order to accomplish this goal, it was necessary to first get our engineering drawings in apple-pie order (part numbers, next assembly, material call-outs, etc.) and then follow by updating the production operation sheets for each part and sub-assembly. This was a tremendous job and a costly one, but one we had to face. We had entered the computer world and there was no turning back.

SAC's average employment for 1974 was 402 workers, and at year end, 416 were on the payroll. (See Appendix 1.) The corporation had a record sales of 7 million dollars, equivalent to about 21 million 1989 dollars. Our average hourly shop rate was $3.90 per hour, and SAC's price for an hour of shop labor was $11.50. Our profit margin for the year was relatively small as a result of inflation, the Teal operating loss, the tornado recovery expense and an additional quarter million dollars that had been invested in the 1-35 project.

During 1975, there was a mild recession in the U.S., and 9.2% of the nation's work force was unemployed. The 12.3% inflation rate of 1974 had dropped to 7.1%. SAC's average labor rate, however, grew by 12%, from $3.91 to $4.39 per hour. Wage increases had been put on hold in 1975 in an attempt to stay in the black. We were attempting to catch up. Schweizer was not alone in this delaying tactic as many commodity prices also grew faster than inflation. The first class letter increased from 10 to 13 cents, and a 10-cent Hershey bar was reduced in size by more than 15%.

In January, SAC's work force grew to 450 employees, and we produced 21 Ag Cats in 21 work days. Grumman American had some concern about the U.S. recession and asked us to hold Ag Cat production at a rate of one ship per day. The Company's profit margin for the first six months of 1975 was over 10% of sales.

Brother Paul was a contestant in the 1-26 Nationals held at Caddo Mills, Texas in August, 1975. After a long six-hour flight,

Paul was unable to complete the task and was forced to land in a cotton field. He remembered setting up his landing pattern—and then apparently passed out on his final approach and crashed. He sustained major injuries, the most serious of which was a skull fracture. Unfortunately, he hit his head on the instrument panel because his shoulder harnesses were loose. They had stretched due to the high "G" load. The accident was thought to be the result of a combination of hot weather, dehydration and fatigue. Paul was hospitalized for two months in Texas and then returned to Elmira and made a miraculous recovery. Six months after the accident, he was back to normal.

After 45 years of accident-free flying, the mishap in Texas was a great blow to Paul. He thoroughly investigated the accident and reported his findings openly to the soaring public. It was his hope that something could be learned from his unfortunate experience.

In the 32 years since the plant was built, we had not experienced problems with flood water. In 1972 during Hurricane Agnes, the water had come within an inch of our plant and we had about 20 inches of water in our warehouses. The Company's problem was minor compared to the serious flooding problems in the Corning, Big Flats and Elmira areas. We felt that the chance of flooding at SAC was an isolated problem that might occur once every 100 years. True, since the 1974 construction of the 900 foot extension of runway 28 to the east we had had four floods from Sing Sing Creek threaten our plant. But none reached it (Figure 86).

In the early morning of Friday, September 26, 1975, a violent cloudburst dumped rain just north of the airport in the watershed area of Sing Sing Creek which flows just east of the plant. Five inches of rain fell in a very short period. The ground was saturated, and the creek was already high from a considerable amount of rainfall during the previous week. At 5 a.m. Friday, the creek crested from the cloudburst. Four inches of water flooded our main plant, and three of our warehouses were under two feet of water.

It was our opinion that the flood was caused by two changes to the county airport. First, a 900 foot extension to runway 28 was added in 1974 which changed the drainage pattern of the airport. It acted like a dam and made the water back up to the north to our plant. Second, the airport built a boundary fence across Sing Sing Creek that filled up with debris and dammed the stream. Because the September 26th flood came without warning and happened at 5 a.m., we were unable to get pictures of the flood when it crested to substantiate our theory.

We complained to airport officials, county supervisors, and the county executive, Morris E. Blostein. The County agreed to take down the fence that crossed the stream and clean out the stream to improve the water flow. They would not, however, assume any responsibility for the September 26th flood. We only had $60,000 of flood insurance, and our damage to inventory and completed aircraft plus the clean-up costs ran well over $400,000. We decided to get attorney Edward B. Hoffman involved and sued the County for damages.

SAC's Ag Cat production continued at a rate of one ship per day until the September flood. With the plant's scheduled summer vacation shut-down and holidays, there would have been 235 work days in 1975. We lost the opportunity to build 17 aircraft due to the temporary shut-down and clean-up period after the flood. This resulted in only 218 Ag Cats manufactured for the year.

The Ag Cat product development and diversification projects were progressing well. The "A" Model with the sealed cockpit and ventilation system was put into production in December 1974 and was well received. The new "B" Model with the longer wings and modified vertical tail was certified and tooled during 1975, and the initial production was underway at year end. The larger "C" Model was expected to make its first flight in the spring of 1976.

The Pratt & Whitney R985 (450hp) and the R1340 (600hp) engines were our current Ag Cat power plants. Large quantities of these engines were built during WWII, but neither engine was still in production. The R985 and R1340 engines used in the Ag Cat were rebuilt to the equivalent of zero operating time. At a cost of six to eight thousand dollars, they made relatively inexpensive power plants for the Ag Cat, since newly manufactured engines would cost over $50,000 each.

In the long run, the dwindling supply of Pratt & Whitney engines posed a potential problem because no radial or in-line reciprocating engines over 400hp were being manufactured.

Therefore, Grumman and Schweizer were looking into alternative power plants including turbine engines. We also looked at 600hp engines made in Poland by Pezetel. Two Polish technicians brought over an engine, and an installation was made on an Ag Cat. All engines made in the West turn clockwise. When we started the Pezetel engine, to our surprise, it turned counter clockwise.

The sailplane business was 17% of SAC's business volume in 1975 and amounted to 1.48 million dollars in sales. There were five sailplane models in production, and a total of 110 ships were sold through our national dealers organization. After being in production for 20 years, with yearly updating for appearance and manufacturing cost reduction, the 1-26 one design class sailplane was still selling. Twenty ships were sold during 1975; the last one was serial number 643. We were pleased to sell 37 of the 1-35 high performance 15 meter class sailplanes. A club version of the 1-35 was introduced to provide a lower-cost ship with high performance. The club version eliminated some of the expensive performance features including the retractable landing gear, water ballast system and flap-aileron integration systems.

The Teal amphibian project was sold to a group of Canadian investors led by an airline pilot who felt there was a Canadian market. The sales price of $135,000 enabled SAC to liquidate inventory and recover our investment. The Teal project was moved to Jacksonville, Florida because of Canadian FAA requirements. If it had been built in Canada, it would have required recertification even though it was acceptable for import to Canada if built in the U.S. The financial transaction took place in January, 1976, and David Thurston, the Teal designer, moved with the project. Unfortunately for the investors, this Canadian/Florida project never got off the ground.

SAC's sales for the year 1975 were 73% Ag Cat, 17% sailplane and 10% subcontract. Our major subcontract customers were Bell Helicopter, Grumman Aerospace and Hardinge Brothers of Elmira. SAC's average employment for the year was 447 workers. (See Appendix 1.) The Corporation's sales were 8.8 million dollars. Profit after the flood loss was $214,000. Our flood claim against the county for $296,623 was scheduled to be in the pre-trial stage by the summer of 1976.

Ernie was going to be 65 years old in April 1976, so we were starting to talk about his retirement and long-range plans for the Corporation. After flying airplanes for over 30 years, I earned my instrument rating at the age of 57. I found it very useful in flying from marginal weather to good but did not use it to intentionally fly into bad weather. My third son, John, the mountaineer and skier, earned his MBA at Dartmouth's Amos Tuck Graduate School for Business. He joined Rossignol Ski Company of Burlington, Vermont as an assistant to the president and, within a year, headed the marketing administration of their ski division. John's wife, Jenny, entered the Amos Tuck Graduate School at Dartmouth the same year John graduated and earned her MBA two years later.

Jimmy Carter was elected 39th President of the U.S., narrowly defeating President Ford. The country was recovering from the recession, and inflation had dropped to 4.9%. The agricultural economy was particularly strong, and 1,000 ag-planes were sold. The world's first scheduled supersonic passenger airline service was inaugurated in 1976, when Air France and British Airways provided Concorde Jet flights across the Atlantic Ocean.

In the spring, Karl Striedieck made the first soaring flight of more than 1,000 miles. He took off at 7 a.m. from Lock Haven, Pennsylvania and flew the Appalachian ridge south 300 miles, then continued by thermal soaring to Oak Ridge, Tennessee and returned to Lock Haven by 8:30 p.m. It was a great flight, but, unfortunately, he flew a German (not a Schweizer) sailplane. However, that same spring Wally Scott, Sr., flew a Schweizer 1-35 to win the Smirnoff (Vodka) transcontinental Derby competing against the best pilots and sailplanes in the world. Each day there was a distance and speed race to a goal, and entrants crossed the country in ten flights. Wally's 1-35 was owned by SAC and after the race was put on display for three years at the National Air & Space Museum in Washington, D.C.

SAC's glider business declined in 1976, and 79 units were delivered. There were numerous reasons for this reduction, but the overriding factor was competition from the sleek-looking fiberglass European imports. Our high performance 1-35, with its all-aluminum structure, provided greater pilot safety and less maintenance, and it had proved able to fly with the best of them. Many U.S. pilots, however, were buying the sleek European ships as a status symbol and because there was a slight price advantage. Another disadvantage for us was that the bulk of our sailplanes were designed for the recreational pilot and for training. These ships were all-metal and lasted almost indefinitely. By 1976 we had pretty much saturated the market. Since 1946, SAC had built over 850 two-place trainers (2-22 and 2-33) and 660 of the 1-26 single-place advanced trainer.

Twenty-two high performance sailplanes were sold in 1976: 1-34 (1), 1-35 (18), and 2-32 (3). One 2-32 went to the prestigious New York City Explorer's Club. Kim Scribner, a senior Pan American Airline pilot talked the club into buying the ship for him to use for high altitude wave exploration. He and his benefactor, a very distinguished looking gentleman, came to Elmira to pick up the 2-32. The ship cost $18,000, and the instruments and radios Kim ordered cost more than the ship. Paul and Tony Doherty were embarrassed to give them such a large bill, but when they did, the gentlemen said, "Kim, are you sure you have everything you need?"

After the 1975 flood, we had strongly requested by letter and through the press that the County take corrective action to protect our plant from future floods. Unfortunately, no significant results were achieved. It was our opinion that county officials understood the problem, but since SAC was suing the county for flood damages, they did not want to admit that the 1974 runway extension had created our recent flood problem. (See Appendix 8.)

On Sunday morning, June 20, 1976, a second flood entered our plant. Again, it resulted in four inches of water in our main plant. This time we were prepared and had an airplane with a cameraman ready to take pictures (*Figure 87*). The flood crested at 10 a.m.

On Sunday afternoon, we arranged to have the county executive, a newspaper reporter and our lawyer come to the plant. They were shown what we believed caused the plant flood and the resulting damage. We demanded corrective action. We pointed out that our current employment was 530 workers—and that if floods like this continued, it would affect our ability to create jobs and stay in business.

On Monday morning, a set of flood pictures was delivered

to the county executive. Within an hour, he declared an emergency and authorized corrective action to start immediately. The engineering firm of Campbell and Weiland, which had been studying the airport flood problem with us during the past year, was called in by the County to design a fix. By the following Monday, large earth moving equipment began excavating the critical area between the east end of the runway and Sing Sing Creek. The dirt was used to build a dike on the north and east boundaries of the plant. This was a quick fix, but it worked. We have not had another flood since. However, we did not think it was the longrange answer, and we made it clear to the County that SAC was looking for further expansion of the dike system around the plant. (This was done in 1988.)

After the 1975 flood, the Company increased its flood insurance to the limit. In addition, all production materials at floor level were raised in the plant and warehouses so the losses were less in the flood of 1976. Because corrective action had been taken by the County, we agreed not to file an additional claim. The 1975 flood claim of $296,623 against the County was still involved in pre-trial hearings and was not yet scheduled on the court calendar. Our lawyer expected the case to go to trial after the first of the year.

In 1976, SAC's Ag Cat production averaged 1.09 aircraft per work day, and a total of 256 aircraft were built including 85 "A" Models, 170 "B" Models and one prototype "C" model. (See Appendix 3.) Our employment peaked at 535 and the average employment for the year was 509. (See Appendix 1.)

The "C" Model made its first flight in late fall. It was the largest Ag Cat produced and had a 500 gallon hopper which held two tons of liquid. The schedule called for having the "C" model tooled, FAA certified, and ready for production by November, 1977. This schedule would allow the new "C" model to be shown in December at the National Agricultural Aviation convention in Las Vegas.

Grumman American also told us to prepare to build 300 Ag Cats in 1977, 350 in 1978 and 400 in 1979. To prepare for this increased volume, SAC needed additional manufacturing space. To help us justify the expansion to the bank, Grumman American gave us a letter of intent in which they stated that they planned to keep the Ag Cat in production at SAC for at least five years. They additionally stated that if there were any changes in their intentions, they would give SAC two years' notice and pay the Company for any purchasing commitments or inventory acquired for the five-year period.

With this Grumman American agreement, two building additions were put in work at SAC. The first was a 60 × 90-foot storage building with its floor level six inches above that of the main plant. It was scheduled for completion in late fall. Secondly, a 10,004 sq. ft. addition to the fabrication department was added to the main plant, with a scheduled completion date in the spring of 1977.

Sales for the year were a record $10.8 million, and profit was about 2.5% on sales. Profit for the year was disppointing because wages increased by 12%, although inflation increased by only 4.9%. The average shop hourly wage increased from $4.39 to $4.95 per hour. This was the result of union pressure and our desire to pay slightly above the area average so we could attract quality workers.

The Grumman Corporation was optimistic about the future of the Ag Cat program, and they became interested in acquiring SAC. We had some exploratory talks with the chairman, and Grumman made us a fair offer, one which would have enabled the three Schweizer brothers, who owned 75% of the SAC stock, to retire comfortably. After much soul searching, we could not bring ourselves to sell the Company and give up our independence. We knew that if SAC became a subsidiary, the profit earned would go directly to the parent corporation. It would make the decisions as to how and where money would be invested, and that might not be in Elmira. We also doubted there would be any future for our sailplane products. We believed that a merger would not be in the best interest of our employees, the community or the pride of the Schweizer family.

My son Paul Hardy was still working at Boeing and making good progress working his way up the corporate ladder. He was expecting to complete his MBA at the University of Washington in January, 1977 and had expressed interest in joining SAC. With three young, aggressive, well-educated Schweizer boys (Leslie, W. Stuart and Paul Hardy) interested in making their future with SAC, we decided to keep the Company a family-owned concern.

86 

87 

88 

***86.** An Ag Cat roars over the expanded SAC facilities in 1974; two years later a storm flooded most of the facility (**87**). **88.** Model "D" Ag Cat with 750hp turbine power plant and 500-gallon hopper.*

13

AG CAT, SAILPLANE AND GENERAL AVIATION 1977–1978

President Carter warned that the energy crisis in the U.S. could result in a national catastrophe, so he established the U.S. Department of Energy. The world's worst aviation disaster happened in the Canary Islands when two Boeing 747 jets collided while taxiing, and a total of 570 people died. That same year, Groucho Marx and Elvis Presley, King of rock-and-roll, died. Who can forget Groucho as Dr. Quackenbush taking a pulse and saying, "Either this man is dead or my watch has stopped."

In 1977, Schweizer was under contract to Grumman American to produce 300 Ag Cats at a production rate of 1.3 aircraft per day. During the spring a softening of the market began to show up. In April, SAC's production rate was six aircraft per week. Finished Ag Cat inventory began to pile up in our backyard, and we unilaterally decided not to increase the production rate to 1.3 Ag Cats per day.

Late in June, Grumman American asked us to cut back the Ag Cat production to one per day or less, if possible. During the first six months of 1977, 141 Ag Cats were manufactured and with our cutback, 93 were built in the last half of the year for a total of 234 airplanes. (See Appendix 3.) In July it was necessary for SAC to lay off 50 people. Piper Aircraft had been building Ag Cat tail surface, but this subcontract was terminated in the fall of 1977. We felt badly about this but had experienced similar cutbacks ourselves.

Unfortunately, Grumman American sold only 207 Ag Cats, so the year ended with 27 completed ships in inventory. A visitor commented that our back yard looked like we were building airplanes for a WWI movie. The Grumman Corporation officials became concerned about the depressed ag-plane market since Grumman American had just invested over a million dollars in the "C" Model Ag Cat. They hired an agricultural consulting firm to study the ag-aviation market and evaluate the Ag Cat's position. SAC was well aware of the problems and real-world situation long before experts came up with their profound observations. They concluded that the demand would level off for a few years and start increasing again in the 1980's. With the new larger "C" Model, they felt the Ag Cat's share of the market would grow from 25% to 30%. It was their opinion that the 1977 decline in sales was the result of too much rain in the farm belt and a depressed agricultural economy. President Carter's reduction in grain shipments to the Soviet Union (because of human rights violations) was part of the reason for the depressed ag-economy in the U.S. As a result of the consultants' report, Grumman American scheduled SAC to build 214 Ag Cats in 1978, despite the obvious problems with the inventory and decreased market demand.

The new 500 gallon "C" Model Ag Cat, which could hold two tons of liquid, was certified and in production by year-end. It was a good airplane with 400 gallons in the hopper, but with 500 gallons, it was under-powered and was not able to perform. Its poor take-off performance restricted its operations to large fields.

Before the "C" Model ever went into production, Grumman management was cautioned by a number of dealers—and the Schweizers—that the aircraft would be a market bust because of its marginal performance. However, after 20 years of continuous success with the program, Grumman failed to correctly evaluate the market or its new product. After a few months of operational experience, it was clear that the "C" Model had little sales potential. This failure lead to turmoil for all concerned.

The only available engine that would be a good match for

the "C" Model was the PT6-34 750hp Pratt & Whitney turbine. It was a lightweight, powerful, reliable turboprop engine that burned low-cost jet fuel and could be run 3,000 to 4,000 hours without an overhaul. However, it was a very expensive engine. The OEM price of a PT6-34 turbine was $85,000 in 1977 compared to the $10,000 price of the 600hp reciprocating radial engine used on the "C" Model. This meant that the "C" Model Ag Cat sales price would increase from $110,000 to $195,000 as a turbine-powered aircraft.

After much discussion, Grumman American management decided to put a PT-6 turbine on the "C" Model design. They also planned to incorporate some additional modifications and call it a "D" Model. Their program called for SAC to work with the Grumman engineers and design and build a prototype. If all went as planned, the "D" Model would be tooled and FAA certified so that it would be ready for the market in 1979 (*Figure 88*). This meant SAC would have four Ag Cat models in production at one time (Models A, B, C & D).

In the meantime, the 2000th Schweizer sailplane was built in 1977 (*Figure 89*). The majority of Americans who have learned to fly sailplanes have done so in Schweizer planes. In 1977, we modified our sailplane manufacturing policy as a result of two conditions. First, the strong American dollar made European high performance sailplanes a bargain. Second, it was difficult for SAC to compete with the European fiberglass contest ships. Our new policy stated that SAC would concentrate its efforts in the training and sport sailplane field and only occasionally build a competitive ship on an experimental basis to keep the Schweizer name in the public eye.

SAC sold 78 sailplanes in 1977. Sixty were trainers or sport sailplanes, and the balance was high-performance contest ships. In the same year were 129 sailplanes imported from Europe and 49 of these were from Eastern Bloc countries whose governments subsidized the industry. These sailplanes were brought into the U.S. under the State Department's "Most favored nation treatment" and hence were duty free. Our Company made a formal protest to the State Department about this unfair competition, but nothing resulted.

Because the Ag Cat market continued to soften as the year progressed, we could spend more time on new business development for diversification. The potential for aerospace subcontract business was still scarce, as it had been since the Vietnam War ended, so other opportunities were being investigated. We had a significant increase in business during 1977 from Elmira's precision lathe manufacturer, Hardinge Brothers. SAC was, at that time, their production source for lathe guards. Because they were fabricated from aluminum and plexiglass, the job was a natural for SAC. Volume increased because OSHA's requirements called for guards on all production lathes to protect operators from hot chips and the splash of cutting fluid. We were making guards for four different Hardinge machines, and our dollar volume of business was approaching $350,000 per year. Bell Helicopter continued to be our largest subcontract customer. Their business ran about $700,000.

In August, 1977, my son, Paul Hardy, joined SAC. The plan was for the three senior Schweizers to become less active in the day-to-day operations of the business and to gradually transition the management and ownership to the three younger Schweizers. Leslie would take over his father's direct organizational functions: engineering and quality control. Paul H. would assume Paul A's line functions: finance, purchasing, marketing and management of the sailplane program. W. Stuart would take over my direct organizational line functions: manufacturing, labor relations and management of the Ag Cat project. All would also gradually work into Company business development, subcontract sales and company-wide management decisions. This management transition plan was important because Ernie was planning to retire at year end 1978, Paul A. in 1980 and I in 1982.

In October of 1977, a three-year agreement was reached with the UAW local which represented our maintenance and production workers. A liberal increase in wages and fringe benefits was granted, but we insisted upon some improved work rules to improve our production efficiency. Employment peaked at 540 in February, and then, with the Ag Cat cutback, it averaged 500 for the year.

Annual corporate sales amounted to $11.2 million which would be about $28 million sales in 1989 dollars. (See Appendix 4.) Our average factory labor rate was $5.38 per hour, and, with a 165% overhead and 10% profit, our rate to the customers was around $15.65 per hour. A reasonable profit was earned in 1977 despite numerous costly plant and equipment changes made during the year to meet OSHA's requirements. The flood damage claim of $296,623 against the County resulting from the September, 1975 flood had still not come to trial. Attorney Edward B. Hoffman said there was sufficient evidence to continue the lawsuit, which was scheduled to come to trial in 1978.

The U.S. population reached 216 million in 1978. The world population stood at 4.4 billion, and was growing by 200,000 people each day. Demographers questioned how long the population of the world could continue to grow at this rate given fixed amount of land and increased demand for food.

In 1978, it appeared to Grumman American and SAC that the market for agricultural equipment like the ag-plane should continue to grow at a steady rate. Aerial application was the most economical way to seed some crops such as rice and to apply certain chemicals for fertilizing, weed retardation and insect control. Despite ecological concerns of the public, it was almost impossible for farmers to economically grow certain crops without chemical treatment.

We believed that the ag-plane business would continue to be a stable segment of the aviation industry and looked for a market demand of at least 200 Ag Cats per year for the next decade. However, in 1978 we started to have some second thoughts when we studied the industry-wide sales record. (See Appendix 3.) Sales for the total ag-plane industry peaked in 1974 at an annual rate of 1207 airplanes. By 1978, demand had gradually decreased to 846 aircraft. Our Ag Cat hit its peak in 1976 with 255 sales and had decreased to 203 units in 1978. SAC built 191 airplanes, so that Grumman's Ag Cat inventory was reduced from 35 to 23 at year end. Grumman projected Ag Cat sales in 1979 to be 200 units, so SAC prepared to build 180 airplanes.

The sales of the new larger "C" Model Ag Cat were a disappointment. Only 34 were delivered in 1978. Ag operators indicated that this aircraft was underpowered, and could not carry a 500 gallon load. Ag pilots like lots of power since they often find themselves in tight places with too little altitude and airspeed. In 1978, Grumman American made the "B" Model available for the first time with the 600hp engine, rather than the 450hp. One hundred fifty-five "B" Models were sold, most of them with the more powerful engine. The "D" Model with the 750hp turboprop was certified in November, and two were delivered before the end of the year.

In the spring of 1978, Grumman American Corp. of Savannah, Georgia, was purchased for $52.5 million by American Jet Industries, which was owned and operated by Allen Paulson. He appeared to be a naive businessman but proved to be just the opposite. His company, American Jet, was only worth one or two million dollars. To buy Grumman American, a very rich friend backed him for $20 million, and he borrowed the balance. After the purchase, he changed the name of his company to Gulfstream American Corp. in order to capitalize on the name of his primary product, the Gulfstream II Airplane. (Paulson sold Gulfstream American Corp. to the Chrysler Corp. in 1986 for $637 million.)

The Grumman Corp. decided to sell their Grumman American division in a hurry because they were in trouble with the U.S. Government for alleged violations of the Foreign Corrupt Practices Act. This happened when many of the African heads of state had bought Gulfstream II airplanes in the late 1970's as a prestige aircraft. Grumman American officials were accused of paying off agents in order to make the sales happen. The allegations were hurting their credibility in contract negotiations with the military for their major business. This unfortunate condition helped Allen Paulson buy the Grumman American division at a "bargain price."

In 1978, Grumman American's major product was the $5 million executive transport airplane, the Gulfstream II. They were also producing a line of small general aviation airplanes competitive with aircraft being built by Beech, Cessna and Piper Aircraft. In addition, the Ag Cat program had been turned over to the Grumman American division by the parent company in 1974.

When we first heard the rumors that the Grumman American division was sold, I called a friend who was on the staff of the Grumman board chairman. I said, "I hope the Ag Cat is not in the deal!" He paused, and then said, "It is in the deal, and I don't think Paulson knew he bought it."

The Grumman line of small airplanes had proven to be a costly and unsuccessful venture. Shortly after Paulson took over, he stopped production and development on the small airplane lines and then put all of the programs up for sale. For the first six months, there was little change in the way SAC operated the Ag Cat program with Gulfstream. In discussions with Paulson during this period, he indicated he would like to sell the Ag Cat program. We told Paulson that if he decided to sell to let us know so SAC could make an offer. We also made him aware of the contract clause that gave us two years' notice before Gulfstream could move the Ag Cat program from Elmira.

In the meantime, a total of 45 sailplanes was delivered in 1978: 1-26 (6), 2-33 (30) and 1-35 (9). The one bright spot was the 2-33 trainer. The 500th unit was delivered in 1978, and demand continued to be strong. The sales of the 1-26 single-place training sailplane, which had been in production nearly twenty years, had dropped off and a replacement model was under consideration.

Ernie's daughter, Sally Lese, who learned to fly sailplanes when she was in high school, was appointed office manager of the glider school. The school continued to attract students from all over the world. When the weather cooperated, from June 15th to September 15th, the school had all the business it could handle. Over 6,000 flights were made in 1978.

One Sunday afternoon, Peg and I drove up to the school, and I went soaring. Peg sat in the waiting area and worked on crossword puzzles. Two young girls sat next to her and asked the usual questions. "How do they stay up?" and "What happens when the wind stops blowing?" One girl asked, "How do you know all about this sport?" Peg said, "I'm Bill Schweizer's wife". The response was, "Oh-oh, can we have your autograph?" Peg reluctantly conformed but said she felt like a "damn fool."

For the first time since the Vietnam War, some aircraft manufacturers were beginning to consider subcontracting airframe work. With the Ag Cat demand slowing down, we turned our attention to subcontracting and increased our efforts in that direction. Stuart and Paul H. each made a number of trips to Seattle because Boeing was accelerating the production of their 727, 737 and 747 airliners. In addition, Boeing had started the development of two new, fuel efficient, quieter airliners, the 757 and 767. Sikorsky Helicopter Company had just won a large long-range contract for the UH-60A Black Hawk (a large military airborne jeep). The general aviation industry (Beech, Piper, Cessna, Lear Jet, etc.) was also having a record year, and 17,811 airplanes were delivered. The more expensive, sophisticated and faster models that could perform cost-effective functions for businesses were selling well.

It normally took from 6 to 12 months from the time SAC received a lead for a new subcontract job until it was put in work, assuming we won the bid. By year end, SAC had bid on a number of new jobs and was waiting for decisions. One important new job put in work was the stabilizer for Bell Helicopter's new 8 passenger executive helicopter, the Model 222. We also received an order from Link-Singer of Binghamton, New York, for a B-52 simulator support structure.

SAC's sales for 1978 were 11.3 million with a profit of $150,000 earned. Our profit was reduced by a large investment in business development. It included a design study and production of a prototype sailplane to replace the 1-26 sailplane, as well as updated manufacturing and computer equipment. As a result of a cost study, we learned that the Company could reduce its group medical insurance expenses by 10% or $40,000 a year by switching from a commercial insurance plan to a self-funded and administrated program. Our average employment for the year was 453 workers. (See Appendix 1.)

At year end, Ernie retired at the age of 66 years. He had made a tremendous contribution to the success of SAC, and it was an adjustment for Paul A. and me to operate without his advice and suggestions. However, he did remain on the Board of Directors and was available to consult on technical problems. His son, Leslie, had been well trained and was prepared to take over his functions in engineering and quality control.

Ernie has many hobbies, including his great interest in wood. He was a member of the International Wood Society, and his collection of wood samples was known throughout the world by wood specialists. At his home, he has a private wood museum, and samples of over 350 varieties of wood on display. Ernie and Eileen also liked animals and had a friendly spirited dog named Tag. Tag got into a fight with a pugnacious dog in a neighbor's yard and chewed him up. Tag went to the pokey and Ernie went to court with a Sayles and Evans lawyer. Ernie got Tag out, and our family suggested that Ernie dye Tag's beautiful red coat black to hide his identity.

We were saddened by the death of Leslie D. Clute, a Director of SAC for 29 years. He was "Mr. Ford" (dealer for over 50 years) and "Mr. Hospital" (President of the Arnot Ogden Memorial Hospital for 24 years) in Chemung County. He was a great gentleman, a true friend of the Schweizer brothers and had a keen sense of humor. I was at a hospital budget committee meeting with Les, and the administration presented a list of equipment for approval to purchase. On the list were six food trucks. Someone doctored up Les's list to read 6 Ford trucks. This got Les's attention.

89 

89. *The second generation of Schweizers take command of what proved to be the last family-owned aviation company in the United States. From left, the sons: Leslie, W. Stuart and Paul Hardy. Aft of the cockpit, the fathers: Ernest, Paul A. and Bill.*

14

THE AG CAT LEAVES AND RETURNS 1979–1980

President Carter had some serious problems in 1979. In spite of new energy legislation, the gasoline shortage grew worse. A nuclear accident took place at Three Mile Island, Pennsylvania, which lead to great public concern about the safety of nuclear power plants. The Iranians took over the U.S. Embassy in Teheran and held a group of Americans hostage for over a year. National inflation climbed to 16%. Only 21% of the American people approved of Carter's presidential performance according to public opinion polls.

It was also a difficult year for SAC. During the previous three years, a minimum of one Ag Cat aircraft had been manufactured each working day, and our employment was over 500 workers. Gulfstream expected to sell 200 ag-planes in 1979, but only 91 were actually sold. To help ease Gulfstream's problem with Ag Cat sales, SAC voluntarily reduced its Ag Cat contract schedule of four ships per week to two during the last six months of the year. SAC manufactured 141 aircraft in 1979, and Gulfstream ended the year with an inventory of 74 completed airplanes.

To our surprise, Gulfstream's Ag Cat project manager did not seem greatly concerned about the large inventory. It appeared to us that Gulfstream might be building a cushion so it could conveniently move the Ag Cat project back to their main facility in Savannah. We also suspected that this might be their project manager's personal goal rather than president Paulson's.

A meeting was held with Paulson to discuss Ag Cat sales and inventory problems. We both agreed that it did not make sense to have two companies that were 700 miles apart each running a phase of the program when the sales picture was so volatile. SAC offered to take over the total program, including the program management and marketing and pay Gulfstream a royalty on all Ag Cat sales. After evaluating our proposal, Paulson responded that he would rather sell the program outright.

We hastily put together an offer to buy the Ag Cat program, which included the FAA approved designs, tooling, manufacturing inventory and 75 completed airplanes. We offered $6.5 million dollars, and Gulfstream countered with a 12 million dollar demand. After two months of negotiations, an agreement was concluded and financing was arranged with our bankers on August 2, 1979. SAC agreed to pay 8.75 million for the project subject to SAC stockholders' approval.

Our rationale for the purchase was that the inventory of completed airplanes, at a 15% price reduction, could be sold in a six month period for 6.5 million dollars. This would mean that the designs, tooling and the manufacturing rights would cost SAC about $2.25 million dollars. In our opinion, this was a bargain price for the Ag Cat program. We believed the program would produce a minimum of five million dollars in sales during the next ten years.

When the Ag Cat purchase agreement was reached in August, the prime rate was 11.5%. One year earlier the rate had been 8%, and then it gradually climbed to 11.75. It remained there for the first seven months of 1979 and then dropped to 11.5% in August at the time the agreement was reached. In September the prime rate started to climb again. By the 29th of October, the day of the SAC stockholders were scheduled to vote on the purchase agreement, the prime rate hit 15.5%.

Because of the volatile economic conditions, SAC financial projections were updated before the stockholders' meeting. The revised studies showed that the new higher interest rate would drastically affect sales and increase our cost of operations. The bottom line was that the project was no longer viable for the following reasons:

The interest cost alone would now amount to over $500,000 for the first year, nearly double of what was projected;

Economists were predicting a recession and they looked for the prime rate to continue to grow. (In March of 1980, the prime rate hit 20%.)

In light of these uncertain economic conditions, SAC's stockholders (the Schweizer brothers controlled 75% of the stock) voted against the Ag Cat purchase proposal.

The next day the result of the vote was reported to Gulfstream. In addition, we told them that with the higher interest rates, the Ag Cat project was over-priced. Gulfstream would not reduce their price and threatened SAC with a formal contract termination. They expected this action would force SAC to purchase the program. SAC had analyzed the alternatives carefully ahead of time, and we surprised Gulfstream by accepting the termination. There were two reasons for the SAC decision: First, the working arrangements with Gulfstream's management personnel were unsatisfactory; second, the termination clause in the contract gave SAC the opportunity to turn a large slow-moving Ag Cat inventory into cash at fair market price.

A formal termination agreement was worked out with Gulfstream in December, 1979. The Ag Cat production would gradually wind down, and the last airplane would be built at SAC in May, 1980. As part of the termination agreement, SAC was to manufacture and ship to Gulfstream a year's supply of spare parts by May of 1980. This would serve as transition inventory and would amount to three quarter million dollars of business for SAC.

To replace the Ag Cat program, an aggressive program was launched to develop new subcontract business. This phase of our business grew from 11% to 19% of total sales in 1979 and was projected to be 50% of sales in 1980. (See Appendix 4.) During this period, we acquired some important new customers including the Boeing Commercial Airplane Company and Sikorsky.

SAC sailplane business held at about the same level as the previous year. Forty-four units were delivered, and 23 of these were the 2-33 two-place trainer. This venerable ship continued to be the standard glider trainer used in North and South America. The U.S. Air Force Academy at Colorado had a dozen 2-33's, and there were over 50 of our two-place trainers in use by the Air Cadet League of Canada for their youth flight training program.

SAC's Engineering Department, headed by Les Schweizer developed a unique all-metal design, the 1-36, to replace the 25 year old 1-26 sailplane. It was expected to have about the same production cost but with a 50% performance improvement compared to the 1-26. The design was FAA certified and tooled by year end, and the first production deliveries were to start in January, 1980 (*Figure 90*).

Tony Doherty, our sailplane sales manager, had an unfortunate incident while visiting a dealer. An attractive couple with a dog was visiting the dealer's glider field. Tony, an animal lover, stopped to play with the dog, and it bit him on the hand. After the dealer put a band-aid on Tony's hand, they returned to the field but the couple and dog had disappeared. The dealer said he had never seen them before, and Tony had to go through painful rabies shots.

SAC sales for 1979 were 10.4 million dollars, and our average employment was 363 workers. In 1979, our 1975 flood suit finally went to trial. The jury awarded SAC $193,000 against our claim of $296,623. After the expense of litigating the claim, SAC netted about $120,000. From an operating standpoint, the year was a breakeven. This was principally due to the Ag Cat schedule reduction, the high cost of developing new business and the 1-36 sailplane.

The Schweizer brothers and sons were a strong unit but each one respected the others' rights to do his own thing. Les, Paul H. and Stu were gradually taking more responsibility at SAC. Ernie was so busy with his various hobbies that he would occasionally come to the plant to rest. Paul A. was still deeply involved in soaring activities. He had been a director of the Soaring Society of America for twenty-five years and had a perfect attendance record at the bi-annual meetings held throughout the country. I had accepted a directorship with the S.F. Iszard Company, a department store with three branches, because I was interested in how other businesses operated, particularly another family-owned organization.

My youngest son, John, also became involved in manufacturing that spring. His employer, Rossignol Corp. of America, manufacturers of winter sports equipment and clothing, wanted to become involved in tennis. This sport was rapidly growing in 1979. Rossignol bought a small Boston-based tennis racket manufacturer, Acro Inc., which employed about 75 people. John was made vice president in charge of this division.

In 1980, the Cold War with the Soviet Union was still very hot. To protest the Soviet invasion of Afghanistan, President Carter announced the U.S. boycott of the summer Olympic Games in Moscow. The first Solidarity strike took place in Poland. After losing three of eight CH-53 Sikorsky helicopters in a sandstorm, the U.S. aborted a hostage rescue mission in Iran. John Lennon, leader of the "Beatles," was murdered in New York City. President Carter lost his bid for second term by a wide margin to Ronald Reagan.

Schweizer Aircraft's product line and organization was also involved in major changes. Prior to the SAC annual stockholders' meeting in April, three members of the board of directors had retired:

Nicholas Haich, a director since 1946 and treasurer of the Company from 1941 to 1972. For 31 years, Nick was SAC's financial watchdog, and his sage, conservative advice was very helpful. Nick was a good balance for three young Schweizer brothers whose love for aviation sometimes exceeded their interest in financial matters.

Alpheus F. Underhill, a director since 1969. Al was the architect responsible for all of SAC's building projects from 1952 through 1980. Al was a leading industrial architect in the Southern Tier region of the state. He was a good friend and very helpful in many ways to the Schweizer brothers.

Edward A. Mooers, a director since 1970. Eddie was an engineer, and during the period 1928-1980, he was President or Chairman of Elmira's Hilliard Corporation, manufacturer of machine clutches and oil purification equipment. He was a WWI airplane pilot and a big supporter of gliding in the Elmira area. Eddie served as president of the Elmira Area Soaring Corp. during WWII when it operated a military glider flight training program in Mobile, Alabama. He was also mayor of Elmira from 1956 through 1962. Eddie was very helpful to us and a great friend.

In addition, we had not replaced Les Clute who died in 1978, so there were four directorships open. At the April annual stockholders' meeting, the three second generation Schweizers: W. Stuart, Paul Hardy and Leslie E., were elected directors and vice presidents of SAC. At the same meeting Boyd McDowell II was also elected a director. Boyd is the son of Robert P. McDowell, who was more responsible than any other individual for SAC's move to Elmira. Like his father, Boyd has been a great booster of Elmira and an effective community leader. He was educated as a lawyer but turned to banking as a profession. He joined the Chemung Canal Trust Co. in 1956 and became president in 1976. (See Appendix 9.)

At the stockholders' meeting two other people whose names were not Schweizer were elected vice-presidents of SAC. These men had made outstanding contributions to the success of SAC during the past 35 years and were still playing important roles in the Company. They were Paul L. Pullen, factory manager, and Donald Quigley, chief production engineer. To simplify things to the outside world, we decided that Paul A. should be chairman and I should be president. The title change did not affect our duties or areas of responsibility. We did, however, turn some of our workload over to the younger Schweizers.

The Ag Cat manufacturing operation stopped at SAC on May 30, 1980. All tooling for four different Ag Cat models plus the inventory of parts, hardware and material were packaged and shipped to Savannah. It required 32 tractor-trailer loads to transport the Ag Cat program. SAC was paid its full manufacturing cost of 1.8 million dollars for the inventory. Gulfstream announced to the agricultural aviation public that they would start building the Ag Cat in Savannah.

SAC's new business was focused on subcontracting. Our volume grew from 1.2 million dollars in 1978 to 4.8 million in 1980. This was a very fast build-up, but it was necessary to replace the Ag Cat production and maintain a critical mass. From an operating standpoint, the fast build-up of new work had a negative effect on earnings. It is difficult to acquire new subcontract work and charge the customer for all start-up costs. Some of the new projects included:

- Boeing 737 and 747 detail parts fabrication which amounted to 1.8 million dollars in sales for 1980;
- Cargo and Airstair door for the Beech Aircraft—King Air 200 transport;
- Wing Tips for the new Boeing 757 airliner;
- Stabilizer Assembly for the new Bell Model 222 eight-passenger business helicopter;
- Gunner Windows for Sikorsky Aircraft's UH-60 Black Hawk Helicopter (*Figure 91*).

Our sailplane volume decreased in 1980, and only 22 new ships were delivered. We attributed this reduction in sales primarily to two economic conditions: first, the high cost of borrowing money, (bank interest loan rates were running from 16% to 18%) and second, the strong dollar made foreign sailplanes a better value for the money. Another negative factor was that the new 1-36 sailplane (*Figure 90*) took five months longer to get into production than anticipated. Our sales department had a backlog of 40 orders but the 1-36 was not FAA certified until October. Only seven 1-36's were delivered in 1980.

Our soaring school business remained strong, and it continued to attract students from throughout the world. One day in August I had a call from the soaring school informing me that the President of Ithaca College, Ellis L. Phillips, Jr. had arrived in a beautiful, large, twin-engine airplane. I had never met Ellis, but I knew he had married LeRoy Grumman's daughter and that he was a director of the Grumman Corp. I showed him through our plant and on the way out offered him a glider flight. I flew the tow and the landing and let him fly the rest of the flight. He did very well. After we landed, I asked him if his pilot would like a flight. "No" he said quietly, "I am the pilot."

When the Ag Cat tooling and inventory arrived at Gulfstream's Savannah plant, the project was not put into work as had previously been announced. In September, Paulson reversed his decision and announced the Ag Cat program was for sale. A number of prospective buyers contacted us about manufacturing the Ag Cat for them. We listened and evaluated their proposals but did not find any that were economically sound from a Schweizer viewpoint. The basic problems were remote management and two profit centers (the new owner and SAC) which made the investment marginal. We believed that the Ag Cat production was over at SAC and concentrated on developing other business.

In November, Allen Paulson called and said the Ag Cat should be built in Elmira and made us an attractive offer. After studying his proposal and working out financing with Chemical Bank of New York City, we made a counter offer to Gulfstream. By the end of November, we had an agreement to purchase the program for 3.3 million dollars and to pay Gulfstream a royalty on all airplanes and spare parts sold during the next seven years. The purchase included the design, FAA certification and tooling for all four models (A, B, C & D) plus the inventory of parts and material. It did not include the inventory of completed Ag Cats which Gulfstream was in the process of selling.

Schweizer's purchase of the Ag Cat was made public the first week in December at the National Agricultural Aerial Applicators Convention at Las Vegas. We told the aviation public that the Ag Cat would return to its one and only home in Elmira and that we planned to have an updated "B" Model back in production by summer of 1981. The Ag Cat dealers and owners were very pleased to hear the news. Cliff Lincoln of Walla Walla, Washington, told the press, "Schweizer is the natural place for the Ag Cat program. The Ag Cat has come a long way since its introduction in 1957, and now our concern is for the future. The sale to Schweizer assures the stability of the program."

The corporation sales for 1980 amounted to 10.5 million dollars and there was a loss of $48,000. The principal reasons for the unprofitable performance were as follows:

- High interest rates (average about 18%) and the strong dollar;
- High cost of developing new subcontract business;
- Tooling and FAA certification of the 1-36;
- Costs associated with purchasing and moving the Ag Cat program.

Paul A. retired in December 1980, but he was always available to consult with the management team. While we were building gliders in the family barn, Paul had the dream of creating an aircraft company. He had also envisioned the National Soaring Museum at Harris Hill. Since Paul had the habit of working to make his dreams come true, he was anxious to get started on his next project, a book about the history of soaring in the United States.

Paul L. Pullen, vice-president and factory manager, retired in the fall of 1980 due to illness. Paul had completed 38 years of service and played an important role in the development of the Company. He was the watchdog of our facilities and equipment and an excellent production cost estimator.

90 

91 

90. *The elegant single-seater, SGS 1-36, which replaced the classic 1-26.* ***91****. Gunners' windows of the Sikorsky UH-60A Black Hawk, made by SAC.*

15

MANAGEMENT TRANSITION 1981–1982

In January, 1981, on the same day that Reagan was sworn in as President, the U.S. hostages in Iran were released after more than a year of imprisonment. Assassination attempts were made on President Reagan in March and the Pope in May, and President Sadat of Egypt was assassinated in December. This was the year that the AIDS disease was first identified. Charles Prince of Wales and Lady Diana Spencer were married in an elaborate cermony in Westminister Abbey. Great progress was made in space travel when the first manned spacecraft took off with a rocket assist and successfully returned to earth as a glider. We were not surprised to learn that NASA required sailplane flying as part of the training for the astronaut pilots of the space shuttle.

As the result of our sailplane experience and association with the Air Force Academy, SAC received an order in 1981 for eight motor gliders from the U.S. Air Force Academy (*Figure 92*). The SGM 2-37 powered sailplane was developed in response to a requirement from the Air Force. The Academy had one of the world's largest glider training programs and over 1000 cadets were trained annually. The 2-37 motor glider's mission was to speed up the training process by reducing the number of training flights (takeoffs and landings) and providing the beginning students with more air work before they flew in a sailplane.

In 1957, the Air Force Academy had purchased five Schweizer sailplanes [two 2-22's and three 1-26's] and had started a small informal program. It appealed to both the cadets and the administration, so it grew rapidly. By the mid 1970's, a sailplane flight training course was included in the Academy's curricula. The administration did not want to expose the cadets to military flight training until after they graduated, but they did want to stimulate the cadets' interest in flying. The Academy's soaring program proved to be a way they could screen those cadets who were qualified and enthusiastic about learning to fly military aircraft. The USAF administration hoped that this would help avoid spending unnecessary military training funds later. From Schweizer's viewpoint, this proved to be a wonderful long-range public relations program. We now find that many U.S. Air Force generals got their first flight experience in our sailplanes. All pilots remember their first solo flight and the ship in which they flew.

Our sailplane sales picked up a little in 1981 as the new 1-36 was in full production. Thirty-eight ships were sold that year, and 31 of them were 1-36's. Because of the strong dollar, the more sophisticated two-place European fiberglass trainers were relatively inexpensive, and their sales cut into our 2-33 sales.

In January, Gulfstream still had an inventory of 44 completed Ag Cats. Because the world ag-plane market was soft, we decided to take the necessary time and make a careful evaluation of each model before it was put back into production. All Ag Cat data, tooling, and inventory and 32 tractor trailer loads were returned, sorted, and stored at SAC by the end of March.

Over the years, we had been impressed by T.C. "Joe" Kosier of Gulfstream's marketing department, and we hired Joe to be our Ag Cat sales manager. SAC inherited Gulfstream's Ag Cat dealer organization, an experienced group of ag-aviation companies which knew our airplane and who had worked for many years with SAC. In February, a two-day meeting with the Ag Cat dealers was held at our plant. Our objective was to determine how to improve the productivity, marketability and service life of our new product line. As the result of this meeting, it was decided to hold up production on the "C" and "D" Models and concentrate on updating and getting the "B" Model back into production. With the improvements, we decided to call it the "B Plus."

SAC went to work and incorporated a number of changes to reduce the Ag Cat's maintenance cost and improve its productivity. The 300 gallon hopper was increased in size to 400 gallons. The gate box attached to the bottom of the hopper was modified so it would provide a wider swath when dispersing solid material. The liquid dispersal equipment was improved to provide a wider spray pattern with a more even distribution. The "B Plus" changes were FAA certified, and production started in September.

On October 12, 1981, a ribbon-cutting ceremony was held at SAC to celebrate the fly-away delivery of the first "Schweizer" Ag Cat. This was the 2,455th Schweizer-built Ag Cat but the first to carry our name (*Figure 93*). It was an important milestone in the history of SAC. Our employees, local dignitaries, FAA officials, plus friends of the Schweizers attended the event. There were also four Grumman officials present: the two men who conceived the original Ag Cat design, Joe Lippert and Arthur Koch; Fred Eckert who originally chose SAC to build the airplane; and Earl Duhame, program manager from 1965 to 1974 (*Figure 94*).

Ten "B Plus" Ag Cats were delivered by year end. In December, the new model was displayed and well received at the National Aerial Applicators Convention in Las Vegas. Gulfstream finally sold all of its Ag Cat inventory, and sales prospects appeared promising for 1982.

A dealer from Central America, by the name of Jose, asked to talk privately with me while at the convention. He wanted an airplane on consignment (he would pay for it when he sold it), but our Company policy would not allow it. The man sitting next to us listened in on our conversation. He obviously had been drinking and toward the end asked Jose, "Where do you come from?" Jose said, "Central America." The drunk said, "I do too." Jose asked, "Where?" The drunk said, "Kansas City."

Sales of commercial airplanes continued to decrease industry-wide, but, fortunately for SAC, our subcontracting business increased again in 1981. Subcontract sales amounted to $6.1 million dollars. Our three major customers were Boeing, Bell Helicopter and Beech Aircraft. Each provided over one million dollars in sales for the year. Our Hardinge lathe guard business amounted to a record sales of $836,184. Two new interesting programs developed during the year; each one amounted to over a quarter of a million in sales and appeared to be an opportunity for long-range product diversification.

Aerolift Cyclo-Crane: D.C. Associates of Bozman, Maryland, was designing and building a new innovative aerostatic heavy-lift vehicle. It was a combination of dirigible and airplane technology. SAC had the job of designing and building the wings and tail for the prototype (*Figure 94A*). D.C. Associates' customer was Canada's Forest Research Institute which was looking for a less expensive way to move a truckload of logs from the forest to the road.

Pheromone Dispenser: SAC teamed with Health Chemical Corp., a major chemical company, to develop an aerial method of dispensing synthetic insect sex pheromones as an alternative to insecticides.

A profit of $108,000 was earned on $9.3 million dollars in sales for the year in spite of extraordinary costs to purchase the Ag Cat, move it back to Elmira, update the product and get it back into production. SAC employment dropped just below 300 for the first time in over ten years. At the annual stockholders' meeting, Thomas Morse, President of LaFrance Equipment Corp., was elected a Director to replace A. Douglas P. Craig. (See Appendix 9.) Doug Craig had opened his own law office in New York City, and, because of time contraints, was forced to resign from our board. We were sorry to lose Doug but were pleased to have Tom join our board because of his expertise in foreign sales.

In October, 1981, Schweizer Aircraft Corp. received the prestigious *Federal Aeronautique International* (F.A.I.) Diplome D' Honneur for its contribution to the progress of aviation over the past 42 years. The award was presented at the annual F.A.I. convention in Japan and was accepted by Paul A. Schweizer on behalf of the Company.

Depressed economic conditions in the U.S. made 1982 a difficult year for SAC. The nation's unemployment rate was the highest since 1941, and 10% of the work force had no jobs. The U.S. budget deficit climbed to $110 billion dollars. President Reagan talked about a tax reduction, but Congress increased taxes by $91 billion. Reagan lifted Carter's restriction on the sale of grain to Russia, but the U.S. did not recover the market. The reversal of the U.S. position was not accepted by the Russians as a friendly gesture. In addition, the value of the dollar had been increasing during the past two years, so our grain was not a bargain to them.

A huge farm commodity surplus had developed in government warehouses, which forced farm prices down. Even the most cost-efficient farmers were not making sufficient profit to invest in new equipment. To compound the problem, the interest rate on business loans was still in the 16% range, so it was a poor environment in which to sell farm equipment or ag-airplanes.

The ag-plane industry sales during the 1970's averaged 802 units per year. The Ag Cat's share of the total market averaged 168 per year or 21%. With the unfavorable agricultural economy (and because we were attempting to be conservative), SAC set its sales goal at 65 units for 1982. At year end, only 36 Ag Cats were sold, and the total industry ag-plane market amounted to only 202 sales. That spring when the demand dried up, our leading competitors, Piper Aircraft and Cessna, stopped building ag-planes. Then, they reduced their prices below cost to convert their inventories to cash. This had a devastating impact on Ag Cat sales.

We looked at this as a short-range problem and hoped for a better market the next year. Our rationale was that SAC was in the ag-plane business for the long haul, and in a year or two, the industry would recover to a level of about 600 units a year. There were now only two other companies manufacturing ag-planes, and it would take Piper and Cessna at least two years to get back in business. Therefore, we decided to continue to invest in product development.

Work got underway in August on the 1983 "B" Model. A number of service improvements were incorporated in the new model, but the outstanding feature was the upper wing which was raised eight inches. The new configuration resulted in a significant visibility and controllability improvement (*Figure 95*).

In addition, with the raised wing, there was some increase in rate of climb which is very important to an ag plane that carries a heavy payload. Having the bi-plane wings farther apart resulted in less air flow interference, so the overall lift was improved. There was also less disturbed air flow towards the tail which made the surfaces more effective. This allowed us to use a smaller and a less expensive fin.

The raised wing Ag Cat was FAA certified in November. This new 1983 bird was called the "Super B" Ag Cat. It was displayed at the NAAA convention in Las Vegas in December and was well received.

One morning in October, I had a call from Ronald Woodard, Foreign Sales Manager of Boeing. He asked if I could have dinner with him that evening in New York City to talk about Ag Cat production in Ethiopia. Then the next morning he wanted to meet with the president of Ethiopian Airlines. Ron told me that Boeing's 767 was competing with France's Airbus 300 for an Ethiopian order for two airplanes which would amount to 80 million dollars in business. The French were also throwing in an ag-airplane design that could be built in Ethiopia, but it would require training and support that was not readily available. Ron wanted to know if there was any way we could help Ethiopia get into the ag-plane business. I told him that to get them started, we could immediately supply kits that did not require a great deal of skill to assemble. As a second phase, we could train Ethiopian personnel in Elmira, so they could progressively build more of the airplane. Then for a fee, we could eventually license them to build the complete airplane. The next morning, we had what appeared to be a successful meeting with Capt. Mohammed Ahmed, the airline president.

When I returned to Elmira, we prepared a preliminary proposal for their general information and to receive their reaction. The captain thanked us for the report and said he would be back with us after the first of the year. I wondered if we would ever hear from him again.

SAC's sailplane business evaporated in 1982, and only six deliveries were made. With the exchange rate of the dollar continuing to increase, the European fiberglass sailplanes were a very good buy. A total of 96 were imported to the U.S. that year. The new 2-37 motor glider project for the Air Force Academy came at just the right time to pick up slack caused by the drop in our sailplane business. In order to keep the 2-37 development costs at a minimum, components from two sailplanes were modified and used. They were the aft fuselage and complete tail of the 2-32 and the wings of the 1-36. The design, tooling and FAA certification for the motor glider were completed by year end, and deliveries of the eight aircraft were scheduled to start in April, 1983. Other uses for the 2-37 such as aerial observation, photo mapping, sport flying, etc., were being studied. SAC decided to build an extra 2-37 to use as a Company demonstrator.

In 1982, SAC's subcontract business volume dropped from the previous year's high of $6.1 to $4.3 million. The military business opportunities improved with President Reagan's defense build-up, but the airline and general aviation businesses were in a depression. Sales of business transportation, agricultural, flight training and pleasure-flying airplanes had decreased from 17,048 in 1979 to 4,266 in 1982. This amounted to a 75% reduction in general aviation's manufacturing volume during a three-year period. In 1982, aircraft manufacturers had sufficient capacity in their own plants and did not need assistance from airframe subcontractors such as SAC. This change was abruptly demonstrated to us by Beech Aircraft Corp.

In the fall of 1981, SAC was chosen by Beech to be one of the candidates to build the forward fuselage of their new Model 1900, a 19-passenger commuter airliner. The manufacturing operation would require about 50 workers. It took about three months to perform the detailed estimate of tooling and production labor plus the materials required to bid a fixed-price to manufacture this new assembly. Our quotation was submitted to Beech in January, 1982. The cost of numerous trips to Wichita, Kansas, plus the estimating crew's time, resulted in an expense of about $25,000 for SAC to prepare the quotation.

In February, Beech announced that SAC won the competitive bid. While the SAC-Beech contract was being prepared, Beech management announced that with the current new sales projections, there would be a shortage of work in their own shop. Therefore, they decided not to subcontract the forward fuselage of Model 1900 project. We were about a week from getting their signatures on the dotted line. Furthermore, two months later Beech announced that when the current order for the King Air 200 Cargo Doors manufactured by SAC was completed in July, the project would be transfered back to their shop in Wichita.

Boeing airliner production schedules were also cutback, which made a one-year supply of parts last an additional six months. This resulted in a decline of our Boeing business for 1982 from $1.1 to $.6 million. Fortunately, SAC had the contract for the wing tip of their new 757 fuel-efficient airliner which was just getting into production and was not affected by the schedule reduction.

SAC's best opportunity for new subcontract business was in the military arena. With careful planning and follow-up, our Sikorsky Army Black Hawk Helicopter business grew from $110,943 in 1981 to $1,163,480 in 1982. In the fall, the Company also received a contract award for a quarter million dollars to build a full-size engineering mock-up of the new Air Force basic jet trainer, the T-46A.

SAC had been working since 1979 with a small specialized development company, Emro Engineering of Summit, New Jersey, building their pilot training motion simulator equipment. In 1982, Emro received an order from the Nigerian Air Force for a vertifuge (disorientation trainer), centrifuge (acceleration trainer) and an ejection-seat trainer, which amounted to a total of about a half million dollars business for SAC.

In our search for diversification, SAC had been investigating the possible purchase of the Hughes Model 300C helicopter program. The Model 300C was the standard training helicopter throughout the world. It was being used by the U.S. Army, numerous other countries and by commercial helicopter operators. Hughes production had averaged between 70 to 100 helicopters per year and total sales was anticipated to be $15 to $20 million per year. Hughes was planning to sell the program because their overhead was too high in their Culver City, California plant. Their major product was building highly sophisticated military helicopters which made the Model 300C project unprofitable.

In spite of the turmoil caused by product changes and adjustments, SAC earned a 2% profit on sales of $9.1 million. Our average employment for the year was 253 workers. As part of our ongoing effort to continually update our manufacturing capabilities, we purchased our first new-generation computerized numerically controlled (CNC) machining equipment that year. With this type of equipment, the computer is programmed to automatically manipulate the machine while the worker monitors the operation. With the CNC machine, the human learning curve is reduced significantly, and the results are manufactured parts of consistent quality starting with the first part regardless of the quantity.

In the spring of 1982, I told the second-generation Schweizers and the board that I planned to retire at year end. Therefore, we had time to work out the smooth transition of responsibilities. When Ernie, Paul and I ran the Company, each one had his own area of responsibility, and we worked as a team on major management decisions and Company policies. Ernie, the oldest, was president, but we actually divided the presidential functions.

Under the new second-generation plan, the chief executive officer's function was to be assumed by the executive committee made up of Les Schweizer (Ernie's son), and W. Stuart and Paul Hardy Schweizer (my sons). The president's title was to be rotated annually, and the president's formal functions would be carried out by that individual. One afternoon in November, the Schweizer boys came to my office, and we drew lots for the SAC presidency. Les won the first year, 1983; Paul Hardy, 1984 and W. Stuart, 1985 (*Figure 96*). Being the last of the senior Schweizers to retire, I was asked to serve as Chairman of the Board. My job was to be available on a part-time basis, and at the request of the executive committee, to assist with special problems and key sales contacts.

My son, John, resigned from Rossignol and with two partners started the Merrell Boot Company. They manufactured and distributed hiking and cross-country ski boots and accessories.

92 

93 

94 

92. *SGM 2-37 powered sailplane fleet at the U.S. Air Force Academy for cadet training.* **93.** *Delivery of the First "B-Plus" Ag Cat, after the whole program was purchased from Gulfstream by SAC, and officials at the ceremony.(***94***).*

94A

94A. *Experimental heavy-lift Cyclo-Crane, with SAC designed-and-built wings and tail, combined dirigible and airplane technology. One proposed mission was to move cut timber from remote sites to logging roads.* DC Associates

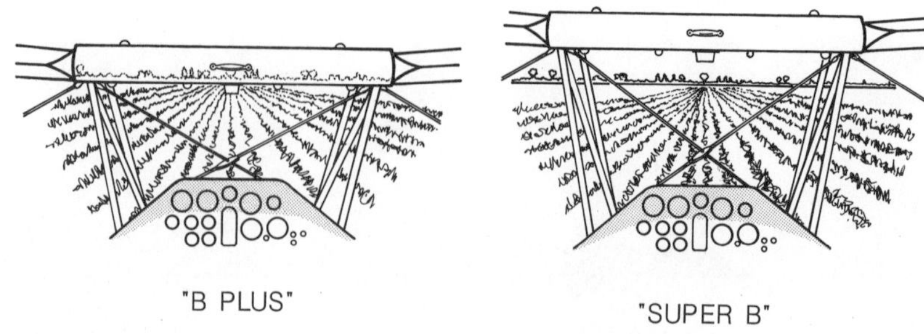

95

95. Improved windshield configuration of the "Super B" Ag Cat (sketches) gave pilots a better view—much needed considering the tight quarters in which they fly (photograph).

96

97

96. *New-generation Schweizer management on the ground, left to right. W. Stuart, Paul Hardy, Leslie, with Bill perched on the cockpit rim.*

97. *Schweizer/Hughes 300C helicopter. In 1983, SAC assumed total responsibility for the product-manufacturing, support, sales and service.*

16

THE SCHWEIZER 300C HELICOPTER 1983–1987

In October, 1983 President Reagan ordered a military invasion of the Caribbean island, Grenada, after rebel forces overthrew the elected government. During the same year, Congress passed legislation designed to keep our Social Security system financially healthy for the next 50 years. It included a new provision that required retired people with higher incomes to pay income tax on 50% of their Social Security benefits. The normal retirement age for Social Security was raised from 65 to 67 effective the year 2003. In 1983, Astronaut Sally Ride became the first American woman to orbit the earth.

The foreign exchange rate or value of the U.S. dollar, which had started to climb in 1980, continued to increase. Foreign goods, including German sailplanes, became more attractive to U.S. buyers. Increasing product liability costs had also grown rapidly and helped make our sailplanes too expensive. As a result, SAC had no sailplane sales in 1983.

The Company's sailplane-derivative business faired better. During the year, SAC delivered eight 2-37 motor gliders to the Air Force Academy at Colorado Springs. As they were completed, ships were flown from Elmira to the Academy by pilots, including five with the Schweizer name (Les, Stu, Paul Hardy, brother Paul A. and myself). The Academy motor gliders had no modern electro-navigation equipment, so we followed the interstate highway system. This was a somewhat new technique because railroad tracks had been the airmen's navigation aid in the early days of aviation.

As I flew the 2-37 motor glider to Colorado in the summer of 1983, I could see acres of untilled fields, the effect of the U.S. Agriculture Department's Payment in Kind (PIK) program. Farmers agreed to idle about a third of the land they normally planted and received in exchange free surplus grain from the government. They were allowed to sell the grain on the open market or use it to feed their livestock. The government's strategy was to reduce the huge commodity stockpiles that had been depressing farm prices. In that respect, the program was successful. However, it had a negative effect on the agricultural-related industries such as seed, fertilizer, fuel, machinery and ag-planes.

In 1983, the total volume of the ag-plane industry continued its downward slide, and only 27 Ag Cats were delivered. In spite of the depressed market, SAC continued the development and FAA certification of the 600hp and 750hp PT6A turbine-powered "Super B" Ag Cats. We felt there would be a foreign market for these aircraft in areas where aviation gas is scarce but turbine fuel is cheap and readily available to support the airline industry. In areas with hot weather and high altitudes, such as in Ethiopia, turbine engines do not lose power like a piston-powered reciprocating engine does. Discussions continued with Ethiopian Airlines, but SAC was not able to finalize an Ag Cat subsidiary manufacturing agreement with them.

The Company's major accomplishment of the year was an agreement reached on November 2 with Hughes Helicopter, Inc., Culver City, California whereby SAC became the licensed manufacturer and product support source for the Hughes Model 269/300C series helicopters (*Figure 97*). With this agreement, Schweizer assumed total responsibility for sales, marketing, product support and manufacturing of the product line. The Model 269/300C family had been in production since 1957, and over 2700 units had been sold throughout the world. During this period, a number of technological advances had been incorporated into the design, and with annual updating, it was (and still is) the world's standard training helicopter. Between

1964 and 1969, the U.S. Army had purchased over 800 of the earlier models for their primary training program.

This new project provided SAC with a third major Company-owned product line to complement the Ag Cat and the high performance sailplanes and motor gliders. The helicopter acquisition required that SAC increase its long-term debt significantly. However, the new young Schweizer management team expected to justify the investment by more than doubling the Company's annual sales. The Model 269/300C series spare parts business alone was projected to amount to $7 to $8 million in annual sales for the next ten years.

Four other organizations competed with SAC for the production rights to this program; therefore, it required a concentrated effort on Schweizer's part to win the program. Paul Hardy took the lead on this business development. He spent about half his time for a year discussing the project at Hughes and SAC, making proposals and working on financing and negotiation details in order to make it happen. The financial support of the New York State Job Development Authority (JDA) and the reputation of the Schweizer Company in the aircraft industry played important roles in the Hughes decision to choose SAC.

After the JDA loan was signed in 1983, New York State Governor, Mario M. Cuomo, visited SAC with the President of JDA, Robert Dormer. After the ceremony, Stuart gave the Governor a sailplane ride which was a big hit (*Figure 98*).

The principal reason why Hughes decided to relocate and eventually sell the Model 269/300C program was because it no longer fit into their helicopter business plan. The bulk of their activity involved the production of the sophisticated AH-6A assault military helicopters, which created a very high cost manufacturing environment in their Culver City plant. The overhead charge on each hour of direct labor made the Model 300C an unprofitable project for Hughes.

It required 32 trucks to transfer the $13 million worth of Hughes inventory, tooling and wherewithal from California to Elmira. Spare parts shipments to customers began soon after the inventory arrived in Elmira. This created immediate income for SAC. Our goal was to deliver our first Schweizer-manufactured Model 300C by the summer of 1984.

Schweizer management continued to place emphasis upon expansion of subcontract business. Unfortunately, despite this effort, the industry-wide recession resulted in a reduction in our sales. Since 1981, our subcontract business had decreased from $6.1 million to $4.1 million. Reagan's defense build-up got underway in 1983, and it started to give military aircraft manufacturers a boost by year end. The bright spot for SAC was that Sikorsky's helicopter business was increasing, and we hoped to benefit from additional subcontract projects.

Our U.S. Army Black Hawk assault helicopter work was increasing because a version of the same design, the Sea Hawk, had been ordered by the Navy for a shipboard mission. This was a very logical cost-saving decision, but a surprise to us because normally when each service has a requirement, they start from scratch on a completely new bird.

In the fall of 1983, we took over a Sikorsky project that had been in trouble at another vendor. It was the production of the auxilary fuel tank support assemblies for the large Sikorsky CH-53E troop transport helicopter. This was the ship that had been used on President Carter's Iranian hostage rescue mission in 1981 that ended in failure after three of the eight helicopters broke down while flying through a sandstorm.

When the bottom fell out of the Ag Cat market in April, employment dropped below 200. This was the lowest level the Company had experienced in 25 years. By year end, as a result of the helicopter project and new Sikorsky business, employment had increased to 246 workers.

In spite of the fluctuation of sales, we had a reasonably good year from a financial standpoint. End-of-the-year helicopter spare parts sales of the Hughes inventory we had just purchased gave our profitability a boost. Our annual sales amounted to $11.2 million and a 4% profit was earned before taxes.

This was my first year of retirement from the day-to-day operations of SAC, so I had an adjustment to make. As a Director, I kept up-to-date on SAC's business activities. I was also asked to assist on some interesting sales and public relations assignments.

After 15 years on the board of the Arnot Ogden Memorial Hospital, I was elected Chairman in February, 1983. (I think they were just waiting for me.) This gave me as much activity as I wanted.

In November, 1984 President Reagan was elected for a second term. He won a large majority of the popular vote and carried 49 states. The New York City subway vigilante, Bernard Goetz, was indicted on gun charges. During that same year, the Union Carbide plant at Bhopal, India developed a gas leak that killed over three thousand people. The ongoing famine in Ethiopia received worldwide publicity, and this resulted in a dramatic acceleration of international help to Ethiopian famine victims. Advisers suggested they acquire agricultural airplanes to help increase food production. This was the reason why the Ethiopians were talking to us about the Ag Cat.

During 1984, Ethiopian Airline personnel, including its president, visited SAC to look over our facilities and the turbo Ag Cat. They also sent an Ethiopian ag-pilot to Elmira to fly and evaluate the aircraft. Because I handled the Ethiopian proposal and negotiations before I retired, I was asked to continue in this role.

In March, Ethiopian Airlines' lawyer visited Elmira and appeared to be interested in working out an agreement. After negotiation sessions during the previous spring, summer and fall, we still had no agreement. The Ethiopians who visited SAC were fluent in English. It is the second language in their country and is used by the educated people. However, their specific interpretation of some of the contract language was different from ours which made it difficult for our lawyer, Kenneth A. Tifft, and theirs to write a legal agreement. After our last meeting in the fall, we were doubtful that we could ever come to an agreement, but they called in December and asked for a meeting in February, 1985.

The Ag Cat sales for 1984 were disappointing since only twenty-seven airplanes were sold. (See Appendix 3.) However, development of the Ag Cat product line continued on a modest basis. Les Schweizer took the lead on this development and emphasis was placed on cost-reduction items to maximize sales. The principal new development was a small Ag Cat with a 450 hp engine and a 320 gallon hopper. The list price for this model called the "B450" was 25% less than that of the 600 hp "Super B" with the 400 gallon hopper. This reduction was made possible because there was a large supply of 450hp surplus engines at a very reasonable price. The new B450 was displayed at the NAAA at Las Vegas in December in hopes of stimulating 1985 sales.

Full production of the Schweizer Model 300C helicopter began in 1984. In June, eight months after the agreement was finalized with Hughes, the first SAC-manufactured ship was delivered to the Baltimore Police Department. A total of eleven helicopters were built in 1984 and accounted for $1.1M in sales. By year end, production had accelerated to a rate of three ships per month.

Getting the 300C helicopter into production was an outstanding accomplishment by Stu Schweizer and the new Schweizer management team. In the past, SAC had built three different helicopter airframe cabins for Bell, but had never tackled the dynamic system (the mechanism between the motor and the main and tail rotors plus the controls) of a whirlybird. It is a highly complex, sophisticated mechanism to fabricate, assemble and inspect. A supply of most of the parts was available in the Hughes inventory, so we could gradually take over the parts manufacturing responsibility.

To do this job, SAC had to take a major step forward in machining and quality control technology. It required over a million dollar investment over the next two years plus the addition of some highly skilled technicians and engineers. The new equipment had benefits for all of the Company's programs and, in some cases, allowed work formerly subcontracted to be accomplished at Schweizer.

With a worldwide fleet of over 2,700 Model 269/300C helicopters in service, the product support became an important and profitable phase of this new undertaking. Before SAC bought the program, our projections showed that we would be able to justify the helicopter buy based on the spare parts business alone. This proved to be correct. Because of the time required for the transaction from Hughes to SAC and the production start-up time, we began 1984 with a spare parts order backlog of $2.5 million. By year end, however, the spare parts backlog had been reduced to $.85 million and critical field shortages had been virtually eliminated. The 1984 helicopter product support business amounted to sales of $7.8 million. The total program amounted to $8.9 million, or 51% of our total corporate sales.

An offshoot of the Company's involvement in the sailplane business has been the development of special purpose, high performance aircraft. Sailplane type aerodynamics technology and existing structural components are often ideally suited to serve as building blocks for this type of airplane. During the 1970's, SAC served as a major subcontractor to LTV Electrosystems, Lockheed, and Martin Marietta for the design and manufacture of three different types of reconnaissance aircraft used by the U.S. Government. Since 1980, SAC made a number of unsolicited proposals to the U.S. military for various versions of reconnaissance airplanes. In 1984, Schweizer received a contract to develop a version of the 2-37 motorglider into a quiet reconnaissance airplane. Les Schweizer's design, called the SA 2-37A, had over twice the horsepower and gross weight of the basic 2-37 (*Figure 99*). This aircraft was powered with a 235hp Avco Lycoming piston engine with a baffled exhaust. When in a cruise mode at 75 to 85 knots and at 2000 feet altitude or more, it is inaudible at ground level to the human ear. Two aircraft were ordered, and this development program created over $2 million in sales during 1984 and 1985. This project opened doors for other new opportunities as well.

All areas of commercial and military aircraft manufacturing continued to remain depressed except for some key military projects which did provide subcontract opportunities for SAC. Our Sikorsky business volume increased from $1M to $2.3M in 1984, although SAC's total subcontract volume remained at about the same level as during the previous two years, $4.3 million.

During 1984, SAC's employment increased by 56 to 312 employees. However, there was still a good supply of capable people available in the job market. In May, Piper Aircraft Corp. announced they were closing their Lock Haven, Pennsylvania plant and moving all of their operations to Vero Beach, Florida. A number of their skilled craftsmen, technicians and engineers who did not want to move to Florida visited our personnel office. With the Piper situation combined with local interest in Schweizer, there was a reservoir of capable people from which to choose.

To support the helicopter program, we required a higher percentage of office type services than had been needed by the sailplane and Ag Cat programs during the 1970's. Therefore, we quickly ran out of office space. During the summer of 1984, a 5,500 sq. ft. office expansion was completed at a cost of $.25 million or $45 per sq. ft. (See Appendix 2.) This was quite a change from 1942 when the original plant was built for approximately $3.50 per sq. ft.

In spite of the various costs of putting the helicopter into production, SAC ended the year with a 1.5% profit before taxes on a record sales of $17.5 million. A large contributor to the profit was spare parts sales. More than 50% of the spare parts we sold in 1984 were from the original inventory purchased from Hughes at a price that allowed SAC a fair return. This helped to offset the high starting-load cost of getting the Model 300 helicopter into full production.

The profit would have been much larger but was reduced because SAC changed its method of valuing inventory from a FIFO (First In First Out) to a LIFO (Last In First Out) system. The principal reason for making the change was to lower the tax expense. (The IRS will only allow a business to change its method of valuing inventory once every seven years.) This was a strategic move in light of the very large Hughes inventory purchased. We were concerned that it might become obsolete before it could be sold.

Paul Hardy completed his year as president of SAC and W. Stuart was elected president at the December meeting to be effective January 1. W. H. Murphy, a management consultant and former executive vice president of Hughes Helicopter Corporation, was elected to the Schweizer Board. (See Appendix 9.) Each year on the evening of the December Board Meeting, the Directors' Dinner is held for the directors and their wives. Traditionally, Ernie Schweizer, the craftsman, makes an exotic gift for each of the women. They are normally made from pewter which Eileen polishes and wraps beautifully. At the 1984 dinner, Paul H. was sitting across from attorney Kenneth Tifft. Ken had a coughing spell and Paul H. thought he was choking. He ran around the table and gave him the "Hug of Life". Ken winced, then smiled and thanked Paul for his concern. Ken had a sharp pain in his side for the next few days. He went to the doctor and found out he had a broken rib from Paul's squeeze.

In 1984 Chemung County held their first annual Distinguished Citizen Award Dinner. I was flattered and somewhat embarrassed to be the first recipient of the award, because I felt many people had done more for the community than I had.

In 1985 Mikhail Gorbachev, the new Soviet leader, met with President Reagan in Geneva. This was the first summit meeting since Carter and Brezhnev met in 1979. They agreed to revive cultural exchanges and to work jointly on airline safety, but no arms control reduction was achieved. Middle East anti-American terrorist activities resulted in the hijack of the cruise ship, *Achille Lauro*. Terry Anderson was kidnapped, and a TWA jet was hijacked with 39 passengers aboard; they were held hostage for 17 days.

Terrorist activities were a concern to SAC management since approximately 40% of our business was with foreign customers who had to be serviced and visited. Our representatives traveled through some of these unfriendly countries, and, as American aircraft manufacturer's employees, they could be a natural targets for the extremists. The U.S. Department of Defense advised American business personnel traveling in foreign countries to act and dress like tourists and carry no obvious company identification.

The U.S. agricultural economy continued to be depressed in 1985. Only 70 new agplanes were delivered by the industry, and, 12 were Ag Cats. The most active sales prospects were in the international marketplace. Many Third World countries wanted and needed agplanes to increase their agricultural productivity; but they lacked the funds. In spite of numerous foreign inquiries received, only two firm orders developed. We sent one ship to New Zealand and one to Bolivia.

The major Ag Cat accomplishment that year was the culmination of a license agreement with Ethiopia Airlines to manufacture the turbine Model B Ag Cat in Addis Ababa (*Figure 100*). Except for Egypt, the Ethiopian airlines' Ag Cat sales territory was limited to the countries in Central Africa. According to our Boeing Aircraft friends, Ethiopian Airlines and its president, Capt. Mohammed Ahmed, had the support of their Chief of

State and had excellent relations with many African countries. We were hopeful that this relationship would open new Ag-Cat sales opportunities for SAC. Surprisingly, Ethiopia was run by a hard-line Marxist leader, yet the airline was run on strict capitalist principles. They worked to make a profit and pay taxes.

The Ethiopian agreement called for a large up-front payment to SAC before the wherewithal to build the Ag-Cat was released. Basically, this consisted of the following:

- Complete set of engineering drawings;
- Technical data required to manufacture and license the aircraft;
- A complete set of assembly fixtures;
- Training for 20 workers (from 2 to 20 weeks) on Ag-Cat technology.

In addition, SAC agreed to sell a completed Model B turbine aircraft and kits of parts required to build complete aircraft. Kits were designed to allow the airline to gradually increase its work scope on each airplane. The goal was for them to with a few exceptions eventually build the complete airplane in Ethiopia on a royalty basis.

The agreement was signed on September 15, 1985 at the Pratt & Whitney Plant in Montreal, Canada for the following reasons: First, the turbine engine used on the Ag Cat is manufactured there, and the airline was buying the engine directly from Pratt and Whitney. The airline's attorney wanted to sign both agreements simultaneously. Second, SAC wanted to make sure the transaction would qualify as a foreign sale so it could be put through our wholly-owned subsidiary, Schweizer International Sales Corp. Kathleen Condon, SAC's Contracts Manager, and I flew to New York City and planned to fly to Montreal with the airline president and his attorney. The attorney got tied up in traffic and missed the flight. The president joined us and both agreements were signed with enthusiasm and a minimum of discussion.

In 1984 Congress passed legislation which allowed U.S. companies to establish Foreign Sales Corporations (FSC) provided their FSC headquarters were located in a foreign country. The goal was to resolve international trade problems created by the previously permitted Domestic International Sales Corporations (DISC) and to increase U.S. exports. SAC established an FSC in January, 1985 with its home office at St. Croix, Virgin Islands. This was done because approximately 35% of our sales was to customers located in foreign countries. The benefits of an FSC to a U.S. company was an approximate 30% reduction in taxes on the profits earned on foreign sales.

That fall Peggy and I vacationed in the Virgin Islands, and I visited our foreign sales office. We were staying at the Caneel Bay, a quiet, low-key resort where the only entertainment was a native steel band which played on Saturday nights. Every time we got up to dance, the floor was crowded. Finally, late in the evening, the band started to play and the floor was empty. So we got up and started to dance. Only after noticing that no one else was dancing did we realize that we were dancing to the "Star Spangled Banner."

The Model 300C helicopter project experienced its second full year of production in 1985. It turned out to be a successful program. The production of helicopters increased from 11 units in 1984 to 23 in 1985, which amounted to $3.3 million in sales. The spare parts phase of the helicopter business turned out to be larger than projected and amounted to $10.1 million.

In June, a 300C Helicopter was delivered to The Cousteau Society to replace their Hughes-manufactured 300 which was based on their oceanographic ship, *Calypso*. The helicopter is used for aerial photography, aerial exploration and ship-to-shore transportation (*Figure 101*). Jean-Michel Cousteau, son of Captain Jacques-Yves Cousteau, accepted the helicopter for The Cousteau Society. I had the pleasure of giving Jean-Michel a ride over Seneca Lake in a 2-37 motor glider. He was interested to hear that Seneca Lake was over 500 feet deep. He said that the Society might possibly be interested in doing some underwater exploration to see what has accumulated on the bottom of the lake since the last glaciation.

Helicopter sales, like commercial airplanes, continued to be soft in 1985. Pilot training and law enforcement provided the majority of our sales. There was some concern at SAC whether we could generate sufficient sales to justify a competitive price in the marketplace. To achieve this goal, we estimated that a production rate of a minimum of one ship per week would be required. Fortunately, in December two contracts were received from the U.S. Army's Foreign Military Sales branch (24 for Thailand and 6 for El Salvador). Therefore, it appeared SAC would sell at least 50 in 1986. This was music to our ears.

In just three years, the helicopter program became 53% of our total business. (See Appendix 4.) Management attempted to develop other diversified aviation projects to keep our business portfolio from getting top-heavy in the helicopter business as it had in the late 1970's with the Ag Cat. SAC had been performing subcontract work for approximately ten companies since 1982, and, in spite of our efforts, the business volume remained at about $4 million. This included our Boeing business which had leveled off at about $.5 million per year. Finally, in 1985 there was a large increase in Sikorsky helicopter work which increased our subcontract volume to $6.9 million. This was the result of two new Sikorsky contracts for the production of external weapons pylons for their U.S. Navy version of the UH-60 helicopter.

SAC had a record sales of $25 million and a 3% profit was earned on sales after taxes. (See Appendix 4.) SAC's employment grew from 312 to 350 in 1985. The closing of the Thatcher Glass Mfg. Company's Research and Production Management Divisions in Big Flats made some key individuals available to help to round out our management staff. There were two departures from the Director/Management Team that year as well. Bill Murphy joined a national accounting firm as a partner and, to comply with their policy, resigned from our Board. Don Quigley, Vice President of Production Engineering, retired after working 44 years for SAC. Both individuals were key contributors to SAC's success and were hard to replace.

Brother Paul A. had spent a great deal of time and effort since 1945 as a director and participant in the Harris Hill Soaring Corp. activities. He had taken the leadership in developing good relations with the Chemung County government, which owns and maintains the Harris Hill facilities. In recognition for his outstanding service, the Harris Hill Soaring Corp. elected Paul A. the Honorary Chairman of their Board of Directors.

In May of that year, I was honored to be selected to join brothers Ernest and Paul as a member of the United States Soaring Hall of Fame. It seems that if you live long enough, all kinds of honors can fall your way. As a complete change of pace in my business career, I was elected Chairman of the Board of the Elmira Savings Bank after twenty years service on the Board. The bank had just converted from a mutual-owned savings bank to a stock bank which created some interesting problems.

This year was full of important happenings. In January, the Challenger Spacecraft, with a crew of five aboard, exploded moments after blast-off. A month later, Marcos fled the Philippines and Carazon Aquino became president. In April, U.S. jets attacked Libya in retaliation for the West Berlin discotheque bombing and other anti-American activities. During the same month, a nuclear catastrophe occurred at the Chenobyl power plant in the U.S.S.R.

In October, President Reagan and Gorbachev held a summit meeting in Reykjavik, Iceland. There was general agreement in favor of a vast cut in missiles and strategic arms. However, there was no accord because the Russians objected to the American "Star Wars" defense plan. In November, Americans were shocked when they heard of the Iran-Contra affair with headquarters in the basement of the White House.

In December, the president of Piper Aircraft Corp., Robert Wyma, announced that their product liability cost averaged $73,000 per aircraft and exceeded their direct labor cost to build the airplane. In 1977 the general aircraft manufacturing industry paid out $24 million in product liability expenses, and by 1985, this cost had risen to $210 million. This was primarily attributed to higher awards to plaintiffs and increased legal expenses. For most manufacturers, the longer they remain in business, and the more products they have in service, the greater the exposure.

According to a 1986 study by the organization that publishes the *Public Safety and Liability Report,* 70% of the product liability payments made by manufacturers was consumed in the litigation process. When combined with the growing product liability cost and the increased costs due to a gradual reduction in the number of aircraft manufactured each year since 1979, aircraft manufacturers had a serious problem. Airplane prices had grown out of range of many prospective buyers so the volume of sales continued to drop. (See Appendix 5.)

SAC had no sailplane sales in 1986, but two high-value sailplane-derivative, special-purpose, 2-37A aircraft were manufactured for the U.S. government. These airplanes were equipped with a sophisticated electronic payload for nighttime surveillance missions.

Only 17 Ag Cats were delivered in 1986. Four additional Ag Cat kits were delivered to Ethiopia, and we were pleased with their progress in setting up a manufacturing facility. In spite of environmental issues relating to chemical use in agriculture, international sales prospects looked somewhat brighter for the Ag Cat, because the U.S. dollar had become weaker during the fall of 1986.

The Model 300C helicopter project proved to be an excellent program for SAC, and 56 were delivered in 1986. The spare parts business continued to be the most profitable phase of the helicopter program and accounted for than 50% of the $17.6 million sales for the total helicopter program. It also appeared that the current spare parts volume would continue into the next decade since there were over 2,700 aircraft of this model manufactured. Helicopters normally require more replacement parts than airplanes or sailplanes and require more frequent inspections. Many of the moving parts on a helicopter have a limited-service life which means that parts are required to be replaced after a certain number of hours of use.

By 1986, SAC had acquired the equipment and technology so it was able to manufacture the majority of complicated machined parts required to build the Model 300C. The exception was the main rotor blades and the tail rotor blades which were still being manufactured by Hughes. (Hughes became McDonnell Douglas Helicopter Company in 1984 when MDHC purchased the Hughes Helicopter Company.) By year end 1987, the manufacturing of the complicated bonded composite tail rotor blade which started in 1986 was successfully transferred to SAC.

In November of 1986, SAC management recommended to the Board of Directors that the Company attempt to negotiate the purchase of the Model 300C program from McDonnell Douglas. The motion was approved by the Board in spite of the large financial commitment because we believed that it was the right time to take this action. This gave SAC the total rights and responsibility for the product line as well as the freedom to carry out independent product development. This was important because the U.S. Army had announced that it planned to retire their aging fleet of primary rotary-wing trainers, the TH-55 (military designation for the original Model 300 family). SAC management wanted a free hand so it could start developing a replacement helicopter trainer for the U.S. Army.

The Company's product base had continually changed since 1940. Schweizer's flexibility is the main reason we are still in business. In 1976, SAC produced 256 Ag Cats and 78 sailplanes, which amounted to 90% of all sales. Ten years later those products amounted to only 17% of our sales. Helicopter sales in 1986 amounted to 65% or $17.6 million of our $26.7 million total business. A record profit of 6.3% on sales was earned after taxes, which helped to justify the purchase of the Model 300C program. Our average employment for the year grew to 357 workers.

In March, Peg and I traveled to New Zealand to visit our Ag Cat and helicopter dealers. Our helicopter dealer, Motor Holdings Ltd., which also handles larger helicopters, had five bases geographically located to service the country. We saw the bases, met the people and with their guidance saw their beautiful country. March in New Zealand is like our September. The mountains in the South Island look like the Swiss Alps. Helicopters are used extensively for personal transportation. There are more helicopters per capita in New Zealand than in any other country in the world. At the time of our visit, there were 89 of our Model 300 family of helicopters in active service.

We found that choppers were providing many interesting services. One dealer said he had a customer who painted bridges with his Model 300. Many sheep farmers in the South Island were branching out and becoming deer farmers. There was a large new export market for deer meat because it had less cholesterol than beef or lamb. The helicopter was used to fly over wild deer and serve as a platform to shoot tranquilizer darts at them. Then the aircraft landed and men put a sling on the deer and used the helicopter to carry the deer to a farm that had ten foot fences.

We spent an interesting day and night on a sheep farm in the mountains. The farmer had 3,000 sheep and 1,000 acres of grazing land. His fields were serviced during the winter by agplanes that applied a superphosphate fertilizer. The farmer said that this treatment is costly, but without it, his fields would only support 1,500 sheep. Each year he must make a major business decision concerning amount of fertilization.

Our nation had two major scandals in 1987. They resulted in the Reverend Jimmy Bakker's resignation from the TV Church PTL, and Senator Gary Hart's withdrawal from the presidential race. At the White House, Oliver North implicated his bosses in the Iran Contra affair. Later that year, Reagan and Gorbachev signed the first pact requiring a cut in nuclear arms. That fall the first half of the NFL football season was lost to a players' strike. On October 19th, the stock market plunged downward 508 points, almost double the 1929 crash, but the disaster did not seem to have a negative effect on SAC's business. During the first nine months of the year, our volume dropped about 15%; but during the fourth quarter, the backlog of orders increased substantially.

The Company's 1987 decrease in business was primarily due to the helicopter program sales dropping from $17.7 million to $13.5 million. Only 41 helicopters were delivered compared to 56 the previous year. The commercial helicopter sales held up, but there were no large, active military orders. The spare parts end of the business also decreased. The U.S. Army parts orders, which had been running over two million dollars a year to keep Fort Rucker's fleet of 150 ships flying, practically stopped when the Army announced that the Fort Rucker's TH-55/300 helicopter fleet would be replaced by the Bell turbine-powered UH-1 Huey in October, 1988. This decision was made because the Army had a large inventory of the UH-1's left from the Vietnam War era, and they wanted a turbine-powered helicopter for primary training.

Schweizer management became concerned about helicopter sales because they still felt that a minimum of one ship per week was essential to make our assembly operation cost effective. Then in December, a second Foreign Military Sale (FMS) order developed for 24 additional helicopters for Thailand. We had been pursuing the sale for over a year. With the other sales commitments, SAC was then able to project a helicopter production rate of one ship every four days for 1988.

The U.S. Army and Thailand were not the only users of Model 269/300 trainers. Military users worldwide included the armed forces of Algeria, Argentina, Brazil, Columbia, El Salvador, Ghana, Greece, Guyana, Haiti, Honduras, India, Indonesia, Iraq, Italy, Japan, Kenya, South Korea, Nicaragua, Nigeria, Sierra Leone, Spain, Sweden, Taiwan, and Turkey.

The U.S. Army's decision to switch to the UH-1 worried us. We were aware that there was a strong feeling among some of the Army brass that turbine-powered helicopters should be used for primary training. Their rationale was that the Army's operational helicopters are turbine-powered; therefore, the training aircraft should have the same type of powerplant. However, it was generally understood that the UH-1 was expensive to operate for this type of mission, and it was not an ideal trainer. The majority of military personnel seemed to agree that a new generation trainer should be developed, and they accepted the fact that it would probably take at least five years before it would become operational. In spite of the Army personnel's desire for a change, we had expected the TH-55/300 to remain the Army's primary trainer until the new generation helicopter was ready to take over.

SAC management faced up to the TH-55 problem and pointed out to the Army that even though there was a surplus of Huey helicopters, they would be very expensive to operate. The Army Training Commmand had already determined a flight operation hourly cost of $107 for the TH-55 and $491 for the UH-1. We suggested to the Army that they take an interim step by upgrading their TH-55 fleet with some 300C helicopters. We soon learned that the Army stood firm on their UH-1 decision, so we backed off and made a serious effort to assist them in determining the requirements for their new generation, turbine trainer. As a result, SAC initiated a Company-financed development program for a turbine-powered training helicopter.

During 1987, Boeing's airline business, which had leveled out during the past few years, started to expand. Their backlog of orders at year end was growing faster than they could accelerate production. Airline passenger service and especially air cargo was on the increase. Services such as Flying Tiger, UPS, Federal Express, etc., had become worldwide, and airline economists predicted continued growth through the next decade. Another factor that also accelerated Boeing's sales was a new concern for airliner obsolescence. This was highlighted by some accidents and aircraft mechanical problems. As a result of Boeing's increased business, our subcontract work for Boeing was growing. In 1987, it was one million dollars, and for 1988, we were projecting $3 million.

In 1987, Schweizer received an order for four additional 2-37 motor gliders from the U.S. Air Force Academy. The original order was for eight ships in 1982. The Academy personnel had been well pleased with the 2-37 aircraft. It was the basic airwork trainer for the cadet glider program before the students were allowed to fly conventional sailplanes. The glider program had become a required course for the second-year class of about 1,100 students.

The Company also conducted a national tour with the SA 2-37A special-purpose aircraft. The goal was to generate interest among military services and government agencies such as Customs, drug enforcement and law enforcement. There were many skeptics who did not believe our reconnaissance aircraft was as quiet as we reported. Therefore, we set out to prove it and received an enthusiastic reception.

In spite of the fact that general aviation's safety record had improved significantly since the 1970's, the cost of product liability in 1987 continued to increase dramatically. During the fall of 1986, the premium for our product liability insurance, which included a very large deductible in the event of an award, increased to an exorbitant level and made the purchase of coverage difficult to accept. In 1987, we were able to plead our own case with Lloyd's of London based upon our good record. Formerly, our rating had been based on industry-wide experience, but our record was better than the aircraft industry average. With a very high deductible, we received a product liability rate we could live with.

The Company successfully reacted to weaker market conditions and earned a 4% profit after a LIFO reserve and taxes on $23 million sales. Our employment leveled off at 350 workers, but due to increase in complexity of our business and development work, a larger percentage of indirect personnel was required. We ran out of office space again and built a 7,000 square foot addition.

After seven years of research and hard work since his retirement, my brother, Paul A. Schweizer, completed his book on the history of gliding and soaring in the United States. It is an excellent book and has been well received by the public. *Wings Like Eagles* was published by the Smithsonian Institution Press.

In August I attended a ceremony organized by our Swedish helicopter dealer, SAAB, to celebrate the delivery of eight Model 300C helicopters to the Swedish Army. This increased their primary training fleet to 26 helicopters. Ten had previously been purchased from Hughes, and eight were ordered from SAC in 1984. In Sweden, the Army Helicopter Flight School also provides the primary training for their Air Force and Navy. At the time of my visit, SAAB had imported over 100 Model 300 helicopters since 1962. About 75 are in use commercially in Scandinavian countries for power-line inspection, reindeer herding, forest work, law enforcement and training.

Our Swedish distributor is a division of the SAAB Corporation, the automobile manufacturer. SAAB was organized before WWII as an aircraft manufacturing company but diversified after the war and got into the automobile business. SAAB did not manufacture helicopters, so it established a sales division that represents foreign helicopter companies in Sweden. The original SAAB aircraft manufacturing division is still active and its basic product is military airplanes. However, since 1982, it has been building a 35 passenger airliner, the Model 340, a turbo prop transport which is used by USAIR and other airlines throughout the world.

The president of the aircraft division took me for a tour of the Model 340 factory. I was surprised to find a great deal of Russian technology and equipment. It appeared to be an efficient operation. The president said that Swedish ecology laws are very strict. They build the airliner from parts that have a protective coating and are primed. When the ship is completed, it is flown to England where it is painted. If SAAB painted the 340 in Sweden, they would need a paint booth large enough to house the airliner, and one that would have all of the latest air purification equipment.

Peg went with me on this trip. The president of SAAB invited us to a cocktail party at his home. We were surprised to see the guests arrive in their cars and then take a taxi to dinner. We asked why this was done and were told that penalties for driving after drinking are so severe in Sweden that most people won't take the risk of being caught.

One night we were sitting by a picture window at the Grand Hotel in Stockholm having dinner when the head waiter came by and whispered that the King and Queen would arrive in about five minutes. They came in two Mercedes and had eight security guards, but no Saab or Volvo. (Incidentally, I remember that the young blond Swedish girls were very beautiful!)

98

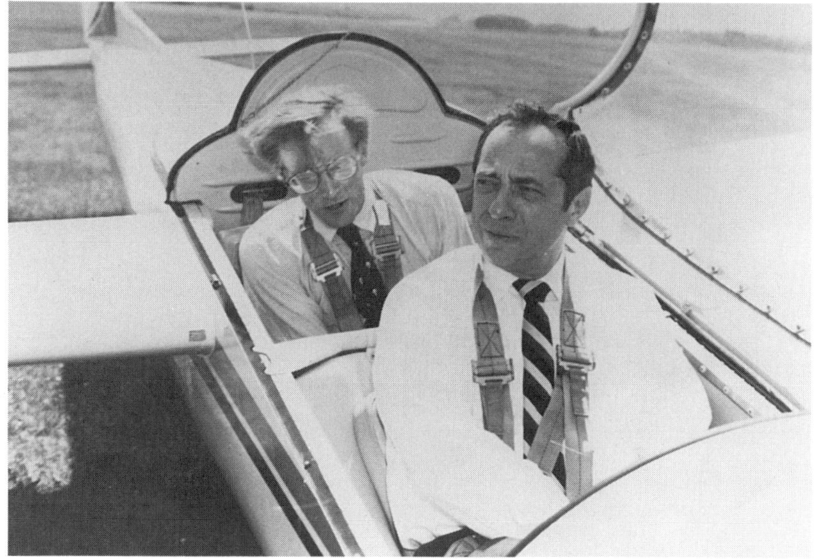

99

__98.__ New York Governor Mario Cuomo takes the front seat of a Schweizer sailplane to fly with W. Stuart. ***99.*** *SA 2-37A, quiet reconnaissance/surveillance aircraft inaudible on the ground when flying at 2000 feet.*

100

101

100. *Capt. Mohammed Ahmed, President of Ethopian Airlines and Bill Schweizer sign an agreement to license building of Ag Cats from kits.* ***101.*** *Model 300C delivered to the Cousteau Society by SAC flies low on a filming mission in Thailand.*

17

THE MODEL 330 HELICOPTER DEVELOPMENT 1988–1989

Finally, in the spring of 1988, the Russians began their withdrawal from Afghanistan. In August, Canada's Ben Johnson was stripped of his Olympic Gold Medal after testing positive for steroids. George Bush was elected President in November. Three days before Christmas, a terrorist bomb exploded on Pan Am Flight 103 over Lockerbie, Scotland. At year end, the president of Boeing Airplane Company announced that his company had a backlog of orders for 1,087 airliners worth more than $53 billion. Deliveries were scheduled into 1995 and the wait for even the least popular models was at least 18 months.

After a series of booms and slowdowns in aircraft orders since 1960, Boeing officials had been reluctant to increase their production rate. However, in 1988 Boeing accepted the challenge and increased their manufacturing rate in spite of the enormous difficulties of adding capacity on the world's largest production lines.

SAC's Boeing subcontract business had amounted to $1 million in 1987, would be $3.2 million in 1988 and was projected to be $6 million in 1989—all music to our ears for two reasons. First, we were working on four different airliners which gave us product diversification. Second, this work was expected to run through the next decade, and Boeing normally does not pull work back from vendors.

The piston-engine commercial airplane business which includes ag planes was still in the doldrums in 1988. Only 15 Ag Cats were delivered, and the program sales amounted to $3.2 million. The new airplane production was not profitable but the Ethiopian kits and spare parts business made the program a break-even. Appendix 5 shows that the high performance, more expensive, turboprop and jet executive business airplanes had been holding their production levels since 1983, while the manufacturers' sales revenue had increased. This is because of the inherent productivity and efficiency of corporate aviation.

The Model 300C piston-powered helicopter deliveries increased from 41 to 55 in 1988, and our backlog of orders increased. By year end, commitments were received for all 80 helicopters planned for production in 1989. The international market was strong, and over 50% of new 300C helicopters were shipped overseas. It appears that even without the U.S. Army business, the Model 300C had a long range place in the world market.

Management's major problem at this point was not selling helicopters but finding ways to increase the production of parts and equipment to support the unanticipated growth in new helicopter and spare parts sales. A great number of the shortages were associated with the dynamic system. Many parts are made from precision castings and forgings and are complex and difficult to fabricate, process and inspect. The production flow time for some of these parts exceeds one year, which means long range commitments by management. SAC development activities, which had started in 1986, related to the U.S. Army's requirement for approximately 200 next-generation turbine-powered training helicopters. This led the company into a new major product area which we hoped would also have a large commercial market. An analysis of the Army's requirements indicated that a helicopter tailored to their specifications could be developed by using the Model 300 proven dynamic systems (main and tail rotor blades, transmissions, drive shafts, and flight controls) with a major modification to the airframe.

Les Schweizer was responsible for the preliminary design of the proposed new trainer. A full size cabin mockup was built in 1987 to work out design details and to assist with the marketing effort. The design and mockup were reviewed and discussed with a number of respected helicopter designers, experienced project engineers and engineering test pilots. It was also shown to the U.S. Army representatives so their informal reaction and input could be received. In line with management's understanding of what the Army would be asking for, the military training version was designed with three seats and three sets of controls. The Army's rationale was that one student could learn a great deal while observing another student flying.

A decision was made during the winter of 1987 to build a flying prototype of the turbine-powered helicopter, the Model 330. The first flight was made in May 1988 (*Figure 102*). Then a month later, in June, the Company hosted a First Flight Ceremony that was attended by many dignitaries including the Commanding General of the U.S. Army's Helicopter Training School at Fort Rucker. Throughout the summer and fall, the prototype design was refined as the result of a rigorous flight test development program. The goal was to come up with a final design by the spring of 1989 that would meet both the requirements of the Army and FAA certification.

In 1988, the U.S. Coast Guard received two Schweizer 2-37A quiet surveillance aircraft from the U.S. Air Force, which they put to work in their Florida coast drug war. The aircraft (*Figure 99*) has a low acoustic signature and requires only 52 hp of its 235 hp Lycoming engine to maintain altitude when in its quiet mode. With its day/night thermal imaging system, it has enabled the Coast Guard to make several important drug busts. In October, SAC received an order for four SA 2-37A special purpose aircraft from another government agency, which amounted to over $1.5 million of business.

The Company's 1988 sales were a record $27.2 million but earned only a small profit of approximately 1% on sales after taxes. This was partially the result of an over two million dollar investment in production equipment, facilities and new product development. Employment grew to 450 workers at year end. Michael D. Oakley, SAC's treasurer, was elected to the Board of Directors to facilitate a closer relationship between finance and management planning. (See Appendix 9.)

Terrell P. Kirk, former Grumman test pilot and Ag Cat sales manager, joined our Company in 1983 after he took early retirement from Grumman. Terrell worked with me on the Ethiopian Ag Cat contract negotiations, and, when the order was finalized, he was appointed SAC's Ethiopian Project Manager. In August of 1988, Terrell and I traveled to Addis Ababa, Ethiopia to look over their Ag Cat manufacturing operation and to consult with Ethiopian airline personnel.

We flew from London to Addis Ababa in an Ethiopian Airline Boeing 767. It was an eleven hour night flight with a stop in Rome. Three border wars were then in progess, and political unrest was prevalent. Even though tourists were not allowed in Ethiopia, Terrell and I had approved visas to enter, but on our arrival in Customs, there was much confusion. At that point, we spotted our friend Taddele Mekuria, who helped us get through their red tape. Taddele had been in Elmira a number of times and was Ethiopian Airline's Ag Cat Project Manager.

We were surprised to find a very obvious Russian presence in Ethiopia. The hammer and sickle insignias were all over, as were pictures of Lenin, Marx and Stalin. Poverty was also greater in Addis than I had expected.

We stayed at the five-story Hilton Hotel in the center of Addis. We were told not to leave the hotel at night without an Ethiopian Airline escort. Our fifth floor rooms were called "Executive Suites". A guard on duty near the fifth floor elevator made sure all people leaving the elevator were hotel guests.

The average temperature in Ethiopia is greatly influenced by the altitude. In August Addis was a comfortable 75 degrees, because the city is 7,600 feet above sea level. On the first day there, Terrell and I became very tired. Then we realized we had to slow down because there is less oxygen at that altitude. The climate on the Red Sea coast, however, is one of the hottest in the world.

Ethiopian Airlines is considered the leading air carrier in Africa and has continually been expanding during the last ten years. It services London, Frankfurt, Moscow, Bombay, Beijing, etc. Their fleet consists of over 25 airplanes, including 12 modern Boeing jet transports. The lack of good roads and railroads has created a great opportunity for Ethiopian Airlines. The Ag Cat was their latest diversified venture intended to assist with increasing the country's food production. In a hard-line Marxist country, it is surprising to see an organization such as Ethiopian Airlines flourish with a free-enterprise system. In my opinion, much of the credit must go to its president, Capt. Mohammed

Ahmed, who is an outstanding leader and diplomat. Although the Chief of State is a dictator, he has, apparently, left the Captain alone, because he has been successful in expanding the airlines and making money for the country. Capt. Ahmed selects his new young employees carefully, trains them well, and they become good, proud employees.

The first day, we were the Airlines President's guests for lunch. He showed us a fax copy of a *New* York Times article dated that day about their Ag Cat project in Ethiopia. We were impressed by the progress they were making in building our airplane. They had completed their fifth Ag Cat and were planning to build six ships a year.

Since my brother Ernie's retirement, he has, among other accomplishments, become an outstanding designer and builder of stainless steel dynamic (moving) sculptures (*Figure* 103). Since 1980, he has created three sculptures in the Elmira area. They are designed for a useful life of at least 100 years. The agency which owns the sculpture also received drawings so replacement parts and equipment plus service instructions are available.

The year 1980 was the 75th Anniversary of the Elmira Rotary Club and the 50th Anniversary of soaring in the Elmira area. Brother Paul, an Elmira Rotarian and a Director of Harris Hill Soaring Corp., wanted to do something to commemorate the 50th Anniversary of Soaring in Elmira. He persuaded Rotary and Harris Hill to work together to build a monument in the center of Elmira. His next move was to get Ernie to design the sculpture. Both organizations liked Ernie's design and talked Ernie into taking the lead in building the monument. With a great deal of time and effort from Ernie, assistance from SAC and volunteer help, the sculpture was built for $50,000. It would have cost at least $200,000 if built by a contractor. Under a similar plan, a sculpture was built near the entrance of the National Soaring Museum in 1982, and at the Elmira-Corning Regional Airport along Route 17 in 1988.

Due to lack of capital for expansion, son John's Merrell Boot Co. became a division of Karhu, Inc. John remained as active head of Merrell with sales of $5 million with forecasted sales of ten million dollars by 1990.

The year 1989 was the fiftieth anniversary of the founding

of our Company. Great advances in technology during the last 50 years had made the world seem smaller, and several of the major news events of the year bore this out.

Japan's Hirohito, emperor since WWII, died in January, 1989. In February, Exxon had a gigantic oil spill in Alaska. During that same month, a Boeing 747 lost its forward cargo door due to a lock failure just after it departed from Honolulu. Nine passengers were swept to their deaths in the Pacific. In April, Iran's religious dictator, Ayatollah Khomeini, died. In June, Chinese students demonstrating at Tiananmen Square were massacred by military forces. That summer Pete Rose was banned from baseball for life. The California coast had a major earthquake just as a World Series game was about to start in San Francisco. The B-2 Stealth Bomber, built from non-metallic material to prevent detection by hostile air defense systems, made its first flight in November. The estimated cost was $500 million each. The unbelievable happened in December; European Communist Regimes were driven out by protests of the masses. The Berlin Wall fell and the Iron Curtain border was opened between the East and West. I never thought I would live to see it happen.

In the fall of 1989, the U.S. Army announced that it would be seeking a new turbine-powered training helicopter. The Army had established a firm requirement for 205 ships and a request for proposal (RFP) was expected by year end 1990. The total contract value is not yet known but is expected to be worth about $100 million. The other known contenders are Enstrom Helicopter, and Aerospatiale.

The new Model 330 engineering prototype was configured specifically to meet the requirements of what we believe the Army will expect in their new training helicopter. At year end, the prototype had made over 500 flights and had logged in excess of 400 hours. As a result of the flight test program, the aft fuselage, tail surfaces, induction and exhaust systems were modified.

Helicopter aerodynamics is not an exact science. Some of the design details must be worked out on a trial and error basis during the engineering flight test phase. A fixed-wing aircraft takes advantage of its forward velocity for flight stability and control and uses the positive air flow for the induction, exhaust and cooling systems of the engine. Helicopters fly forward, backwards and sideways and hover at zero airspeed. In all modes, the engine must receive air and control the flow of it to support the power plant operation. This must be done without affecting the flight controllability and without creating unacceptable vibrations or buffeting. This is one of the many reasons that the development program for the 330 has been so extensive and has taken close to two years.

By year end, management and our helicopter consultants felt the 330's flight characteristics were outstanding and will satisfy the U.S. Army. The next step is to finalize the design, tool for production and build the production prototype for FAA certification. SAC's goal is to have the ship in production by the fall of 1991 (*Figure* 104). The Company has limited the number of orders and deposits for the commercial version of the Model 330 until the U.S. Army contract is decided.

The thirteen-foot main rotor blades (which provide lift for the helicopter similar to an airplane wing) were the only major components of the Model 300C Helicopter that SAC was not manufacturing. SAC had a contract with McDonnell Douglas Helicopter Company (MDHC) calling for them to supply blades to us through 1990. At that point, SAC will take over this manufacturing operation and become independent from MDHC. This move is important to SAC, because the Model 300 blades will also be used on our new turbine Model 330 Helicopter. Management also believes it will be cost effective to build the rotor blades in-house. Not only will this help make the Model 300C Helicopter more competitive, but the replacement blade business amounts to over a million dollars a year. The FAA requires the 300C main rotor blade to be replaced after 5500 flight hours.

The blade assembly is composed of metal parts that require very close control during fabrication and processing. They are progressively bonded together under pressure in a controlled environment. The bonding area must be dust free and requires strict humidity and temperature controls. In order to meet the requirement, a 7,500 square foot shop addition was built in 1989 which increased our total floor space to 187,500 square feet (*Figure 105*). (See Appendix 2.) The major part of the new building was scheduled to become a dedicated bonding manufacturing area for the main and tail rotor blades with room for product expansion. The Company's goal was to set up and prove out the assembly bonding operation during the first eight months of 1990, then start production in the fall so there will be an inventory of SAC-manufactured blades by year end.

Our fiftieth year in business was a record year in sales, profit and employment. Sales totaled $33.8 million, and 5% profit was earned on each dollar of sales after a LIFO inventory reserve and taxes. Helicopter sales amounted to 56% of our total business in 1989. (See Appendix 4.) Seventy-eight Model 300C choppers were delivered which brought the total built at SAC since 1983 to 267 units. Our product line was diverse and strong.

In spite of the U.S. Army's phase out of the TH-55, the market demand of the 300C continued to increase throughout the year. Apparently, our relatively low-cost, versatile, and proven piston-powered helicopter had become the industry leader for training, aerial photography, power line and traffic control and many other commercial roles. By the fourth quarter, sales commitments were on hand for all 90 ships planned for production in 1990.

Our work force grew to 552 employees at year end and averaged 525 for the year. (See Appendix 1.) This surpassed our previous high of 540 and 509 average for the year in 1976. At year end, the Company occupied 187,000 square feet of office, factory, and warehouse space. (See Appendix 2.)

A highlight of 1989 was the celebration of Schweizer Aircraft's fiftieth anniversary. The major events were:

The construction and flight demonstration of a replica of the first Schweizer glider, the SGP 1-1;

A Regatta for Schweizer-built sailplanes at Harris Hill in July;

An anniversary party held in December for all employees, retirees, and their families.

The building and flying of the replica of the first Schweizer glider, the 1-1, (one passenger and first design) was a great thrill for all of the Schweizers. Ernie's original sketchy drawings had been lost and the original ship had been destroyed when our barn burnt down. Ernie redrew the plans from memory and about 50 employees volunteered to help build the 1-1.

Ernie was assisted by his son, Les, in organizing and monitoring the project. I was assigned the elevators and stabilizer which I built in my cellar with some help from Stu and Paul H.

The general plan, which was Paul A's original idea, was to fly the 1-1 and then put it on display at the National Soaring Museum. It would be part of the Schweizer 50th Anniversary Exhibition which was scheduled to open a week before Memorial Day.

The 1-1 created a great deal of interest among the employees, friends of soaring, and the press when they heard that it was under construction. Everyone wanted to see it fly, so we scheduled a public flight demonstration on Saturday, May 20th. The project fell behind schedule, so there was a big fire drill to get it finished on time. The credit must go to Ernie for getting it built properly and on time.

On Thursday the 18th, the 1-1 was ready to fly, and the FAA stopped by to inspect the ship and give us an experimental license to fly it. Late that afternoon when there were just a few people around, we decided to make sure the 1-1 would fly properly. We were pleased to see that it flew well and that the control system was responsive, so we decided to go through with the public demonstration on Saturday.

The crowd and press assembled. Ernie decided not to fly because he had not been actively flying in recent years. Paul A., 75, took the first flight and carried some Air Mail "First Flight" letters. At age 71, I made the next flight (*Figure 106*) and then Les, Stu and Paul H. followed. Afterwards, we took the 1-1 back to the hangar and turned it over to the museum.

As I left the plant that afternoon and looked at the Schweizer name over the entrance, I had mixed feelings—both great pride and humility for the success we had experienced since our first flight in Peekskill fifty-nine years earlier.

102

103

104

***102.** Prototype of SAC Model 330 turbine-powered helicopter on an engineering test flight.* ***103.** It seems a long way from sailplanes, here commemorated in a sculpture designed by Ernest Schweizer* (Tony Fusare), *to the production version of the 330 (**104**).* Kevin Proaper

105 

106 

***105.** The SAC plant in the fall of 1989.* Kevin Proaper *As part of SAC's 50th Anniversary Celebration, volunteers built a replica of the original SGP 1-1, and Bill Schweizer flew it (**106**).* Kevin Proaper

18

THE FUTURE

In 1899, ninety years ago, the Director of the U.S. Patent Office, Charles H. Duell, said, "Everything that can be invented has been invented." It is obvious he was incorrect. There is no future for individuals or companies that are not open-minded to change. Therefore, our future depends upon making adjustments and making things happen.

I think this is the principal reasons why Schweizer Aircraft Corp. has survived the first fifty years as an independent aircraft manufacturer. As far as we know, our Company is the only aircraft manufacturer whose roots go back to World War II whose ownership is still in the control of the original family. The other family-owned companies have either merged, been swallowed up by a conglomerate or gone out of business.

The business cycle of our industry since World War II has ranged from a volatile-booming demand to unpredictable slowdowns and has included drastic product changes. I don't expect that aspect of the aircraft industry will ever change. The Schweizers have had a number of crises and we have made our share of mistakes. But apparently none were bad enough to force us to lose control of the Company. We have learned the hard way that the Company must remain flexible, work for diversification and keep up with the new technology so it can adjust to new phases of aviation.

Over the past 50 years, we have been fortunate to be able to attract an outstanding group of people to the Schweizer team. The Schweizer family's second generation management team is in place; and from my knothole, I think they are doing an excellent job (*Figure 107*). It will be interesting to see what new projects develop in the future and what the Company will look like fifty years from now.

107

107. *Two generations of Schweizers take it easy—for just a moment—in the 50th year of Schweizer Aircraft Corporation: June 5, 1989.* Kevin Proaper

APPENDEXES

1. Schweizer Aircraft Corp. Employment Record, 1940–1989
2. Schweizer Aircraft Corp. Floor Space Growth, 1940–1989
3. Record of the Free World Ag-Plane Sales and the Ag-Cat Program
4. Schweizer Aircraft Corp. Sales Breakdown 1965 to 1989
5. U.S. General Aircraft Manufacturers' Sales and Billings (Airlines and Military Aircraft are not Included)
6. Schweizer Aircraft Corp. and Surrounding Area in 1966
7. Schweizer Aircraft Corp. Employees as of December 31, 1989
8. Schweizer Aircraft Corp. Retirees as of December 31, 1989
9. Historical Record of Schweizer Aircraft Corp.'s Board of Directors
10. Schweizer for Half a Century the Quiet Soldier
11. Schweizer Sailplane Family

SCHWEIZER AIRCRAFT CORP. EMPLOYMENT RECORD
Annual Personnel Average
600
500
400
300
200
100
0
Number
of
Employees
76
204
277
382
331
Ten Year
Average
509
525
1940
1950
1960
1970
1980
1989

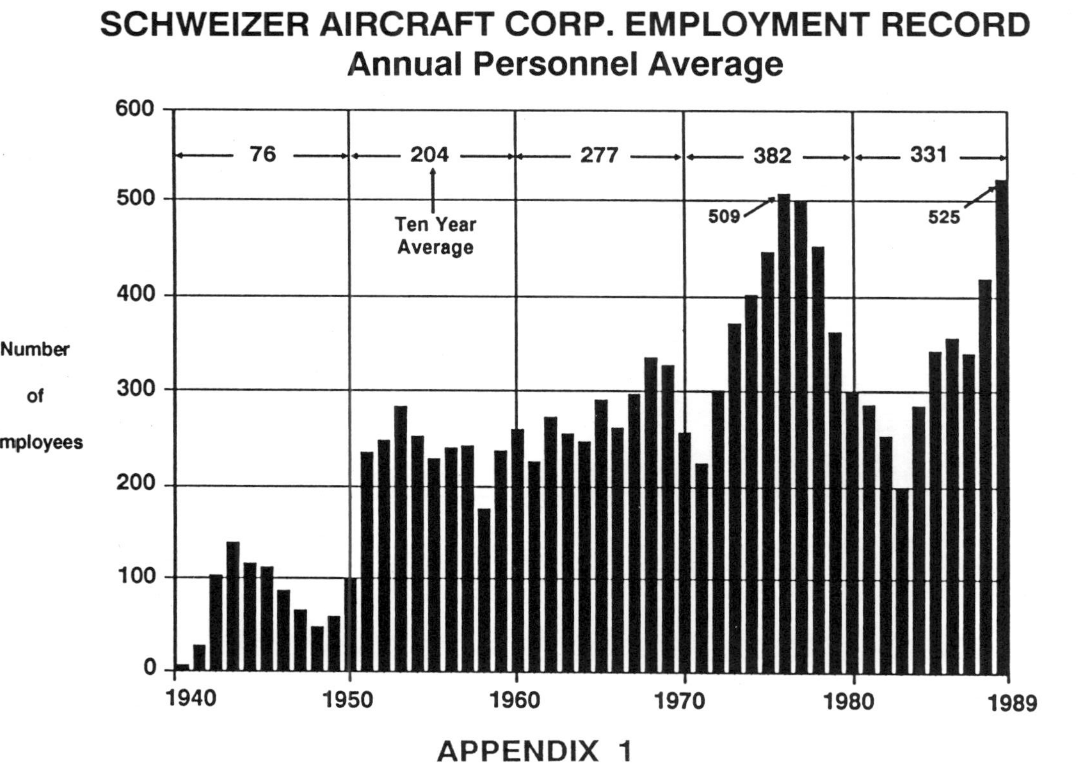

APPENDIX 1

SCHWEIZER AIRCRAFT CORP.
Floor Space Growth

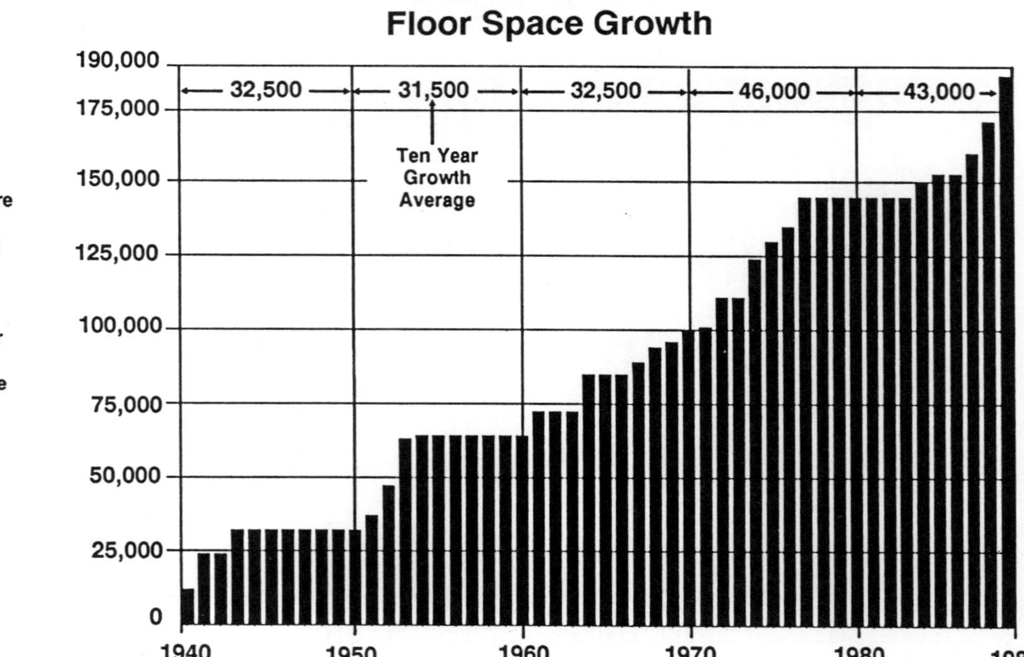

APPENDIX 2

FREE WORLD AG PLANE SALES
Number
of
Planes
1300
1200
1100
1000
900
800
700
600
500
400
300
200
100
0
1965
1970
1975
1980
1985
1989
YEAR
INDUSTRY WIDE
SALES
AGCAT
SALES

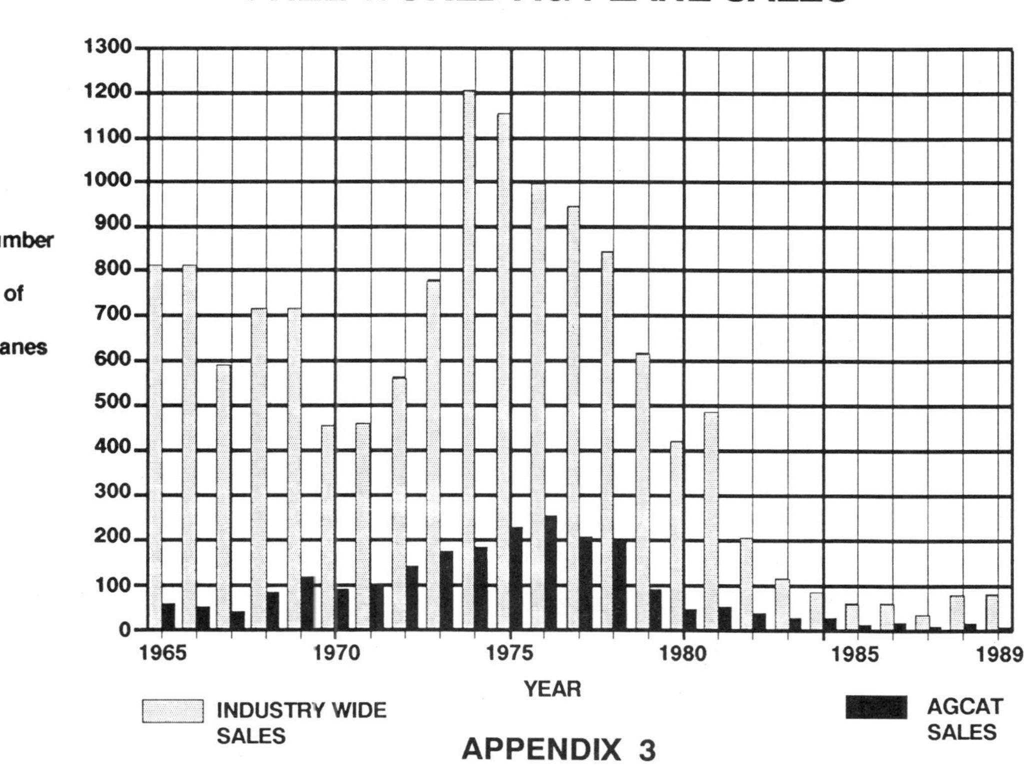

APPENDIX 3

SAC SALES RELATIVE TO EMPLOYMENT AND PRODUCT LINES

Sales dollars are affected by the dollar value of purchased material and the amount of labor in products plus the compounded general inflation rate. Inflation alone has caused the value of a dollar of sales to increase over 100% for each 10 year period. A dollar of sales in 1965 would be worth $4.04 in 1989.

YEAR	TOTAL EMPLOYMENT	TOTAL SALES	HELICOPTER: AIRCRAFT & SPARE PARTS	AG-CAT: AIRCRAFT & SPARE PARTS	SAILPLANE MOTOR GLIDER & RECON AIRCRAFT	SUBCONTRACT & OTHER BUSINESS
			%	%	%	%
1965	292	3,248,000	0	33	14	53
1966	262	2,785,000	0	30	16	54
1967	298	3,593,000	0	17	19	64
1968	336	4,332,000	0	33	19	48
1969	328	4,292,000	0	54	17	29
1970	257	3,587,000	0	50	21	29
1971	224	4,188,000	0	46	15	39
1972	302	4,793,000	0	63	16	21
1973	372	5,653,000	0	69	17	14
1974	402	7,032,000	0	70	16	14
1975	447	8,822,000	0	73	17	10
1976	509	10,821,000	0	79	11	10
1977	500	11,310,000	0	80	10	10
1978	453	11,334,000	0	81	8	11
1979	363	10,510,000	0	72	9	19
1980	300	10,504,000	0	46	7	47
1981	287	9,366,000	0	23	11	66
1982	253	9,111,000	0	46	5	49
1983	196	11,272,000	26	27	11	36
1984	286	17,543,000	51	22	2	25
1985	343	25,253,000	53	9	9	29
1986	357	26,728,000	66	16	3	15
1987	341	23,354,000	58	11	6	25
1988	419	27,202,000	59	12	2	27
1989	525	33,380,000	56	10	4	30

APPENDIX 4

Schweizer Aircraft Corp. Sales Breakdown 1965–1989

(Airliners and military aircraft are not included.)

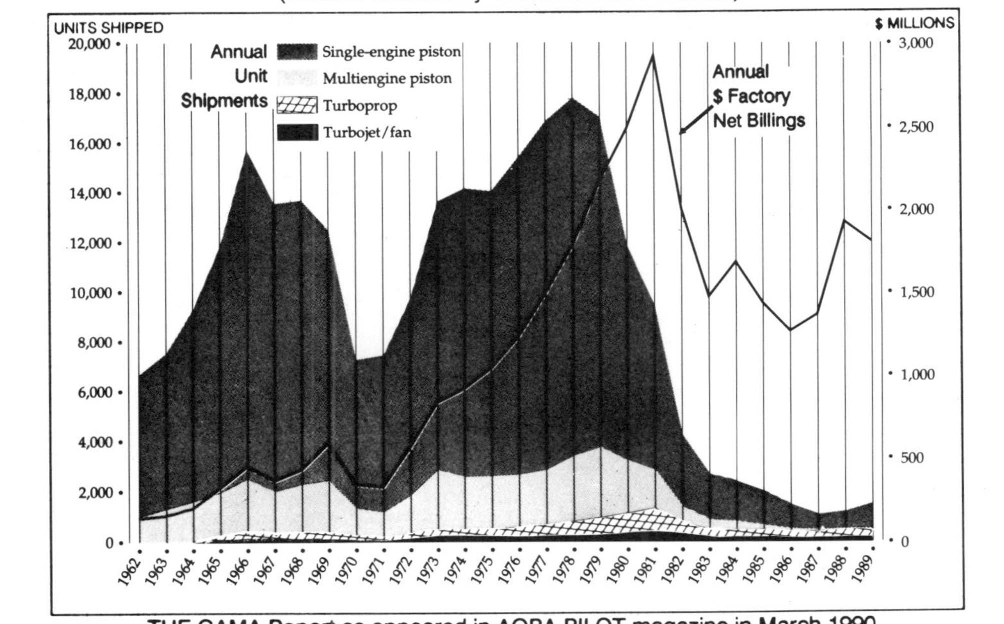

THE GAMA Report as appeared in AOPA PILOT magazine in March 1990.

Net dollar billing for the industry has grown in spite of fewer units sold because the majority of airplanes purchased are the more sophisticated and expensive business transportation aircraft.

APPENDIX 5

SCHWEIZER AIRCRAFT CORP. AND SURROUNDING AREA IN 1966

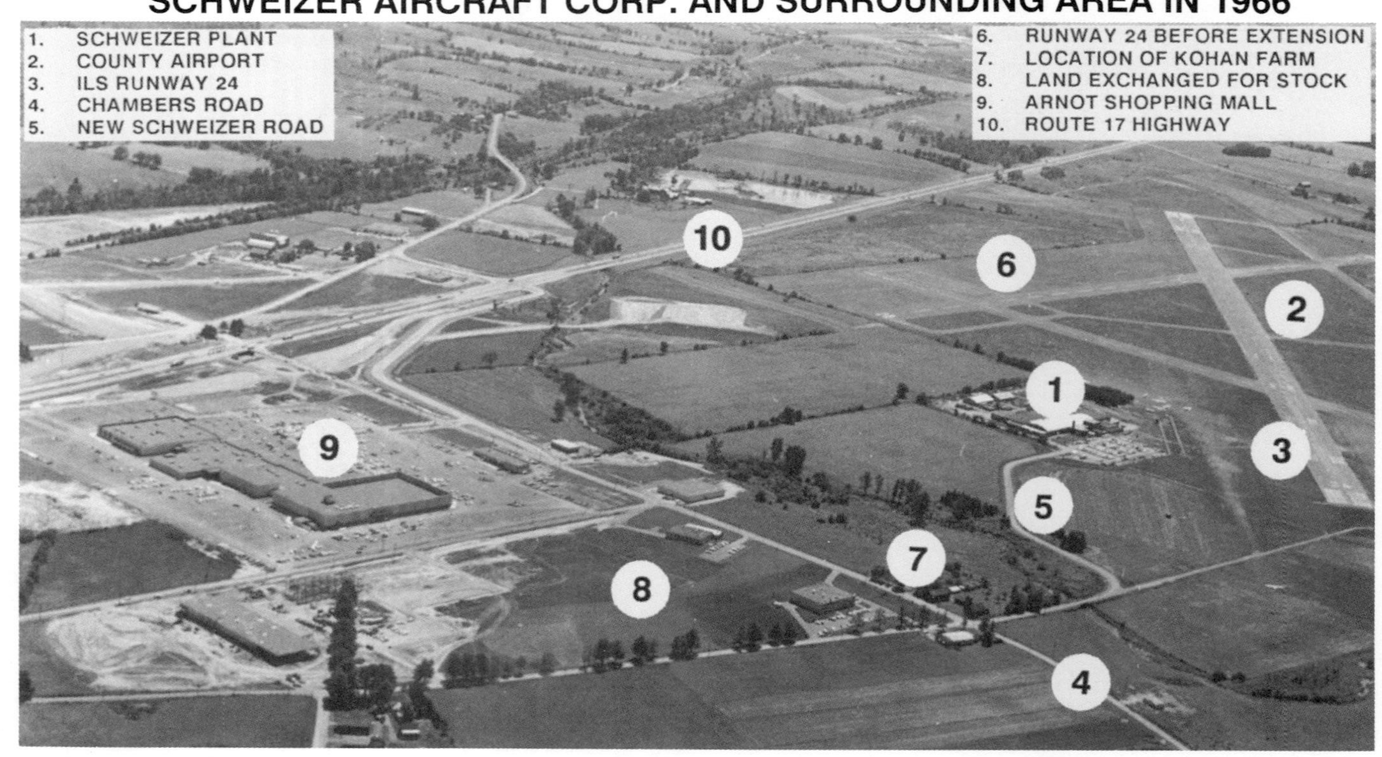

APPENDIX 6

SCHWEIZER AIRCRAFT CORP. EMPLOYEES

AS OF DECECMBER 31, 1989

ACKER, MELVIN
ADAMS, CHARLES B.
ADAMS, DAVID C.
ADAMS, ERIC
ADAMS, ROBERT
AGAN, JAMES F.
AIKMAN, THEODORE
ALLYN, WILLIAM
ANDREWS, RAYMOND J.
ANDRUKAT, KEVIN A.
ARCHER, RICHARD A.
ARMSTRONG, EDWARD
ARNETT, JOSEPH
ASKINS, DAVID H.
ATHERTON, LEE R.
AUMICK, CHARLES
AYERS, CAVANAUGH R.
BACKUS,MARY
BAKER, BARBARA
BAKER, CHARLES
BAKER, MAXINE
BALDWIN, ROBERT K.
BALLINGER, TERI
BANKER, RONI E.
BARRETT, WILLIAM P.
BARTSCH, GUENTER
BAXTER, GERALD
BEACH, WALTER
BEAN, KENNETH W.
BEAUCAGE, JOSEPH
BECKER, RUSSELL S.
BEHAN, JOSEPH T.
BELT, ARTHUR
BENEDICT, ROBERT I.
BENJAMIN, RONALD G.
BENNETT, BEVERLY
BENNETT, HARRY E.
BENNETT, JOHN H.
BENNETT, STEVEN H.
BENTLEY, J. WILLIAM
BERNARD, PAUL R.
BESLEY, MICHAEL L.
BIERY, RICHARD P.
BLACK, RICHARD W.
BLACKMAN, IVAN J.
BLAKE, HENRY CALVIN JR.
BLIM, NORMA M.
BLUNDELL, FRANK
BOARDMAN, RICHARD
BOGART, JOHN
BOGLE, DAVID E.
BOGLE, ROBERT B.
BOLDEN, CURTIS W.
BONNING, RICHARD P.
BORDEN, BETH ANN
BORDEN, PERRY D.
BORN, DOUGLAS
BORN, JUDITH
BOSTWICK, JOHN M.
BOUILLE, MICHAEL P.
BOWES, ERNEST A.
BOWMAN, PAUL F.
BOYLE, DAVID W.
BRADSHAW, ROBERT
BRICK, JAMES E. JR.
BRICKA, JACK I.
BROCK, DEVON V.
BROCK, DINYL
BROOKS, LARRY
BROOKS, SAMUEL L.
BROWN, DAVID L.
BROWN, FRANKLIN J.
BROWN, KAREN J.
BROWN, LAWSON L.
BROWN, LLEWELLYN
BROWN, MICHAEL
BRUTSMAN, RICK A.
BRYINGTON, WILLIAM J.
BUCHHOLZ, DAVID M.
BUCHTEL, DAVID M.
BURDICK, DAVID M.
BURGIT, JEROME
BUSHOR, ROBERT K.
BYERS, EDWARD E.
CALICHIO, DOREE
CAPARULA, ARTHUR F.
CARD, OWEN
CARPENTER, COLIN G.
CARRIS, BERNARD M.
CARSON, JOHN L.
CARSON, ROBERT C.
CASE, ERNEST D.
CASE, ERNEST L.
CEVETTE, JEFFREY, L.
CHABOREK, MARK J.
CHAMBERLAIN, MARVIN
CHAPMAN, KEN
CHAPMAN, THEODORE
CHEUNKAO, JURAI
CHREPTAK, PAUL
CLARKSON, JOHN
CLARKSON, MICHAEL D.
CLATE, ANTHONY
CLEMENS, BUDDY
CLEMONS, ALAN R.
CLINE, KENNETH A.
COATES, MARK A.
COLLIER, WILLIAM J.
CONDIE, TED G.
CONDON, KATHLEEN
CONGDON, PAUL
CONSIDINE, ROBERTA
COOK, BOBBIE SHARON R.
COONEY, GERALD L.
COURTRIGHT, HANS
CRAMER, JAMES A.
CROTEAU, FRANCIS L.
CULLEN, EDWARD J.
CUMMINGS, TIMOTHY
DALEY, WILLIAM S.
DAMIANI, RAYMOND
DANN, RAYMOND
DAUDELIN, PAUL M.
DAUM, CAROLE M.
DAUM, JAMES E.
DAVIS, BARBARA L.
DAVIS, RICHARD E.
DEATS, PAULINE
DEHAAS, KELVIN
DEHAAS, MARK L.
DERSHAM, JAMES E.
DEWOLFE, ROGER
DIBARTOLOMEO, BARBARA
DIVEL, JOHN
DIXSON, KANDI M.
DOMINICK, GARY
DONAHUE, JOHN F.
DONAHUE, KEVIN M.
DONAHUE, PATRICK
DONOVAN, JOSEPH
DORN, KEVIN
DOUTY, RONALD E.
DOVE, SUSAN K.
DUANE, KENT
DUANE, KENNETH E.
DUNHAM, JACK R.
DUNTON , DONALD
EARL, STEPHEN
ELLIOTT, JOHN
ELWOOD, FRANK E.
ELWOOD, JEFF
ERGOTT, RONALD L.
ERHARD, ROBERT
ERNEST, KENNETH
ERNEST, ROBERT O.
ESTEP, JAMES
EVINGHAM, DONALD
FARNHAM, RICHARD G.
FARR, DONALD G.
FIALA, TIMOTHY
FISH, DANNIE SR.
FISHER, KEVIN
FISK, JOHN F.
FLANAGAN, JOHN
FLEMING, DAVID R.

APPENDIX 7 (1 of 4)

SCHWEIZER AIRCRAFT CORP. EMPLOYEES

AS OF DECEMBER 31, 1989

FLICK, KENNETH
FLINT, WAYNE B.
FORD, VICTOR D.
FOSTER, WALTER
FOX, FRANK EDWARD
FRACCHIA, BARBARA
FRAZIER, PAUL JR.
FRENCH, HARRY L.
FROST, DALE
FROST, MICHAEL
FRUITT, DANIEL E.
GAUGHAN, ANN E.
GIAMMICHELE, ROBERT
GILL, JOHN
GITCHELL, WILLIAM H.
GLEASON, STEVEN L.
GOLDEN, ELIZABETH
GOODMAN, HENRY I.
GORSKI, DONALD
GORTON, CHARLES J.
GOULD, DONALD
GRACE, ARTHUR
GRAHAM, AUDREY
GRANGER, DALE C.
GREEN, DAVID F.
GREEN, TIMOTHY A.
GREEN, WILLIAM R.
GRIDLEY, JEFFREY
GRINNELL, FRANK N.
GROFF, DONALD D.
GROOVER, DUANE
GROOVER, KENNETH
GROVER, BRADLEY
GUBLO, THEODORE
GUNNING, CLAIR LAVERN
GUSTIN, DALE L.
HAIGHT, ROBERT A.
HALL, GERALD B.
HALL, HERBERT L.
HALL, JEFF
HALL, STEVEN M.
HAM, KENNETH W.
HARRIS, DAVID H.
HATHERILL, BRADLEY
HEATH, JOHN M.
HEIMER, CRAIG T.
HENRY, MICHAEL E.
HENSON, PAUL K.
HERBER, GENE
HERLOCHER, CLAIR L.
HERRICK, ROGER L.
HILL, CLIFFORD
HOEFFERLE, LYNNE
HOEFFERLE, HERBERT F.
HOFFMAN, DEAN E.
HOFFMAN, STEVEN E.
HOFMANN, JEFFREY
HOLLENBECK, DONALD
HOOK, URSULA
HOOPES, TERRY D.
HORTON, LARRY W.
HOWARD, RICHARD
HOWE, STEVEN
HRASDZIRA, ROGER
HUBBARD, LARRY G.
HUCKLE, ROBERT
HUGHES, JOHN
HUGHES, JOHN R.
HUGHES, MONTY J.
HUGIC, KEVIN T.
HUGILL, KATHRYN L.
HUNT, THOMAS R.
HURLBURT, JONATHAN
HURSH, WILLIAM
HUSTED, JOEL
IRWIN, GARY
JENKINS, LUCINDA
JENKS, DEBORAAH
JOHNS, CHARLES E. JR.
JOHNS, LU ANN
JOHNSON, ALAN
JOHNSON, ANDREW C.
JOHNSON, JOSEPH E.
JOHNSON, MARY J.
JOHNSON, MICHAEL
JOHNSON, PAUL V.
JONES, DANIEL C.
JONES, ERWIN F.
KALLENBORN, DAVID
KAMBEITZ, RICHARD
KASICK, BRUCE P.
KEACH, MICHAEL A.
KELLOGG, DONNA
KENT, RICHARD
KETCHUM, ROBERT
KINGREY, JACQUELYN
KIPFERL, HOWARD D.
KIPFERL, JEFFERY
KIRK, TERRELL
KISHBAUGH, ROBERT A.
KLINE, CARL
KODGER, DONALD
KOEHLER, KATHLEEN M.
KOSIER, TRUMAN C.
KRISE, ALLAN
LAFRITZ, RONALD L.
LAFRITZ, LAVERN
LANCASTER, CYRAL
LEAR, THOMAS
LEONARD, JAMIE
LESE, SALLY
LEWIS, JEFFREY H.
LIDDIARD, BROOKS
LIDDIARD, JANET E.
LOTT, DOUGLAS
LOUD, DORIS L.
LUCAS, RUSSELL
LYON, WILLIAM L.
MADISON, WALTER D.
MAGLIOCCA, JOSEPH
MALONEY, PEGGY
MANNING, THOMAS W.
MANWARING, J. E.
MAPSTONE, RONALD C.
MASONE, EDWARD F.
MASONE, JEANIE
MASSEY, WALTER
MASTERS, HAROLD R.
MATTESON, EDWARD
MAY, CHARLES R.
MAY, GARY F.
MAY, JOHN L. JR.
MAY, LEIGHTON
MCINERNY, BRIAN
MCCARTHY, BRIAN F.
MCCARTHY, BRIAN J.
MCCAULEY, RICHARD H.
MCCHESNEY, JEFFERY
MCCRACKEN, WILLIAM D.
MCCRAY, THEODORE D.
MCGUIRK, THOMAS
MCKEOWN, STEVEN
MCKIVISON, DALLAS
MENTUCK, MARK
MERRILL, RICHARD
METCALF, STEPHEN J.
MILLER, ARNOLD G.
MILLER, CHRIS
MILLER, DAVID
MILLER, ROBERT J.
MILLER, WILLIAM
MOORE, BENJAMIN
MOORE, WILLIAM
MORGAN, DUANE
MORGAN, RAY
MORRIS, DAVID
MORTENSEN, LORING
MOSHER, BONNIE
MOSHER, PHILIP E.
MOSHER, LEONARD
MULLEN , ROSS
MURPHY, CLAYTON E.
MURPHY, SANDRA J.
MYERS, WAYNE S. JR.
NAILOR, EUGENE

SCHWEIZER AIRCRAFT CORP. EMPLOYEES

AS OF DECEMBER 31, 1989

NEELY, HAROLD A.
NEVINS, NORMA J.
NICHOLS, DREW
NICOLO, MICHAEL A.
NIVER, FRANK
NOVOTNY, BRETT
NOVOTNY, EMMA R.
NOVOTNY, GEORGE M.
NOVOTNY, PAUL E .
O'BRIEN, SHARON E.
OAKLEY, MICHAEL D.
OCHAB, CHARLES E.
OLSON, CARL N. JR.
OSBORNE, JOAN
OSBORNE, JOHN
OSBORNE, KEITH H.
OVERHISER, CARLGENE
OVERHISER, JAMES
OVERHISER, MARION J.
PARADIS, JOSEPH A.
PARSONS, GLENN
PARVEL, ALAN
PATELUNAS, EDWARD J.
PAUGH, RONALD
PECK, RICHARD C.
PERSONIUS, MICHAEL
PETERSON, CHARLES E.
PHENES, LESLIE L.
PHILLIPS, TIMOTHY
PIERCE, DAVID L.
POLLOW, LARRY
POTTER, RICHARD
POWELL, RICHARD
POWERS, GARY E. SR.
POWERS, JOHN S.
PRESUTTI, DANA L.
PROAPER, KEVIN
PULVER, DOROTHY
QUERRY, MICHELLE A.
QUERRY, WILLIAM B.
QUINN, SEAN
RANDALL, DANA B.
RAPLEE, SAMUEL
RARICK, CLARENCE
READ, JOHN R.
REED, SHARON K.
RIBBLE, JOSEPH
RICHARDSON, WAYNE D.
RINEBOLD, RAYMOND D.
ROBBINS, DAVID E.
ROBBINS, THERESA M.
ROBERTS, CORNELIA J.
ROBERTS, MICHAEL R.
ROBINSON, JAMES
ROBINSON, NORMAN L.
ROCK, EDWARD W.
RODABAUGH, LEONARD
ROEMER, DAVID JAMES
ROLLS, DEBORAH
ROLLS, JAMES
ROSEKRANS, WARREN
ROSELL, RICHARD
ROSH, JENNIE
ROTHCHILD, DAVID B.
RULAND, SHAWN
RUMMINGS, SCOTT H.
RUMSEY, FREDERICK J.
RUMSEY, MICHAEL A.
RUOCCO, JOSEPH A.
RUSSELL, GARY
SALTSMAN, GARY
SALTSMAN, JANICE
SALZER, JOHN R.
SAMPSON, DOUGLAS
SAMPSON, RALPH E.
SAXBURY, RICHARD
SAYRE, SANDRA A.
SCHALL, GEORGE W.
SCHIFFEN, DONNA S.
SCHIFFERLE, PAUL T.
SCHILL, JOHN L.
SCHIRALDI, KIM L.
SCHLAUFMAN, ROBERT
SCHNAUTZ, CHARLES C.
SCHRINER, DURWOOD
SCHWEIGER, WALTER
SCHWEIZER, LESLIE
SCHWEIZER, PAUL HARDY
SCHWEIZER, STUART
SCOTT, TIMOTHY M.
SEMPLER, ROBERT W.
SHAW, GEORGE B.
SHEARER, RICHARD
SHEARER, RONALD
SHEEHAN, DANA
SHEETS, LEON
SHERMAN, LAWRENCE
SHERMAN, ROBERT D.
SHERMAN, STEWART A.
SHOREY, STELLA
SIMPSON, CHARLES
SIMPSON, EDWARD
SIMPSON, MARJORIE
SKINNER, KIM A.
SLINGERLAND, CARL E.
SMITH, MICHAEL L.
SMITH, STANTON
SMITH, WADE H.
SNYDER, HARRY A.
SNYDER, BARRY W.
SONNER, DIANE M.
SONNER, LOLA
SOSNOSKI, ROBERT D.
SOURS, CLAUDE
SPAGNOLO, MARGARET M.
SPECIALE, PAUL A.
SPENCER, SEWARD
SPIVEY, JOE
STAGE, ROBERT L.
STANTON, MICHAEL
STARKWEATHER, CHARLES
STARNER, GREG
STEINER, WALTER
STEVENS, CHARLES T.
STEWART, KEITH R.
STEWART, MARY A.
STILES, DONALD
STOCK, DARREL
STOCK, DAVID
STOCUM, ROBERT E.
STONER, JAMES
STRAIT, SHERRY L.
STRAIT, LEWIS M.
STROMAN , ALICIA R.
SUTTON, WILLIAM A.
SWAN, FREDRICK
SWARTHOUT, TIMOTHY D.
TALADA, EARL G.
TARBY, JOHN
TENNY, DOROTHY
TERWILLIGER, CHARLES
TERWILLIGER, RICHARD K.
TESKE, LORRIE
THOMAS, LESLIE O.
THOMPSON, KEITH
THORPE, TIMOTHY
THRALL, EVANGELINE
THURSTON, KENNETH
TIBBENS, ROBERT M.
TIFFT, LAWRENCE
TINKER, DOUGLAS R.
TIPTON, MARGARET
TITUS, EARL A.
TOLBERT, MARK
TOWNSEND, KARL J.
TRIMM, CHARLES
TULLER, RICHARD
TURNER, GEORGE E. JR.
TWEEDT, BARBARA
UPDIKE, RICHARD
VAN AMBURG, RAY
VAN AMBURG, RAYMOND J.
VAN DEBOGART, JAMES
VANALSTINE, DAVID
VANDERHOFF, ALAN L.

SCHWEIZER AIRCRAFT CORP. EMPLOYEES

AS OF DECEMBER 31, 1989

VAVRASEK, DEBORAH
VELIA, DANIEL J.
VOLINO, NICHOLAS
WAIT, JOSEPH L.
WALBORN, ROBERT
WALKER, BILLY L.
WALKER, LYLE O.
WALLLACE, REGINALD A.
WALTON, THOMAS R.
WARD, BRIAN
WARD, MARSHALL
WARD, MARTIN R.
WARD, RALPH P. JR.
WARDWELL, JOHN C.
WARNER, EDWARD R.
WARWICK, LYNN M.
WATERS, JEFFREY B.
WATTS, HAROLD M.
WEAD, DELBERT R.
WEAD, DONALD J.
WEAVER, ROBERT L.
WEED, CONSTANCE D.
WEEKS, RONALD G.
WEIDEMAN, ROBERT JR.
WEIDEMAN, ROBERT SR.
WEILAND, BRUCE A.
WELLES, DAVID
WENCK, LARRY H.
WESTERVELT, DARRICK
WESTLAKE, DWIGHT E.
WHITE, ALVIN J.
WHITE, JOSEPH D.
WHITFORD, MICHAEL
WILCOX, DOUGLAS J.
WILCOX, JOHN
WILCOX, LARRY D.
WILCOX, THOMAS
WILDE, ROBERT F.
WILLIAMS, CLIFFORD G.
WILLIAMS, DONALD
WILLIAMS, DOUGLAS
WILLSEY, ARNOLD
WILSON, EVERETT E.
WILSON, JOHN K.
WINSLOW, ROBERT L.
WOOD, KENNETH E. JR.
WOOLEVER, THOMAS I.
WYLIE, MARK R.
YAWGER, THOMAS
YUSKO, MARK
ZAHRADKA, LISA A.
ZAHRADKA, MICHAEL A.
ZEGILLA, MICHAEL
ZOERB, SCOTT
ZUNIGA, JOSEPH

SCHWEIZER AIRCRAFT CORP. RETIREES* AS OF DECEMBER 31, 1989

Name	Years	Months	Date Separated	Reason
Zeigler, Joseph	9	10	5/29/56	Deceased
Young, Nelson	3	5	11/07/59	Deceased
Schutz, Harold	16	5	8/03/62	Retired
Isabel, Heller	15	6	1/04/63	Retired
Crawford, Clark	12	6	1/24/63	Deceased
Budnar, Joseph	1	11	2/20/63	Deceased
Williams, Donald	4	8	2/20/64	Deceased
Ward, Ruth	10	11	5/01/64	Retired
Olin, Pinneer	13	9	1/01/65	Retired
Yohn, Russell	17	8	12/28/66	Deceased
Ward, Ralph Sr.	16	11	4/28/67	Retired
Knapp, Ross	15	0	3/06/68	Retired
Bardwell, Eugene	27	0	3/31/69	Retired
Bennett, Glenn	18	4	8/29/69	Deceased
Overstrom, Arnold	1	10	5/01/70	Retired
Seafuse, Charles	27	5	8/14/70	Retired
Preston, Lowell	4	5	9/04/70	Retired
Hamlin, Carl	28	4	4/01/71	Retired
Watson, Richard	19	6	4/18/71	Deceased
McKenna, William	29	9	7/01/71	Retired
Adams, Roy	5	9	10/01/71	Retired
Driscoll, Verna	21	2	12/01/71	Retired
Congdon, Leon	17	8	3/07/72	Deceased
Landon, Joseph	19	5	8/31/72	Retired
Walmsley, Vernor	19	5	8/31/72	Retired
Sassano, Edward	5	7	10/01/72	Retired
Coward, Fred	22	8	3/01/73	Retired
Eggersdorf, Marian	18	5	3/12/73	Deceased
Brown, John	15	7	4/01/73	Retired
Eichorn, Bertron	30	7	8/01/73	Retired
Finch, Myron	30	7	11/01/73	Retired
Finch, Vernadean	10	7	11/01/73	Retired
Eisenhart, Mark	14	5	1/01/74	Retired
Molloy, Bernard	31	2	4/01/74	Retired
Stow, Edgar	26	4	4/01/74	Retired
Clack, Lewis	15	5	8/01/74	Retired
Sadler, Dorothy	14	11	8/01/74	Retired
Campanelli, Alfred	14	8	9/01/74	Retired
Youngman, Ernest	15	9	10/19/74	Deceased
Commisa, Anthony	22	7	11/01/74	Retired
Cook, Clyde	23	5	12/01/74	Retired
Hay, Dean	6	6	2/25/75	Deceased
Miller, Garfield	25	0	11/01/75	Retired
Peterson, Siegfred	15	9	1/01/76	Retired
Parker, Rudolph	10	11	3/31/76	Retired
Ernest, Lawrence	25	5	4/05/76	Deceased
Eastham, Arthur	8	2	4/30/76	Retired
Whidden, Muriel	7	11	7/30/76	Retired
Mills, Gordon	14	5	9/01/76	Retired
Jones, Robert	2	1	12/10/76	Deceased
Starkey, Mark	5	0	10/18/76	Deceased
Bassett, James	25	5	1/01/77	Retired
Pullen, John	12	1	3/01/77	Retired
Thomas, Leslie	25	0	5/20/77	Retired
Hauck, Atlee	37	9	9/01/77	Retired
Hess, Karl	36	2	8/01/77	Retired
Dunton, Donald	35	9	8/05/77	Retired
Swisher, Orvis	26	8	8/01/77	Retired
Watts, Lillian	22	4	9/01/77	Retired
Griswold, John	35	8	11/01/77	Retired

SCHWEIZER AIRCRAFT CORP. RETIREES* AS OF DECEMBER 31, 1989

Name	Years	Months	Date Separated	Reason
Whidden, Ernest	35	7	1/01/78	Retired
Henley, James	3	10	10/18/77	Deceased
Strader, Kenneth	27	4	6/01/78	Retired
Cokely, Lyman	27	6	7/31/78	Retired
Lewis, Clara	24	0	8/31/78	Retired
Schweizer, Ernest	39	0	1/01/79	Retired
Jack, Hugh	36	3	1/01/79	Retired
Aston, James	27	10	1/01/79	Retired
Monroe, John	13	9	1/01/79	Retired
Donor, Alton	25	7	3/20/79	Deceased
Sanscharowski, Victor	4	2	5/08/79	Deceased
Yakimovich, Peter	29	4	12/31/79	Retired
Yellott, Robert	38	5	3/21/80	Retired
Cullen, Robert	30	4	3/21/80	Retired
Olin, Floyd	27	1	6/30/80	Retired
Gerwin, William	12	8	5/20/80	Deceased
Shon, Joseph	27	10	8/15/80	Retired
Chorney, Genevieve	16	1	10/01/80	Retired
Dassance, William	7	11	10/01/80	Retired
Schweizer, Paul A.	41	0	1/01/81	Retired
Pooley, Kenneth	21	6	1/01/81	Retired
Bush, Otis	29	2	1/01/81	Retired
Harper, Edwin	30	3	1/01/81	Retired
Roe, Rita	19	1	1/01/81	Retired
Harper, Elizabeth	29	1	2/01/81	Retired
Condon, Donald	30	8	3/01/81	Retired
Pullen, Wealtha	15	2	4/01/81	Retired
Van Alstine, Gerald	8	6	4/01/81	Retired
Ochab, Alexander	8	1	2/01/81	Retired
White, Herbert	21	10	5/01/81	Retired
Dassance, Richard	36	10	5/01/81	Retired
Good, Charles	8	1	6/01/81	Retired
Patrick, Gordon	19	8	8/01/81	Retired
Schmick, Marjorie	18	3	10/01/81	Retired
Smith, Charles C.	35	5	12/05/81	Deceased
Doherty, William	22	10	2/01/82	Retired
Swisher, Eva	25	1	9/01/82	Retired
Fox, Carlyle	31	7	1/01/83	Retired
Rounds, Erwin	32	4	1/01/83	Retired
Schweizer, William	31	8	1/01/83	Retired
Semski, Donald	40	0	2/01/83	Retired
Pullen, Paul	40	1	4/01/83	Retired
Courtright, Milton	29	9	7/01/83	Retired
Merrill, Frank	32	2	11/01/83	Retired
Blackman, Manley	36	5	11/01/83	Retired
Parmelee, Gladys	27	4	1/01/84	Retired
Flood, John	33	3	1/01/84	Retired
Firenze, Paul	10	10	2/01/84	Retired
Hadley, Harlen	10	3	2/01/84	Retired
Horning, Robert	34	4	3/01/84	Retired
Everson, Paul	34	6	3/01/84	Retired
Mosher, Philip L.	32	8	7/30/84	Deceased
Rumsey, Ralph	17	6	9/23/84	Deceased
Miller, Leslie	20	0	10/01/84	Retired
Ayres, Chris	10	6	1/01/85	Retired
Griswold, Holman	22	10	1/01/85	Retired
Kroczynski, Joseph	28	2	1/01/85	Retired
Solometo, William	34	0	2/01/85	Retired
Hancock, Alfred	10	10	5/01/85	Retired
Moylan, James	11	9	5/01/85	Retired

APPENDIX 8 (2 of 3)

SCHWEIZER AIRCRAFT CORP. RETIREES*
AS OF DECEMBER 31, 1989

Name	Years	Months	Date Separated	Reason
Palmer, Vernon	18	3	9/01/85	Retired
Ward, Robert	34	2	11/01/85	Retired
Vanderpoel, Doris	13	4	11/01/85	Retired
Sutherland, Richard	10	8	11/15/85	Deceased
Rose, Charles	17	2	1/01/86	Retired
Quigley, Donald	44	4	1/01/86	Retired
Carris, Bernald	32	9	3/01/86	Retired
Sharp, Edwin	34	6	3/01/86	Retired
Kilmer, Neal	35	0	4/01/86	Retired
Gray, Karlyle	10	0	4/01/86	Retired
Kilmer, Laura	22	0	5/01/86	Retired
Ewsuk, Gabriel	27	7	9/04/86	Deceased
Snyder, Dorothy	10	6	9/01/86	Retired
Gould, Richard	35	1	11/01/86	Retired
Bowers, Merrill	35	10	11/01/86	Retired
Ellsworth, Jack	34	5	12/01/86	Retired
Mc Inerny, Thomas	32	2	12/01/86	Retired
Morgan, Vernon	27	7	12/01/86	Retired
Peckham, Francis	24	2	12/01/86	Retired
Powers, Jack L.	10	11	3/05/87	Deceased
Jones, Erwin	27	1	4/01/87	Retired
Bennett, Lynn	23	0	7/01/87	Retired
Moat, Carl	20	3	7/01/87	Retired
Martin, Douglas	21	3	11/01/87	Retired
Blackman, Mary Ann	27	5	2/01/88	Retired
Patterson, Mary	22	5	4/01/88	Retired
Bierwiler, Carroll	45	1	4/01/88	Retired
Drake, Francis	14	5	4/30/88	Deceased
Pitt, Rose Mary	15	2	5/29/88	Deceased
Bryant, Willard	34	10	9/01/88	Retired
Rice, Emerson	20	11	1/01/89	Retired
Tagliaferri, Americo	37	6	1/01/89	Retired
Thompson, Robert	35	2	1/01/89	Retired

*No Records before 1956

APPENDIX 8 (3 of 3)

MEMBERS OF SCHWEIZER AIRCRAFT CORP.
BOARD OF DIRECTORS

	Name	Position	Years
1.	Ernest Schweizer	SAC Executive	1940-
2.	Paul A. Schweizer	SAC Executive	1940-
3.	Harry M. Moseson	Lawyer - Represented Elmira, Industries	1940-1970
4.	Robert P. McDowell	General Counsel of SAC and Secretary	1940-1968
5.	William McGrath	General Manager of Eclipse Machine Co.	1940-1941
6.	Douglas G. Anderson	President, Hardinge Brothers	1941-1948
7.	Nicholas Haich	SAC Treasurer	1946-1979
8.	Leslie D. Clute	President, Clute Motor Co.	1949-1978
9.	Alexander G. Long	Vice President of American La France Foamite Corp.	1949-1955
10.	William Schweizer	SAC Executive	1951-
11.	George Chamberlain	Sales Representative	1951-1959
12.	Thomas G. Craig	President, Chemung Valley Savings Bank	1955-1968
13.	Kenneth A. Tifft	General Counsel of SAC and Secretary	1968-
14.	Alpheus Underhill	Architect	1969-1979
15.	A. Douglas P. Craig	General Counsel of U.S. Industries	1970-1980
16.	Edward A. Mooers	President, Hilliard Corp.	1970-1979
17.	W. Stuart Schweizer	SAC Executive	1980-
18.	Paul H. Schweizer	SAC Executive	1980-
19.	Leslie E. Schweizer	SAC Executive	1980-
20.	Boyd McDowell, II	President, Chemung Canal Trust Company	1980-
21.	Thomas Morse	President, LaFrance Equipment Corp.	1981-
22.	William H. Murphy	Management Consultant	1984-1985
23.	Michael D. Oakley	SAC Vice President; Treasurer	1988-

APPENDIX 9 **(1 of 3)**

MEMBERS OF SCHWEIZER AIRCRAFT CORP.

BOARD OF DIRECTORS

Harry M. Moseson

Robert P. McDowell

William McGrath

Douglas G. Anderson

Nicholas Haich

Leslie D. Clute

Alexander G. Long

George Chamberlain

Thomas G. Craig

APPENDIX 9 (2 of 3)

MEMBERS OF SCHWEIZER AIRCRAFT CORP.

BOARD OF DIRECTORS

Kenneth A. Tifft

Alpheus Underhill

A. Douglas P. Craig

Edward A. Mooers

Boyd McDowell, II

Thomas Morse

William H. Murphy

Michael D. Oakley

Schweizer
for half a century the quiet soldier.

Building for the future through a history of excellence.

For five decades, Schweizer Aircraft has been a quiet but important part of the Army team.

We are committed to broadening this relationship in the next decade with SEMA aircraft, UAV's, and training helicopters.

Today, in particular, Schweizer is focused on the Army requirement for a next generation training helicopter. The turbine-powered TH-330 is configured specifically to meet this need.

Schweizer, a quiet partner, committed to the future of Army Aviation.

1940's

TG-3A Army/Air Force training glider

1950's

OH-13 Production source for cabin and frame assemblies

1960's

YO 3 A Quiet observation aircraft—operational in Southeast Asia

1970's

UH-60A Production source for gunner windows and other assemblies

1980's

TH-55/TH-300C Product support of Ft. Rucker fleet/Manufacturer of Model 300C product line

APPENDIX 10

SCHWEIZER SAILPLANE FAMILY

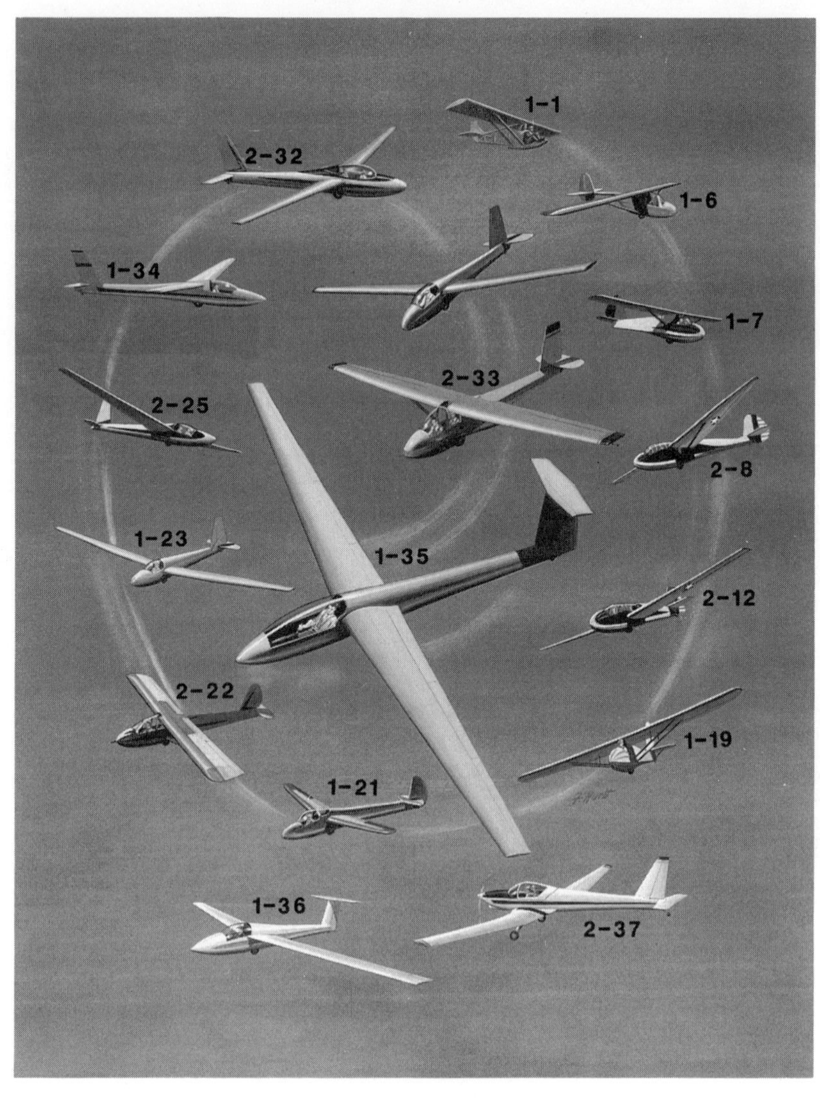

APPENDIX 11 (1 of 2)

SCHWEIZER SAILPLANE FAMILY

MODEL	FAA CERTIFIED	PRODUCTION YEARS	NUMBER MANUFACTURED
SGP 1-1	No	1930 & 1989	2
SGU 1-2	No	1932	1
SGU 1-3	No	1933	1
SGU 1-6	No	1937	1
SGU 1-7	No	1938	2
SGS 2-8	Yes	1938-1942	57
SGS 2-12	Yes	1942-1943	114
SGU 1-19	Yes	1944-1946	50
SGU 1-20	No	1949	1
SGS 1-21	No	1947-1948	2
SGS 2-22	Yes	1946-1967	258
SGS 1-23	Yes	1949-1969	74
SGS 1-24	No	1950	1
SGS 2-25	No	1954	1
SGS 1-26	Yes	1954-1981	689
SGS 1-29	No	1960	1
SGS 2-32	Yes	1967-1976	87
SGS 2-33	Yes	1967-1984	579
SGS 1-34	Yes	1969-1979	93
SGS 1-35	Yes	1973-1982	101
SGS 1-36	Yes	1980-1982	43
SGS 2-37	Yes	1981-1987	12
		TOTAL	2,170

APPENDIX 11 (2 OF 2)

SOARING WITH THE SCHWEIZERS

Composed by Blue Heron, Inc. in Palatino text and display.

Printed offset by Thomson-Shore, Inc. on 60 lb. Boise Cascade, and bound by them in Holliston Roxite B grade cloth. The paper on which this book is printed carries acid-free characteristics for an effective life of at least three hundred years.